D1165698

Books of Merit

INWARD JOURNEY

The Life of
Lawren Harris

JAMES KING

THOMAS ALLEN PUBLISHERS
TORONTO

Library and Archives Canada Cataloguing in Publication

King, James, 1942–   Inward journey : the life of Lawren Harris / James King.

Includes bibliographical references and index.

ISBN 978-1-77102-206-4

1. Harris, Lawren, 1885–1970.   2. Painters—Canada—Biography.
3. Group of Seven (Group of artists)—Biography.   I. Title.

ND249.H36K55   2012   759.11   C2012-904217-X

Editor: Janice Zawerbny
Cover design: Angel Guerra
Cover image: Detail from Lawren Harris, *North Shore, Lake Superior*, 1926.
Oil on canvas. The National Gallery of Canada.

Published by Thomas Allen Publishers,
a division of Thomas Allen & Son Limited,
390 Steelcase Road East,
Markham, Ontario L3R 1G2 Canada

www.thomasallen.ca

ONTARIO ARTS COUNCIL
CONSEIL DES ARTS DE L'ONTARIO

Canada Council   Conseil des Arts
for the Arts   du Canada

The publisher gratefully acknowledges the support of
The Ontario Arts Council for its publishing program.

We acknowledge the support of the Canada Council for the Arts, which last
year invested $20.1 million in writing and publishing throughout Canada.

We acknowledge the Government of Ontario through the Ontario
Media Development Corporation's Ontario Book Initiative.

We acknowledge the financial support of the Government of Canada
through the Canada Book Fund for our publishing activities.

1 2 3 4 5 16 15 14 13 12

Text printed on a 100% PCW recycled stock

Printed and bound in Canada

For Patrick and Jackson

CONTENTS

LIST OF
ILLUSTRATIONS

CHAPTER THREE

Page 26. Max Liebermann. *Jewish Quarter in Amsterdam.* 1905. Oil on canvas. Wallraf-Richarz Museum, Cologne.

Page 27. Lawren Harris. *Street in Berlin. Circa* 1907. Pencil drawing on cardboard. Private Collection.

Page 28. Franz Skarbina. *View from a Berlin Studio Window on to a Backyard in Winter. Circa* 1895–1905. Oil on fibreboard. Private Collection.

Page 29. Walter Leistikow. *Grüewaldsee. Circa* 1895–1905. Oil on canvas. Staatliche Museen, Berlin.

Page 29. Caspar David Friedrich. *The Monk by the Sea.* 1808–10. Oil on canvas. Alte Nationalgalerie, Berlin.

Page 30. Ferdinand Hodler. *Der Niesen.* 1910. Oil on canvas. Kunstmuseum Basel, Switzerland.

Page 31. Lawren Harris. *Buildings on the River Spree.* 1907. Watercolour on paper. The Art Gallery of Windsor.

Page 35. Lawren Harris. "Over the Old Route into Egypt" (book illustration) from Norman Duncan, *Going Down to Jerusalem* (1909).

CHAPTER FOUR

Page 43. Trixie Phillips. Photograph. Undated. Private Collection.

Page 45. Lawren P. Harris (Lornie), four years old, Trixie and Margaret Knox (Peggie), one year old. Photograph taken November 1914. Photographer J. Kennedy. Private Collection.

Page 45. Lawren P. and Peggie Harris with Nanny Stevenson. Photograph. Private Collection.

Page 46. Lawren Harris. *Laurentian Farm. Circa* 1908. Oil sketch. Private Collection.

Page 47. Lawren Harris. *Little House. Circa* 1911. Oil on paperboard. McMichael Canadian Art Collection.

Page 48. Lawren Harris. *House in Toronto. Circa* 1908. Pen and ink drawing. Private Collection.

Page 49. Lawren Harris. *Top of the Hill, Spadina Avenue.* 1909–1911. Oil on canvas. University of Toronto Art Collection.

CHAPTER SEVEN

Page 100. Lawren Harris. *Decorative Landscape.* 1917. Oil on canvas. National Gallery of Canada.
Page 107. Lawren Harris. *Waterfall, Algoma.* 1918. Oil on canvas. Art Gallery of Hamilton.
Page 107. Lawren Harris. *Algoma Woods II. Circa* 1918. Oil sketch. Private Collection.

CHAPTER EIGHT

Page 112. Lawren Harris. *Woodland Snow, Family Outing. Circa* 1918–21. Oil sketch. Private Collection.
Page 113. Lawren Harris. *Red House, Barrie. Circa* 1918–20. Oil. Private Collection.
Page 114. Lawren Harris. *Hurdy-Gurdy. Circa* 1919–20. Oil. Private Collection.
Page 115. Lawren Harris. *Old Houses, Toronto, Winter.* 1919. Oil on canvas. Art Gallery of Ontario.
Page 116. Lawren Harris. *Shacks.* 1919. Oil on canvas. National Gallery of Canada.
Page 117. Children in Price's Lane. Photograph. *Circa* 1912; Arthur Goss, photographer. City of Toronto Archives.
Page 118. Lawren Harris. *January Thaw, Edge of Town.* 1921. Oil on canvas. National Gallery of Canada.
Page 120. Lawren Harris. *Billboard (Jazz).* 1920. Oil on canvas. Imperial Oil, Ltd.
Page 122. Lawren Harris. *Black Court, Halifax.* 1921. Oil on canvas. National Gallery of Canada.
Page 122. Lawren Harris. *Elevator Court, Halifax.* 1921. Oil on canvas. Art Gallery of Ontario.

CHAPTER NINE

Page 128. Arthur Lismer. *Lawren Harris.* 1920. Charcoal on paper. Art Gallery of Ontario.

CHAPTER TEN

CHAPTER ELEVEN

CHAPTER TWELVE

CHAPTER THIRTEEN

CHAPTER FOURTEEN

CHAPTER NINETEEN

CHAPTER TWENTY

ACKNOWLEDGEMENTS

For assistance in researching and writing this book, I am grateful to Lynn B. Bertrand, Imperial Oil; Rochelle Boehm, Art Gallery of Alberta; Tobi Bruce, Hamilton Art Gallery; Belma Buljubasic, National Gallery, Canada; Janine Butler, McMichael Canadian Art Collection; Cyndie Campbell, National Gallery of Canada Archives; Louise Caron, National Library, Canada; Janet Cauffiel; Felicia Cukier, The Art Gallery of Ontario; Danielle Currie, Vancouver Art Gallery; Cecilia Esposito, Plattsburgh State Art Museum; Jill Godfrey; Juliet Graham, University of Lethbridge Art Gallery; Sue Hayter, St. Andrew's College; Laurie Klein, Beinecke Library, Yale University; Nicole McCabe, Art Gallery of Windsor; Rebecca Martz, Beinecke Library, Yale University; Lia Melemenis, The Glenbow Museum; Linda Morita, McMichael Canadian Art Collection; Grant Parker, Imperial Oil; Heather Darling Pigat, University of Toronto Art Centre; Lisa Quirion, Winnipeg Art Gallery; Mary Reid, School of Art Gallery, the University of Manitoba; Susan Richie; Denise Ryner, Hart House Gallery, University of Toronto; Jay Satterfield, Dartmouth College Library; Clemencia Sheppard; Betty Carol Smith; Gordon Smith; Richard Sorensen, The Smithsonian Institution; Leon Tuey; Kelly-Ann Turkington, Royal British Columbia Museum; Robert Ware, Raymond Jonson Collection, University of New

Mexico; Margaret Zoller, Smithsonian Archives of American Art.

I am much obliged to the art historians who provided much-needed assistance: Gregory Betts, Joan Murray, David Silcox and Ian Thom. In this regard, I am particularly indebted to Peter Larisey and Dennis Reid for meeting with me and answering my questions.

Although there has never been a biography of Lawren Harris, there has been some outstanding published scholarship on him. In this regard, I am beholden to the published writings of Jeremy Adamson, Charles C. Hill, Peter Larisey, Larry Pfaff, Dennis Reid and Maria Tippett. Hill's *The Group of Seven: Art for a Nation* (1995) and Ross King's *Defiant Spirits: The Modernist Revolution of the Group of Seven* (2010) provide excellent accounts of Harris's interactions with Tom Thomson and members of the Group of Seven. Very kindly, Charles C. Hill and Larry Pfaff read the manuscript of this book and made many useful suggestions to improve it.

I began *Inward Journey* about fifteen years ago, when I consulted the holdings of the National Archives. I also met with the late Lawren P. Harris, Lawren's eldest son, at his home in Ottawa; he encouraged me to write this book and supplied me with a great deal of useful information. When I contacted Margaret Knox, Lawren's daughter, she told me that she did not wish a biography of her father to appear. She did not state her reasons, but she was an exceptionally dutiful daughter who had strong protective feelings for her father.

Three years ago, I approached Stewart Sheppard, Margaret's son, about reviving this project. He told me that he would very much welcome a life of his grandfather. From that time, Stew and his sister, Toni Ann Chowne, have assisted me in every possible way. They have been exceptionally generous with their time and energy on behalf of this book.

PREFACE

On March 20, 1970, two months after his death, the ashes of Lawren Harris and his wife, Bess, were buried on an ice-splattered hillock outside the McMichael Collection near Kleinburg, Ontario. The ashes had been shipped from Vancouver to Ontario in plain pine chests bearing only the names and dates of husband and wife.

The day was bleak and windy. In the near distance, pine and fir trees stood against the flat grey countryside—much like a stylized Harris landscape. Two years before, Harris had asked Robert McMichael, the founder of the gallery, to find him and Bess a burial plot nearby. The idea of a consecrated area for the members of the Group of Seven had been A.Y. Jackson's. He wanted the members of the Group to be brought together near the gallery that had been founded to celebrate their accomplishments.

The only member of the original Seven still alive was a frail, tottering Jackson, and he was very distressed that day. He recalled: "Harris was the doer. He was the Group's moving spirit. He helped everybody, but he just did it without any fuss. He never acted like a financier. He was always for a Canadian school of painters. Everything was for the country; he didn't want anything for himself." In his customary wry and sardonic way, Jackson also observed that the tribute by the speaker from the Theosophical Society "was too long." A.J. Casson, one of the later members of the Group, added that Harris was the kind of man who "got you worked up no matter where you were. I used to say you'd come home from a party at Lawren's at 12:30 at night and want to paint. Lawren was that way."

As bleak as the day might be, Harris had welcomed any kind of encounter with nature throughout his long life. Although his reputation as a Canadian iconic painter tends to be focused on his Lake Superior, mountain and Arctic canvases, it had taken him a long time to reach that particular stage in his career. Before that, he had painted a series of urban canvases that highlighted the plight of the underclass; he had also painted a series of delicate, decorative snow pictures; and he had undertaken a small number of portraits, all of an exceptional quality.

After completing his Arctic canvases in 1930, he felt duty bound to explore the geometric shapes he had encountered in the monumental icebergs in a series of abstract paintings. At first, those images inhabited a kind of halfway point between abstraction and realism. He tried to rid himself of figurative elements, and he finally reached that summit in the last years of his life, when he painted canvases that revealed his own subjectivity in a way he had never before been able to realize.

Moreover, he was the only member of the Group of Seven to become engaged with Modernism in a protracted manner. He had been the Group's most significant apologist; and after the Group disbanded, he attempted to align himself with a variety of European and American forms of Modernist expression.

In addition to his paintings and sketches, Harris bestowed upon Canadians another legacy. He constantly reminded them—even when they tried to keep their eyes and ears closed—that Canada has its own distinct culture that must be preserved.

He was a deeply spiritual man, although not a religious person in the usual definition of that word. Moreover, he was a man who cultivated his internal landscape and attempted to externalize that terrain in his paintings.

The life of Lawren Harris is the story of his epic encounter with the vital forces of life, which he used to express, in his art, the fullness of existence. In part, his search was a hidden one. The drama may have been within, but he found a way, in a series of extraordinary paintings, to dramatize and thus externalize those struggles.

I have called this biography *Inward Journey* because it centres on Lawren Harris's search for inner meaning and fulfillment in his life through his art. Harris's life was devoted to the making of art, and he constantly challenged himself to find deeper, more intense ways of creating images. He had a restless soul and a concomitant streak of ambition. He longed to express his soul's engagement with the universe, and his encounter with spiritual values underwent many changes.

Metaphors associated with mountains and mountain climbing are also especially appropriate for Harris, because he was an avid mountaineer; he envisioned mountains as sacred places connected to the divine. Having arrived at a plateau—often with considerable difficulty—he knew instinctively that he had to ascend farther.

This narrative is centred on the motif of the quest, because that was precisely how Harris saw his life on earth. For him, to be alive was to be engaged with locating the divinity within himself, and then to find ways of making meaningful images out of that experience.

In his writings about art, Lawren Harris spoke in strong and eloquent language about his own work and that of his contemporaries. He was much more reticent in writing about or discussing personal matters. In order to write a biography that does justice to Harris's inner thoughts and feelings, I have begun each chapter with a brief section in italics that attempts to re-create his emotional life at that time. In every instance, I have relied on the available evidence.

1

EARLY JOYS
AND SORROWS

(1885–1894)

Confined to his bedroom for what seemed like endless hours, the little boy would fidget. Readjusting his pillows every few minutes, he would sit up abruptly and then as quickly place himself prone upon the mattress. Even when he managed briefly to escape his bedroom, he would be routinely returned to quarters. He simply could not go outside, the ambition of any self-respecting male of five years of age.

Lawren had been born a sickly child, and his mother would fret about the countless invisible microbes that might infect him if he was allowed to play outdoors. Her son, she had been informed soon after he was born, had a tricky heart and a frail constitution. Such children required close supervision, she was instructed. Sports were an exertion that could not be part of his daily existence. Instead, he was encouraged to collect stamps and was even taught to knit.

Lawren, dutifully accepting the privations imposed by well-intentioned protectiveness, had to find some way to make the weary hours pass. His solution was to draw "what he could see out the window, objects in his room, illustrations of the stories *that were read to him, and endless sketches of his family and friends who came to see him."¹ Making a virtue of necessity, Lawren forced his eyes to examine every aspect of his young existence. From early on, he trained his hands to render what his eyes beheld.*

His high spirits found expression on paper. Throughout his life, in this manner, he obtained solace—and salvation. Whether downcast or elated, drawing and painting released him from this mundane world into another, in which he embraced life. In this way, he learned to replenish himself.

L AWREN'S MOTHER, Annie, remembered that the doctor attending his birth in Brantford, Ontario, on October 23, 1885, had unsuccessfully tried, after he was delivered, to "bring him to life, then simply put him aside to look after [Annie]." The loyal family attendant "Little Auntie," ready for such an emergency, "worked over the baby until he began to breathe and cry."² The delay of a few minutes, Annie felt, accounted for his frailty in his early years.*

His mother and father, who had married on November 28, 1884, were a bit indecisive about his name. Father wanted to call the boy Lorne whereas Mother favoured Lawrence. They "compromised and named him Lawren Stewart."³

He may have begun life with an ardent disposition, but that spirit was often stronger than his body. Robust he may not have

---

*Lawren Harris's childhood home (and birthplace) was likely on Brant Street. The City of Brantford directory for 1883–86 lists "Harris T M, book-keeper, Brant Avenue [Street]." This was Thomas Morgan Harris, Lawren's father.

The home of Thomas and his family may have been in close proximity to 150 Brant Street, a property acquired by Alanson Harris, Lawren's grandfather, in 1883; this residence was owned by him until 1892, at which time the deed to the land was transferred to Eleanor Popplewell, his daughter and the widow of Alfred Popplewell. There is a possibility that 150 Brant was Lawren Harris's birth residence.

Before his marriage, Thomas would have lived at his family's home at 133 Market Street; the office of A. Harris & Son was on Colborne Street near the rail station.

been, but Lawren was decidedly headstrong. His first experience with paints "was a near disaster," he later told his daughter. "He received a set of watercolours in little cubes of such pretty colours that he ate several of his favourites and was violently ill."4

(left)
Tom Harris, Lawren Harris's father.

(right)
Annie, Lawren Harris's mother, with her sons Howard (left) and Lawren. *Circa* 1887–88.

(left)
Lawren (left) and Howard. *Circa* 1889.

(right)
Lawren (top) and Howard. *Circa* 1891–92.

The household into which Lawren was born was one of wealth and its accompanying privileges. His father, twenty-three-year-old Tom, born in 1862, was secretary of the family-owned implement business, Harris, Son & Company. That firm, founded in Beamsville in 1857 by Tom's father, Alanson (1816–94), and his brother, John, moved to Brantford in 1872.

Alanson Harris was the son of John Harris, often referred to as "Elder John," a circuit-rider preacher, and his wife, Catherine Duggart or Dygert (1794–1872). They emigrated from New York State's Mohawk Valley shortly after the War of 1812 ended, settling in Ingersoll in Upper Canada, where Alanson was born. At the age of thirteen, he was apprenticed to a sawmill operator. Later, father and son went into partnership operating a sawmill at Whiteman's Creek. In 1839, at the age of twenty-three, Alanson married Mary Morgan.

"Elder John" had been resourceful, inventive and restless. He was a gifted preacher, but he could not make his living that way. Instead, he turned his hand to farming, a profession that he disliked. To relieve the tedium of tilling the land, he invented machines such as a revolving hay rake, a device that would make tending the land easier and more productive.

At the age of forty, Alanson sold the sawmill and moved to Greensville, where he began manufacturing farm implements. Later, Alanson took his son John (1841–87) into partnership and moved to Beamsville and then Brantford, where they invented the Brantford Light Binder, a harvesting machine that cut grain and bound it into bundles.

By 1885, 69-year-old Alanson was a wealthy man. He was renowned for his "great inventive ability and [the] wonderful energy" that "laid the foundation for one of the largest agricultural manufacturing establishments on the continent."[5] Successful businessman though he may have been, he placed even greater stock in his strong religious beliefs. He had been "converted at a revival service held in Boston, Ontario, when eighteen years of age, and at once joined the Baptist Church."[6] He later gave a plot of land worth $8,000 to the Walmer Road Baptist congregation in Toronto, where one of his sons, Elmore (1854–1911), was the pastor. He and his wife had six sons and six daughters, but by 1891 only three were living (Tom, Elmore and one daughter, Eleanor).

Lawren's mother, Anna (often called Annie), born in 1865, also came from a distinguished family, one in which Alanson would have taken special pride. She was the daughter of the Reverend William Boyd Stewart (1835–1912) and his wife, Augusta Kilborne.

Stewart, who was born in the village of Ecclefechan on the southern border of Scotland, was educated at the Annan Academy and the University of Glasgow. He immigrated to Canada in 1856 and three years later was ordained a Baptist minister at Beamsville. He taught Greek, Latin and Hebrew at the Canadian Literary Institute in Woodstock and ministered in Brantford and Hamilton. He also served as joint proprietor and editor of the *Canadian Baptist*. In 1882, he accepted the presidency of Roger Williams College in Nashville, Tennessee; and two years later became principal of the Collegiate Academy in Winchester, Kentucky. In the autumn of 1889, when he spoke at Berea College, in Tennessee, one onlooker described him as "tall, straight as a West Point cadet, [with] square shoulders, neatly dressed. A touch of gray to an abundance of hair. Thoughtful, affable, courteous and capable."[7] In 1890, he became president of Berea, but he remained for only two years. He returned to Canada, where he taught at the Toronto Bible Training School.

Stewart abandoned his life as a minister, teacher and writer in Canada to take an active part in social reforms, working in the American South in educational institutions that were fiercely pro-black. In fact, the students at Berea College consisted of an integrated community of blacks and "mountaineers" (poor white students from Appalachia). Stewart, who was the victim of sectarian politics at Berea, spent eight years in the United States attempting to put his religious beliefs to the test in practical ways.

Like Stewart, Alanson Harris felt that his material success obliged him to use his wealth to manifest God's presence in human affairs.

One contemporary account recalled, "There are few men in the land who have given more money to the cause of Christ than Mr. Harris. The majority of the weaker Baptist churches in Ontario have felt the benefit of his warm heart and ample capital."[8]

For Alanson, Brantford, located at the deepest navigable point on the Grand River, was an ideal spot to conduct business. It was a railway hub for southern Ontario, which meant it possessed both waterpower and reliable transportation. The small city had quickly abandoned farming in favour of manufacturing, and had become the number-three locale in Canada in terms of the cash value of manufactured goods exported. Brantford was known at that time as "the Telephone City" because a former resident, Alexander Graham Bell, had made the first distant telephone call from nearby Paris, in 1876.[9]

Brantford was in the vanguard of young Canada's surge towards industrialization. In 1877, it achieved city status, having doubled its population in ten years to ten thousand. Immigrants from the United States and the British Isles flocked there. The city became known as a place loyal to Britain but infused with Yankee know-how. The stamp "Made in Brantford" that appeared on Tisdale iron stoves, Slingsby Mills wool blankets, T.J. Fair cigars and Lily White Gloss starch came to be associated with quality products.

In 1860, Edward, Prince of Wales, was served a sixty-dish luncheon at the Kerby House Hotel in Brantford. When it opened in 1854, it claimed to be the largest hotel in Upper Canada. There were subsequent visits by Prince Arthur, Duke of Connaught, Governor General Lord Dufferin, and then his successor the Marquess of Lorne. The city had two daily papers (the *Brantford Courier* and the *Daily Expositor*), and from 1854 the city had its own rail link, the Buffalo and Brantford, to the United States. There were even cultural activities: a Philharmonic Society and a Mendelssohn Society.

Along Colborne and Dalhousie Streets, costly plate-glass windows were installed at Frank Cockshutt's Dry Goods Store, Lester's Candy Store, Robertson's Drug Store, Hawthorne's Sporting Goods, and Mason and Risch's Music Shop.

All in all, Brantford was a wonderful place to be born in late nineteenth-century Canada, especially if one's parents were well-to-do. Lawren's parents may have been economically blessed, but they also felt enriched by the deep spirituality they had imbibed from their parents. For them, material prosperity went hand in hand with godliness. They were both humble people who did not feel they had done anything remarkable to deserve such blessings, but they nonetheless treasured the prosperity that came their way.

By 1861, there were thirty-one factories (mostly foundries) in Upper Canada producing agricultural implements. Alanson Harris had to do everything in his power to stay ahead of Hart Massey (1823–96), one of his most successful rivals in the manufacturing of farm implements, who had moved most of his operations to Toronto and Hamilton by the early 1880s. Daring and vituperative, Massey was a genius at advertising his wares and acquiring patent rights. In a crowded, cutthroat marketplace in which they were the key players, Harris and Massey fought each other vigorously.

Massey was resolved to sell his firm to a company in England, but the deal broke down. Harris also considered selling his business, but then he introduced an innovative, open-ended binder capable of cutting grain to any length. Upon reviewing the new equipment, Massey initiated negotiations with Harris to merge their two companies. Massey-Harris was formally incorporated on July 22, 1891, resulting in a firm that was easily able to outdistance its much smaller rivals.

The kind of manufacturing carried out by Massey-Harris was deeply rivalrous; a great deal of cunning and conniving was necessary to keep on top. It was also an industry, heavily dependent on the abundance of arable land in pastoral Canada, that was vigorously attempting to give Canada a competitive edge among industrial nations. However, although he was a ruthless businessman, Alanson maintained his strong religious convictions.

Lawren's father, Tom, inherited these principles. Although Lawren and his brother, Howard Kilborne, only fourteen months younger, absorbed a great deal of religious earnestness from their father and grandfather, they were quite often extremely naughty. Sometimes their lives were the ordinary ones of boys at that time: "swimming in the Grand River in summer, skating and hockey in the winter, and rubbing against types of all grades of society at the public school."[10]

Pauline Johnson (1861–1913), who would later become a celebrated poet and performer, of Mohawk and English ancestry, was one victim of the pranks of the nefarious twosome. Fourteen years older than Lawren, she and her widowed mother moved from their mansion, Chiefswood, to a modest home in Brantford in 1884, when she was at the outset of her remarkable career. No respecter of their elders, the two Harris brothers—nine and eight at the time—tormented the twenty-three-year-old woman, who lived behind them and shared the back fence. "One of their tricks was to wait until she had a line of washing hanging out to dry in her back garden and then make up a supply of mud balls and aim them at the sheets with slingshots. They were cured of this when one day she caught them, came over, and paddled them both with a stick."[11]

Attendance at church was a "stifling burden" to the two rascals. There were prayers at home every morning and evening, and attendance at church three times on Sunday. Although Baptist religious beliefs were sometimes socially progressive, the two youngsters did not enjoy the fire-and-brimstone aspects of the faith. Card playing was forbidden, as was dancing. On Sundays, the children had to bear the additional burden of not being able to play; nor were they allowed to read anything but the Scriptures.

A rigid formality held sway over the Harris family. Grandmother Augusta Stewart always addressed her husband, William, as Mr. Stewart. "When asked [by one of her granddaughters] why she did not address him by his first name, [she] replied 'Because I have too much respect for him!'"[12] As a youngster in a strict Baptist household, Augusta had not been permitted even to put a ribbon in her hair because that would signify vanity.

Sometimes, when the two brothers were deemed to have been disobedient, they were not allowed out of the house to attend church. They remained at home to reflect on their misdeeds. On one occasion, the castaways rebelled.

> The boys thought of dressing up in their parents' clothes. Howard put on a dress of his mother's, a fur neckpiece and hat; Lawren, aged about seven, wore a suit and hat of his father's. Thinking they looked very handsome, they decided to go out. Down the street they walked, straight to the church, in the door and down the aisle, right in the middle of the sermon. There were horrified gasps, and sounds of muffled giggles; finally the entire congregation became convulsed with helpless laughter. The boys, frightened by the reaction they'd caused, were hustled out in disgrace by their mortified parents. The punishment was severe and included a personal apology to the minister.[13]

Mother and father decided that they had to find a suitable way of dealing with the high spirits of two adventurous, prank-inclined youngsters, and they soon hit upon a solution: the two could do whatever they wanted as long as they were willing to accept the consequences of their actions. Harris's daughter would later write: "After repeatedly having to pay one way or another for hasty judgments, they were usually able to think ahead and use some self-discipline."[14]

Despite Lawren's sometimes frail health, the early existence of the two boys was largely idyllic. Their world was soon shattered, however, when their father became ill in about 1891. Lawren was about six, Howard five. Tom fell victim to Bright's disease, a kidney ailment first described in 1827 by the English physician Richard Bright. Today, this condition is called acute or chronic nephritis. The symptoms are severe: back pain, testicular pain, elevated blood pressure, vomiting, fever, edema and restricted breathing. The diagnosis was made in 1894, three years after the onset of symptoms. Before his diagnosis, and in great pain, Tom travelled to California and various parts of the American South in search of a cure.

Like most businessmen, Tom was away from home a great deal, and his sons missed him. Tom, who seems to have been much warmer and gentler than his own father, Alanson, was a diligent businessman, and his public life was centred on worthy causes, especially those devoted to the welfare of young people. When he received the diagnosis of Bright's disease and knew he would not live long, he was direct with the news. He told Lawren and Howard that he expected the two of them to be both self-sufficient and responsible; most of all, he encouraged them to look after their mother. To Annie, he was equally forthright: she would have to cope with two headstrong youngsters on her own.

Tom faced death without fear. He was resolute in his determination to die bravely. The cruel irony was that in the final month of his life he visited Dr. J.H. Salisbury in New York City, who, in the early 1890s, had introduced new diagnostic techniques, a special diet of pulped steak (cooked rare in patties) and rest in a new kind of hospital bed. "For some time," a contemporary account states, "the change of air and the efforts of Dr. Salisbury seemed to afford Mr. Harris considerable relief. The fears entertained for his recovery vanished, and it seemed as if he would soon be restored to excellent health. The improvement was not of a permanent character, and soon signs of the ravages of the disease made themselves apparent."[15]

Annie and Elmore travelled to New York, and as his end approached Tom asked his wife to send a message to those back home. She replied: "I will write it for you. What shall I say?" Tom replied that he was ready to meet Christ.[16] He died on August 30, 1894.

The children were not with their father when he died. Their mother was not at home either. These cruel privations added to the tragedy of their father's early death. Compounding their grief, Alanson Harris, who was too infirm to attend Tom's funeral, died only a few weeks afterwards, on October 3.

On the one hand, to his advantage, Lawren was left with a sense of the benefits of earnestness and religiosity; his father had been a role model of how virtue could be practised. Decades later, he claimed: "I have not yet [1954] succeeded in emancipating myself from some of the effects of my clergyman forbears and so remain inclined to point a moral whenever the opportunity offers."[17] To his detriment, though, at a crucial time in his development, he had experienced a profound loss. He would never be the same again.

Lawren was wounded by his father's death and remained a deeply vulnerable person throughout his life. Well aware of his father's commitment to assisting others less fortunate, Lawren also carried the burdens associated with noblesse oblige.

Like his father, Lawren Harris the adult disdained materialism. He was friendly, charming and erudite, but from an early age he rejected the acquisition of money and power in favour of the peace and rejuvenation he found in the realms of art and unorthodox religious beliefs. Certainly he was a wealthy man who could easily live comfortably, but to argue from such a premise would be to miss the point. Emotionally, Lawren was fated to spend the rest of his life questioning the values of the world and learning to find solace within.

2

YOUTHFUL
AMBITION

(1894–1903)

---

*Lawren disliked school. That fact was evident to all his teachers.
He was averse to rote learning and did not like to recite in uni-
son. Anything that resembled slogging was anathema, mathematics being particularly hostile territory. He hated irregular
verbs; nor did he wish to store large chunks of Shakespeare and
the Bible in his memory.*

*He was not what was considered a "serious" student unless
his imagination was engaged. The exploits of great men and
women from the past—Charlemagne, Joan of Arc, Napoleon—
were fascinating to him, as were facts about foreign countries
such as the various colonies that constituted Africa. He luxuri-
ated in the pleasures of reading because it allowed his mind to
wander freely among the imaginations of others.*

*During classes from which he felt disengaged, he often
cut out "little paper figures representing teachers and friends,
drawing faces and clothing on them. He would chew bits of paper
to pulp, add a little pine gum stored in his pocket, attach the
cut-outs to the gum with thread, and shoot them by slingshot to
the ceiling. They usually stuck, and by the end of the lesson there*

would be several paper people dangling from the ceiling."[1]

Rejecting his mother's belief that he suffered from poor health, he began to rebel against her strictures. He was keen on sports and became an excellent swimmer, and later an outstanding diver, taking special delight in launching himself from great heights. Like many youngsters who have endured privation, he spent his childhood trying to rid himself of heavy thoughts, and for the most part he was successful.

SOON AFTER Tom's death, Annie wanted to be near her parents, whose emotional support she desired and needed. She and her two boys moved to 123 St. George Street in Toronto, the city where her parents lived. Lawren and Howard were enrolled at Huron Street Public School starting in the autumn of 1894.

There were many gleeful childhood moments for the boys in Toronto, but Lawren always retained one sorrowful memory, which directly connected his life to art. As a child in Brantford, he had made Christmas cards for his family. He "had a friend named Billy Davison who lived on the same street. He and Billy worked together [making] pictures of all the houses in the neighborhood." Soon after he was settled in Toronto, Lawren learned that Billy had died in Brantford at the age of twelve.[2]

Toronto was a big change from pastoral Brantford. The city was born during the American Revolution, when Upper Canada's first governor, John Graves Simcoe, decided that the village should occupy a position that would assist in warding off the Americans. Simcoe laid out the community, which he called York, by the harbour. Soon he was using it as his capital.

Yonge Street, the main thoroughfare, was created in 1796. During the War of 1812, American forces briefly held the city. After the war, immigrants from the United Kingdom began to arrive. Toronto quickly became a city of merchants who supplied retailers in the surrounding hinterlands; of necessity, it also became the banking centre for Upper Canada. In 1834, the fast-growing town of nine thousand was incorporated as a city. As the

1800s advanced, steamboat activity increased, streets were paved and gas-lit, and rail lines connected the city to New York, Montreal, Detroit and Chicago. At Confederation in 1867, the city was made the capital of the new province of Ontario. By 1891, the city was rapidly expanding in size and population.

Publicity releases from the Government of Ontario described Toronto as an idyllic city of stone and brick, with clean sidewalks, paved streets and up-to-date streetcars. Lake Ontario provided a natural harbour, and the Don and Humber Rivers bisected the city, which was filled with parks, stately residences and rugged ravines. Second only to Montreal in population, the city hummed with factories specializing in clothing, printing, metal fabricating and metal polishing.

Toronto was proudly and defiantly British. Canada was part of the British Empire and, of course, Canadians were British subjects. Children studied from British schoolbooks; British pageants and plays were eagerly watched; British music-hall songs were committed to memory.

In the late 1890s and early 1900s, Toronto was both admired and reviled. To some, it was a place of considerable wealth, an ambitious new metropolis. Like many other cities of similar size, it craved the mantle of respectability and quickly moved to attract the best singers and actors willing to perform there. The University of Toronto, founded in 1827, attempted to become the Harvard of the North.

By the time Lawren arrived in Toronto, it had become a High Victorian city, architecturally speaking. The city had many detractors, who felt that it succumbed too quickly to superficial blandishments. Such disparagers labelled the city the creation of greedy bankers and industrialists who simply wanted to exploit newcomers from the United Kingdom, Europe and the Far East. For such people, the nickname "Hogtown" seemed appropriate, especially considering that livestock of all kinds, including pigs, offloaded at the railway yards, could sometimes be heard lamenting their fates.

One area was called Cabbagetown because the gardens of its poor Irish immigrants were filled with potatoes and cabbages, stock items necessary for their survival. In contrast, the ravines and parklands of the city's wealthiest inhabitants enjoyed the name Rosedale. St. George Street, where the Harrises lived, was in the neighbourhood near the university, often referred to as the Annex. Not very far away was the rundown Ward (St. John's Ward), home to the city's Jewish, Italian and Chinese immigrants.

Lawren and Howard left Huron Street Public School in the spring of 1898. Since neither boy displayed the eagerness for education that their grandfather, William Boyd Stewart, would have liked, he pressured his daughter to enrol the two at the newly established St. Andrew's College, in Rosedale, in its inaugural year. Lawren entered the Second Form, the equivalent of grade eight, in September 1899, more than one full year after leaving grade seven at Huron. It is likely that he lost this year due to illness; St. Andrew's records indicate that he had a tutor before coming to them. His new school's records also reveal that he spent two years in the Third Form (grade nine), graduating from the Fourth Form (grade ten) in 1903. Clearly, Lawren was still physically frail, and he was not a diligent pupil.

Chester Harris (cousin), Howard Harris, Lawren Harris, Fred Popplewell (cousin). *Circa* 1900.

Lawren was good at hockey and cricket, however. He also made some important connections at this period in his life. One contemporary at St. Andrew's was Vincent Massey (1887–1967), of the other family making up Massey-Harris; Massey later became Governor General and was the author of the Massey Report (1951), which made many recommendations that strengthened and expanded Canadian culture. Lawren also met Frederick Broughton Housser (1889–1956), who was to become a close friend and an ally in the national movement in Canadian painting.

Lawren Harris, George Porter, Morgan Harris. White House, Lake of Bays, Muskoka. 1902.

Photographs reveal Lawren the teenager in two guises. In one group photo, he looks ahead with an air of modest pride, whereas his brother has a glum, shyer and more serious look. In another photo, he stares a bit petulantly at the camera. His countenance is that of a rebellious young man. If he was, this would not have fazed his mother, Annie.

As discouraged as Annie often felt, she was never defeated. "She exuded," her granddaughter recalled, "love and a sense of well being, as though at peace with herself and the rest of the world."[3] Annie was also open to innovation. She was one of the first people in Toronto to purchase a "horseless carriage," an endeavour into which she was prodded by her two sons, who "ached"[4] to have a motor car and thus retire the family horse and carriage.

Lawren (left) and Howard holding up "Little Auntie." *Circa* 1903.

When the car was delivered, the salesman briefed the boys on its use. Neither had driven one, nor had Annie. While she was in the house attiring herself in dustcoat, driving boots and hat with motoring veil, Lawren and Howard had a fist fight on the front lawn for the honour of being first to drive the car. With considerable aplomb, which she very much needed since some snickering neighbours had gathered to behold the spectacle, Annie announced: "That will do, boys. Lawren will drive first, as he is the eldest, and Howard, you may drive us home." The brothers quickly put on their motoring goggles and, after "much cranking and backfiring, took off in a series of jerks."5 In queenly fashion from the back seat, Annie waved goodbye to her nosy neighbours.

In the autumn of 1903, Lawren enrolled at University College at the University of Toronto. This is a mysterious matter, as he had graduated from St. Andrew's the previous June with only grade ten. His university application form asked for the date of his matriculation, but that line was crossed out. The likely explanation is that Annie Harris (or another family member) had requested that Lawren be granted special permission to matriculate at university because of his age (he was eighteen), and that permission was extended, perhaps as an experiment to see how he would fare.

Much later, Fred Housser provided this account of Lawren's time there:

In the course of a conventional education we find Harris at Toronto University filling his notebook with pencil sketches of his fellow freshmen and various members of the faculty instead of listening to professional lectures. One of these illustrated notebooks was left by accident in the classroom where it was picked up by a professor intelligent enough to see that this student was wasting his time at college. He called at the family residence and stated his opinion, and the incident ended by Harris being sent to study painting in Germany.6

A.T. (Alfred Tennyson) DeLury (1864–1951) was the professor who found the notebook. He may have been in the mathematics department, but he had a great deal of interest in literature and the arts.7 Possessing an excellent eye, DeLury informed Annie that her son should study in Europe (the choice of Berlin was Annie's).

Apparently, Harris had already been to Europe once, at the age of nine, shortly after his father's death, with his mother and brother. The trip had been organized by his grandfather Stewart, who was attempting to distract the young widow and her offspring from their grief.

Lawren was vaguely aware that he was destined for some sort of new experience, although he remained deeply unsure of himself as a person. His only surviving early work of art is a short story entitled "Jack Brown," published in the *St. Andrew's College Review* in 1902, when he was seventeen. In the story, Jack, a farmer's son, is an inventor, mainly of farm machinery. However, he eventually goes well beyond farm equipment and succeeds in producing a battery-powered flying machine. "Jack Brown continued his inventions, not to better his father's farm, but to better the world," the narrator observes.

In his story, Lawren appears to be paying tribute to his father's family and the machinery—such as the Brantford Light Binder—that had made the Harrises rich. At the same time as it celebrates the inventiveness that characterized the Harris men, however, the story also suggests that Jack has altogether nobler, loftier ambitions. Unconsciously, the teenager may have been suggesting that he was born to different, perhaps greater, things than his ancestors. He had inherited his creativity from his father, yet he would use his talents to venture into art rather than farm equipment.

3

THE ARTIST AS A YOUNG OBSERVER

(1904–1908)

Before he arrived in Berlin, Lawren was increasingly, and somewhat embarrassingly, aware that while he had the ambition to become an artist, he hadn't fully taken into account what his chosen vocation entailed. In his daydreams, he had fantasized in fuzzy, romantic ways about how wonderful it would be to dedicate his life to this profession, one that seemed to suit his devil-may-care attitude. Unlike Howard, who had turned into a serious student and was on his way to becoming a lawyer, Lawren did not feel like dedicating his life to one of the conventionally acceptable professions for men of his class.

In Toronto, the wisdom of channelling his energy into art seemed self-evident, but in Germany his feelings changed. He quickly realized that becoming an artist was a time-consuming, arduous enterprise. Only the most dedicated apprentices became successful artists. The Biblical adage was as true in art as it was for a spiritual calling: many are called, few are chosen.

> *Soon, Lawren's new-found clarity about his future was accompanied by a host of surprising feelings. First, he discovered he had a strong streak of ambition. Strangely, he had never been in contact with this side of himself before. He also understood that he wanted to put his own sensibility on to paper and canvas, which brought his reflections full circle: he would have to work long, tedious hours to master the tools of his vocation. If he wanted to become successful, he could no longer be a dilettante. Lawren had, with all the determination he could muster, decided to become a genuine artist.*

FREE SPIRIT though she may have been, Annie was not inclined simply to permit Lawren to go anywhere he wished in Europe. Some curbs had to be placed on her slightly wayward son. Her recently married younger brother, William Kilborne Stewart, an instructor in German at Dartmouth College in New Hampshire, and his wife, Ethel, were planning to be on study leave in Berlin from the autumn of 1904. William, who had studied at the University of Toronto and Harvard, would be able to keep an eye on her son, Annie reasoned.

Uncle and nephew were accustomed to playing chess and had gone on canoe trips together. William had taught at Harvard from 1897 to 1899 before he was appointed at Dartmouth; he knew exactly how to speak to younger men of Harris's generation—and to stimulate their intellects. Moreover, William and Ethel—who were only ten years older than Lawren—shared the same interest in culture. All in all, Annie's decision to send Lawren to Germany was an excellent one. The trio, who lived in the same *pension* in Berlin, got along extremely well during their time together.

In 1905, the traditional training ground for young artists in Europe was Paris, but Annie resisted this option because she hoped her brother would provide some gentle paternal guidance for her son. Berlin was an excellent choice for Lawren in another regard as well: he played the violin, and he intended to study that instrument while in Germany. His stay in Berlin unleashed his deep and abiding love of music. For Lawren, great music was a "moving and emotional experience. He went to all the great operas and concerts"[1] with the friends he made in Germany, who were mainly music students from North America.

Early twentieth-century Berlin was a much less starchy place than Toronto. Yet, compared to Paris, it seemed drab. Baudelaire once described his city as "rich in poetic and marvellous subjects. We are enveloped and steeped as though in an atmosphere of the marvellous; but we do not notice it." Sharing this outlook, Charles Huard, the French travel writer, in *Berlin comme je l'ai vu* (1907), expected a great visual spectacle when travelling on Berlin's famous street, Unter den Linden: "I anticipated an admirable avenue decorated with magnificent trees, bounded by the palace and frequented by princely carriages. To be sure, I found a large avenue, but it was planted with ordinary trees, unwelcome chestnut and linden trees, topped and stunted; unsightly hired carriages drawn by emaciated, decrepit horses . . . Dense, inelegant crowds of people halted at the intersections."[2] To be sure, some French chauvinism can be glimpsed in Huard's disappointment. Nevertheless, Berlin was shapeless and arbitrary in comparison with the dramatic vistas of Paris's boulevards, parks and monuments.

Moreover, Berlin was suffering growing pains: it had expanded from a town of 170,000 inhabitants in 1800 to a city of two million a hundred years later. To many Germans, it was a city of shabby tenements, a place of fervent materialism and a terrain that was visually and emotionally barren. "The Armies of Work," an article in the *Berliner Illustrierte Zeitung*, provides additional ammunition for seeing modern Berlin as an urban nightmare:

Day has hardly dawned, when the legions of workers from the outlying districts begin their march to the shops and factories . . . The masses make their way to the commuter stations. People, people, and more people as far as the eye can see . . . In no time at all the special trains for the workers, which only have a third class, are overfilled . . . Though the trains follow one another in short intervals, the crowding does not let up until seven in the morning. Then the huge army of white-collar workers marches out. They only have different faces and [are] better dressed, but en masse they have the same effect.[3]

For many, the overcrowded, poverty-ridden German capital became a kind of Whore Babylon in which modern man could see extremely clear reflections of his disjunction from the natural world and religious beliefs. Certainly, the city's vaudeville houses and cabarets came to be associated with louche forms of sexual expression. The decadence was palpable.

Lawren was certainly attracted to the idea of the artist as a free spirit and a bohemian, but he never partook of the aesthetic of profligacy in either his professional or his personal life. He would soon abandon Christianity, but he would remain intensely religious; he always retained a strong sense that a spiritual existence underlies all material appearances. Harris's belief in a mystical underlining to all human endeavour was one way he kept in touch with his father. As a young man, he consciously imitated his father's behaviour. Like Thomas, he was kindly, considerate, honest, above board and compassionate.

Berlin's art world was clearly divided into two camps in 1904. On one side was the Kaiser, William II, who proclaimed:

> But when art, as often happens today, shows us only misery, and shows it to us even uglier than misery is anyway, then art commits a sin against the German people. The supreme task of our cultural effort is to foster our ideals . . . That can be done only if art holds out its hand to raise the people up, instead of descending into the gutter.[4]

In contrast to the safe academic art espoused by the Kaiser was one that rigorously displayed and thus critiqued the ethical stalemate in which Germany existed.

In the spring of 1892, 106 painters and sculptors resigned from the Munich portion of the Allgemeine Deutsche Kunstgenossenschaft to form a new association, the Vereingung Bildender Künstler Münchens—the Munich Secession. Six years later, a similar group was formed in Berlin. These new associations challenged the values enshrined in the salons that produced works of art favoured by William II; the Secessionist groups wanted to concentrate their efforts on paintings and sculptures that displayed what Germany had become—not what it had been. These artists wanted to live in the present tense. However, Secessionism was not simply a movement that advocated social realism—although it most certainly did that—but one that also espoused inner spiritual values. In that sense, its impetus was derived from nineteenth-century German Romanticism as much as from 1890s Modernism.

Max Liebermann (1847–1935) was the leader of the Berlin Secession. The son of a businessman, Liebermann first studied law and philosophy at the University of Berlin, but abandoned those disciplines to become an artist. In 1872, he was in Paris, and in the Netherlands in 1876–77. He used his inherited wealth to build a collection of French Impressionist paintings. As an artist, he eventually specialized in portraits that resemble those of Édouard Manet.

At their first show, Liebermann attempted, somewhat discreetly, to highlight what the Berlin Secessionists wanted to accomplish:

> In selecting the works for our exhibition, talent alone, whatever its style, was the determinant . . . We do not believe in a single, sacred direction in art. Any work, whatever its style, that expresses feelings honestly seems to us to constitute art. Only craftsmanlike routine and the superficial production of those who regard art as a cow to be milked are excluded on principle.[5]

Art produced only to make money was categorized as unacceptable, but Liebermann was really saying that his group disdained work that reflected bourgeois values and avoided the depiction of "misery." Liebermann's own practice as an artist extended to depicting the lives of those sometimes not celebrated, such as the inhabitants of the vital Jewish section of Amsterdam.

Max Liebermann.
Jewish Quarter in
Amsterdam. 1905.

As someone in the teething phase of his career, Harris in 1904 Berlin was more concerned with learning the mechanics of his art than with analyzing the place of art in the modern world. In this respect, being in Berlin rather than Paris was not necessarily a handicap, as his training in Paris would have been almost identical to that he was receiving in Berlin. In both places, students usually spent two years drawing from casts, still lifes and models in order to acquire technical competence. Work in watercolour and oil paint usually came only after a student had achieved an acceptable level of draughtsmanship.

Morning and evening sessions in pencil, charcoal and watercolour sketching were spent in large, private studio classes. Afternoons, as Harris later recalled, were spent out of doors: "I went to the older parts of the city along the River Spree and painted houses, buildings, etc.—small water colours. Also went the rounds of the public and dealers' galleries. My whole conditioning was academic."[6] His mind swarmed with impressions of what he beheld. What might have been mistaken for physical robustness was actually an exuberant "nervous vitality."

As artists, his teachers were perfectly competent, if not overly exciting. Fritz von Wille (1860–1941) had studied at the Dusseldorf Academy from 1879 to 1882 but considered himself self-taught. He was a regionalist painter. In 1903, a reviewer said of his work: "It is not houses, not haystacks, not manure piles or similar things, nor little genre episodes that von Wille gives us in his painting, but Nature with her vastness and grandeur."[7] Adolf Schlabitz (1854–1943) studied in Berlin and at the Académie Julian in Paris. His work was strongly influenced by Impressionism. The paintings of Franz Skarbina (1849–1910) occupy the

Lawren Harris.
Street in Berlin.
Circa 1907.

middle ground between the salon and the Secessionists. During the 1880s and 1890s, his work focused on poor and working-class people.

Although he labelled himself "academic," Harris was allowing his mind to expand by reading the American Transcendental writers Ralph Waldo Emerson (1803–82) and William James (1842–1910). The young man's interest in these two writers was instigated by his uncle, who knew of the parallels between German idealist philosophy and the Americans. In Emerson especially, Harris discovered a kindred spirit, a man interested in a level of being beyond the mundane. In beautifully articulated sentences, Emerson earnestly voiced his convictions: "There is a correspondence between the human soul and everything that

Franz Skarbina. *View from a Berlin Studio Window on to a Backyard in Winter.* Circa 1895–1905.

exists in the world; more properly, everything that is known to man . . . The purpose of life seems to be to acquaint man with himself . . . The highest revelation is that God is in every man." According to Emerson, man often blinds himself to these spiritual values because he sees material existence as the only reality.[8]

At this stage in his career, Harris was absorbing a great deal. He did not know exactly what he wanted to accomplish as a painter, but he was very much immersing himself in the artistic milieu that confronted him. He may have noticed how Max Liebermann concentrated on the facades of houses and that he often chose his subjects from the poor sections of Berlin, especially the Jewish quarter.

Harris would also have seen the regionalist landscapes of Walter Leistikow (1865–1908) every time he attended an exhibition of the Berlin Secession. Indeed, it was the rejection of Leistikow's painting *Grüewaldsee* by the Grosse Berliner Kunst-Ausstellung in 1898 that had provided the catalyst for the avant-garde to form the Secession. Leistikow's contrast between the wall of dark green forest and the luminous orange light that fills the sky and invades the water is meant to stir the viewer's strong feelings in an almost nostalgic way, as if this were a landscape from a forgotten dream.

In 1906, Harris would have visited the enormous exhibition Ausstellung Deutscher Kunst aus der von Zeit 1775–1875, which included a large selection of the works of Caspar David Friedrich (1774–1840). Up until that monumental exhibition, Friedrich's reputation was not high. Harris must have been moved by a major landscape such as *Monk by the Sea* from 1810, in which

Walter Leistikow.
Grüewaldsee.
Circa 1895–1905.

Caspar David
Friedrich. *The
Monk by the Sea.*
1808–10.

the tiny figure is overshadowed by the unknowable and mysterious ocean. That juxtaposition of the paltry human figure and the power of nature more than hints at the sublime.

Harris's sensibility was being exposed to a wide variety of art. The great Norwegian painter Edvard Munch (1863–1944) lived in Berlin from 1902 to 1908 and frequently exhibited with the Secession. The young Canadian may also have seen the mystically inclined landscapes of the Swiss painter Ferdinand Hodler

Ferdinand Hodler.
Der Niesen. 1910.

(1853–1918). Moreover, Harris had ample means to visit Paris, where he looked at canvases by Van Gogh and Gauguin, artists he fervently admired.

In the summer of 1905, Harris returned to Canada, but he was back in Berlin by the autumn. The next summer he did not return to Canada but went on a walking and sketching tour in the Austrian Tyrol with Adolf Schlabitz and had his first experience of Alpine climbing near Brixlegg in Austria. The following year he took another walking tour with Schlabitz, during which he met the poet, philosopher and regionalist painter Paul Thiem (1885–1922), whose nonconformist ideas deeply impressed him.

Harris described his encounter with Thiem as "shocking and stirring." He was not really talking about the German artist's paintings so much as a conversation that introduced him directly to theosophical beliefs. The likelihood is that Thiem, who may have been a theosophist, told Harris about the German section of that movement. Of course, Harris, whose religious education had been largely traditional, was aware of conjectures about the transcendental from reading Emerson and James. Thiem may

Lawren Harris.
*Buildings on the
River Spree.* 1907.

have made him aware that a form of religious belief could be elucidated from such speculations.

In the career of most artists, there is a treacherous in-between time when a significant gap exists between what the artist wants to do and what he can actually accomplish. This phenomenon is clearly discernible in Harris's early work.

The sombre watercolour *Interior with a Clothes Closet* (1906) probably depicts Harris's own bedroom in Berlin. With this subject, a stock item in the repertoire of young artists at the time, Harris is obviously showing off what he has learned. A winter cape, starched shirt collars, and some sketches or watercolours occupy the left-hand side of the closet. The Secession's interest in the mundane and the ordinary is reflected in this composition, in which the apprentice painter shows a special aptitude for distinguishing between shiny and dull surfaces.

Buildings on the River Spree (1907) may mirror the Secession's preoccupations, but its strength lies in the careful layering of restrained colours in three buildings of contrasting heights, and its emphasis on forcing the viewer's eye to confront the flatness in the resultant picture plane.

Harris's first surviving works amply demonstrate how much he had learned during his time in Germany. He had mastered many facets of his chosen profession. His hand was steady, his eye accurate. He had been exposed to a wide variety of isms in modern art—so many that he had trouble knowing in what direction he wanted to venture. If Harris had been trained in France, his colour palette might have extended far wider. He would later exploit that seeming fault with a preference for restrained, sombre colours.

When he returned to Canada, Harris would paint many street scenes in Toronto and, later, Halifax. As a child, he and Billy Davison had made drawings of all the houses in their neighbourhood in Brantford, so this was clearly a natural preoccupation. It would thus be a mistake to view the urban images of the 1910s and 1920s as mere academic exercises continuing Harris's training in Berlin. And this would also miss the crucial point that the artists Harris was imitating were genuine Secessionists, breaking away from prevailing bourgeois values. In following their lead, he too was critiquing the prevailing social values of members of his own class. In this important aspect of his career, Harris was decidedly a rebel.

From his time in Germany, he also imbibed the notion that the creation of a distinctively national art was a vital project. In France, he might not have been so strongly exposed to such an idea. Moreover, in Germany, Harris was made to understand, through the work of artists such as Friedrich, Hodler and Leistikow, that landscapes can be infused with the kind of spiritual meanings he had discussed with Thiem and read about in Emerson.

Upon finishing his training, Harris was inclined to wander. He likely returned to Canada at the end of the summer of 1907. By late November, however, he was in Damascus with the Canadian popular writer Norman Duncan (1871–1916), who had been born in Norwich, Ontario. As a roving correspondent, Duncan had been commissioned by *Harper's Monthly Magazine* to write a series of eight travel articles about the Middle East (Harper & Brothers of New York would issue this material as a book, *Going Down from Jerusalem*, in 1909). His new friend asked Harris to provide illustrations to accompany the articles and book. The young artist was delighted to accept, and remained in the Middle East until at least February 1908, when he returned home.

Harris had met Duncan in the summer of 1907 in Italy. The connection was strengthened by the fact that Duncan, in his high school years, had worked for the *Brantford Beacon*. Later, he attended the University of Toronto, where he may have known William Stewart, Lawren's uncle, who was four years younger than himself. Duncan, who left the University of Toronto without taking a degree, had been a friend there of William Lyon Mackenzie King, the future prime minister of Canada.

From 1897 to 1901, Duncan was a reporter for the *New York Evening Post*. He also taught at Washington and Jefferson College in Washington, Pennsylvania, and at the University of Kansas. His real career, however, was in his adventure books, which included *The Way of the Sea* (1903), *The Adventures of Billy Topsail* (1906) and *The Cruise of the Shining Light* (1907).

In the autumn of 1907, the two friends met in Damascus and then went on to Jerusalem to assemble their caravan: twenty-five camels, a dozen camel drivers and supplies for a two-month journey southwest to Cairo. In his description of their adventures, Duncan provides an account of twenty-two-year-old Harris as a self-assured, fun-loving young man, whom he calls *Khawaja*:

> "Catch me!" shouted the younger *Khawaja*. Here was a familiar game; the challenge, though spoken in English, needed no interpretation. They reached to seize him; but the younger *Khawaja* leaped from the quick hands of the muleteer, dodged the catspring of the Sudanese, buffeted [Towfic] Aboosh, overturned the Bedouin, and darted off into the moonlight with a whoop like a shriek of a disappearing locomotive. They were after him in a flash.[9]

The self-confidence that Harris had gained in Berlin had found an outlet. If he was ever a retiring, uncertain young man, he had now shed those sides of his personality. He was self-assured, charming and, when he was in the mood, playful. When Duncan, Harris and their entourage made their crossing from Palestine into Egypt, "all at once, the younger *Khawaja* spurred his horse to a gallop; and the whole caravan, with much shouting and noise of bells, clattered down the hill at a furious pace and crossed the boundary."[10]

Harris could also be insensitive. There was an incident where he insisted that a man who had called him "a Christian lout" be handed over to the authorities. When Duncan protested, Harris stood firm. Duncan remarked, with a great deal of sarcasm, that the man's crime had been "the unpardonable offence of lifting a hand against the Anglo-Saxon . . . in an eastern land occupied by the English."[11] What is surprising about the anecdote is that such colonial attitudes were largely absent from Harris's makeup. In fact, his social conscience was, and would remain, highly developed. In Damascus, Harris returned one day to where he and Duncan were lodging. "The young *Khawaja* burst in, as though escaping pursuit, his eyes at the widest, his cap askew on the back of his head, his cane waving in a frenzy of emotion." Harris was distraught: "'I tell you it was fearful—terrible—horrible!'" The

Lawren Harris. "Over the Old Route into Egypt" (book illustration) from Norman Duncan, *Going Down to Jerusalem* (1909).

young man had been distressed to see a blind man reduced to tending a furnace in the city bath.

Later, Lawren formed a friendship with the head camel driver, Aboosh, a young Arab from Mesopotamia. Harris wrote Annie telling her that he wished to bring the young man back to Canada with him and send him to college. He added that Aboosh was much too intelligent to remain a mere camel driver. Annie reminded him of their family pact: he could do anything he wished as long as he accepted responsibility.

This experiment in international relations turned out to be a dismal failure: Aboosh, who could not adapt to life in the New World, cheated and stole, and was soon expelled from the college.[12]

Years later, Harris would scoff at the work he did for *Harper's* ("the world's worst"), but he was not being completely fair to himself. The fifty-nine illustrations for the magazine articles (only a selection of which were used in the book) give even more convincing evidence than his early sketches and watercolours of just how wide-ranging were Harris's abilities in the use of light and shade and how effective he was as a portraitist. The contrast between the mauve sky and the pinks and sand tones of the desert is effectively rendered in "Over the Old Route into Egypt"; the two camel drivers and their mounts are very much in the spirit of Howard Pyle (1853–1911), the doyen of the stable of illustrators employed by *Harper's*.

Harris's time in Berlin had been well spent. Although considerably more worldly than when he had arrived, he had still not identified his artistic personality, that special something that distinguishes the competent from the good and the great. One thing he did know, though: de Lury had been correct in his estimate of him. He was a born artist.

4

SPIRITUAL
REALITIES

(1909–1910)

He was glad to be back home in Canada, but Lawren was grow-
ing ever more aware that he did not know how to focus his train-
ing as an artist. He was not completely lost, but he remained
deeply uncertain of what the future held.

He had acquired a public manner, one that concealed the
inner man. He had a broad smile, a warm handshake; he spoke
much more confidently than he felt. On the outside, he remained
a wealthy young man who could mix freely in the highest echelons
of Toronto society; on the inside, he was beginning to think of his
destiny in spiritual terms. As one friend later remarked: "He was
not in on the game of empire-building and money making, and
had no reason for joining it."[1] Lawren was now entranced with
mountain climbing, "never losing the urge to get to the top of
everything," and yet he was unsure of who he wanted to become.

Y EARS LATER, discussing his first sketches and paintings
after his return to Canada in 1908, Harris pasted over his
initial reaction to being back home: "When I returned
from Germany and commenced to paint in Canada my whole

interest was in the Canadian scene. It was, in truth, as though I had never been to Europe. Any paintings, drawings or sketches I saw with a Canadian tang excited me more than anything I had seen in Europe."² These claims are not only inaccurate but also tinged with myth making, an activity in which he sometimes later engaged in order to bolster the status of Canadian art and his place within it. The sad truth was that Harris was cut off from a great deal. In Berlin, it may have been true that the German artists with whom he was involved were making their marks in relative isolation. However, in that city, as well as in Paris and London, he had had the opportunity to see a great deal of cutting-edge, truly experimental art.

In Germany, Expressionism was just beginning to emerge. This angular, distorted and violently emotional art, exemplified in the work of Ernst Ludwig Kirchner (1880–1938) and his depiction of women, was the Teutonic equivalent of Cubism, the abstract art form with which Picasso and Braque were still experimenting. In 1910, the first Post-Impressionist Exhibition was held in London. That same year, Gaudí's extravagant, flowing apartment complex Casa Milà was completed in Barcelona. The Blaue Reiter group was founded in Munich in 1911. Although he did not publish *On the Spiritual in Art* until 1912, Wassily Kandinsky by 1910 had reached the point of pure abstraction.

In comparison, Canadian art seemed provincial and backward looking, responding tamely to the Modernisms being unleashed in Europe. In terms of the marketplace, it behooved young artists to recognize that the prominent collectors in Toronto and Montreal favoured pastoral landscapes in the style of the Hague School, sometimes facetiously referred to as the Grey School because of its penchant for sombre colours.

Like Harris, Edmund Morris (1871–1913) was independently wealthy. He was born in Perth, Ontario, moved to Fort Garry (Winnipeg) when his father became lieutenant-governor of Manitoba, and then to Toronto, where he studied painting. He later studied at the Art Students' League in New York City and at the Académie Julian. As a young man, he tended to work in Holland during the summers. Particularly successful in evoking the elemental forces in nature, he was also adept in his use of reds and blue-blacks to infuse his landscapes with a poignant melancholia.

Curtis Williamson (1867–1944) was born in Brampton, Ontario, and studied in Toronto before going briefly to the Julian. He worked mainly in the village of Barbizon for almost three years after leaving Paris. When it was first shown, *Fish Sheds, Newfoundland* (1908) was seen as startling: it is free of anecdotal detail and integrates its various passages (boat, earth, sky and sheds) in an unsentimental, understated manner.

In 1907, Williamson and Morris, dissatisfied with the stodgy, academic painting of most of their contemporaries, were among those who formed the Canadian Art Club, a private exhibiting society supported by lay members. Professional memberships were by invitation. Most of the members recruited from Ontario resigned from the Ontario Society of Artists (founded in 1872), which was seen as a bastion of conservatism.

The career of James Morrice (1865–1924) followed a different trajectory. The Montreal-born painter produced most of his work outside Canada, and he had a fierce loyalty to French Modernism. In 1910, he wrote to Morris about Cézanne: "His is the savage work that one would expect to come from America—but it is always France that produces anything emphatic in art."[3]

Harris, who desperately wanted to produce "emphatic" art, was inclined not to abandon Canada. Throughout his career, he championed the idea of his native land as a nation that could produce great art. He possessed the conviction that he would find his true self in such a pursuit. He also saw himself as patrician—a person upon whom money and social standing had been bestowed, and who therefore had an obligation to show others the correct path. If others got in his way, he would debate them. Sometimes, as an older man, he would become autocratic, the refuge he resorted to when his sense of entitlement was challenged.

His decision to focus much of his time on landscape painting has to be seen in the context of how a young artist in early twentieth-century Canada could envision making his mark. Until the end of the nineteenth century, history painting was hailed as the most significant genre in Europe and North America. In Canada, the shift towards the landscape genre had been firmly established by the early twentieth century.

In theory, a great artist was a person who could portray accurately and incisively the look of his native land. Such a person did not necessarily attempt to overlook such issues as the existence of the Aboriginal peoples or to evade social responsibility by concentrating on picturesque or sublime views. Rather, landscape was the genre in which to make one's mark. As a calling, this was a demonstration of oneness with the spirit of the entire land. There was a crucial patriotic dimension: to be a proper country, a nation needed to have its own distinct landscape, and it required painters to enshrine it.

There was another key factor. To venture into the land, particularly its wilderness, demanded a certain kind of man. Such a person was strong, determined and virile. In Canadian landscape painting, a correlation is frequently established between manliness and the ability to render the landscape effectively.

In Harris's case, there was an added complexity: he chose at the outset of his career to try to establish himself as a landscape artist *at the very same time* as he was depicting the plight of the underclass. This was an ambitious project, demonstrating that he had both a social conscience and a nationalistic agenda. This dual purpose was unusual at the time. Urban landscapes in the Berlin Secessionist tradition are concerned with the plight of the underclass; in the early twentieth century, many German landscape artists were attempting to enshrine the appearance of their nation. But for a single artist to deal with both things was daring.

Well aware of these issues, Harris was also of the opinion that an artist in the 1910s had to find a distinctive Modernistic style in which to encapsulate landscape and urban views. By any standard, this was a daunting enterprise, one with which Harris would grapple for many years. Certain of his vocation, though, he was willing to undergo yet another rigorous apprenticeship.

As he wrestled with the direction to take in his work, Harris rented a studio over Giles' Grocery Store on Yonge Street near Cumberland Avenue. However, still living the life of a young man of means, he frequently left these modest quarters to attend Albert Edison Austin's strawberry teas on the terrace of Spadina, the splendid mid-Victorian mansion set on the hilltop above the corner of Spadina Avenue and Davenport Road.

This house had been built in 1836 by William Warren Baldwin, who called it Spadina, a name derived from the Aboriginal word *espadining*, "a sudden rise of land." In 1866, James Austin, the founder of the Dominion Bank and Consumers Gas, purchased the property, which covered eighty acres. He sold off forty acres in 1889, and three years later he turned over the house and twenty acres to his son, Austin William Austin. Immediately east stood Ardwold, the Italianate palace and estate of the department store magnate Sir John Craig Eaton. Just around the corner, on the lot adjacent to Spadina, Major-General Sir Henry Mill Pellatt would construct the castle-like Casa Loma in 1911.

Lady Eaton remembered the Austins as "friendly, open-handed hosts, of the type who would never let any disparity in age stand in the way of friendship . . . Mrs. Austin was one of the leading hostesses in Toronto's music circles . . . she entertained visiting artists. Just before Christmas she always gave a party for the young people of their connection and acquaintance."4

Lawren's friend Albert Edison Austin was three years younger. Together with his father, Austin competed in golf at the 1904 Summer Olympics in St. Louis, Missouri. Another frequent visitor to Spadina was Vincent Massey, Harris's former schoolmate at St. Andrew's. And it was probably at Spadina that Lawren met Beatrice Phillips (1885–1962), always called Trixie. The couple married on January 20, 1910.

Trixie's father, Francis (Frank) John Phillips (1847–1910), was a self-made millionaire. Born in Kinneigh Parish in County Cork, Ireland, he immigrated to Canada in 1856 and settled in Kingston, Ontario, but by 1864 he had moved to Toronto, where he worked for John McGee, an iron founder. Frank's wife, Annie, née Bacon, was born in Brockville, Ontario, and married Phillips, on August 20, 1872. The couple had eight children: six girls and two boys.

In partnership with John Bacon, his father-in-law, Phillips purchased Hurd Leigh Company, a crockery and china business. The firm's name was changed in 1876 to Phillips Thorne and Company when John Bacon retired and C.E. Thorne became a partner. The firm, located at 23 Front Street in Toronto, mainly imported fine china.

This arrangement lasted only two years, and then Phillips became manager of C.G. Cobban Company, which became Cobban Manufacturing Company in 1880. By 1893, Phillips was president. The company manufactured, among other things, picture frames, plate glass, mouldings and curtain poles; they also imported plate glass and picture glass from Belgium and England. The company moved to Lake Street in 1901. During the great Toronto fire of 1904, Phillips and a worker ran from woodpile to woodpile with a garden hose to keep the timber free of the flames.

When Lawren and Trixie married, the firm was at 258 Carlaw Avenue. The Phillipses lived at 63 Queen's Park Crescent, an imposing Romanesque Revival mansion a short distance from the Ontario Legislature. They also owned Wistowe, a ten-acre island on Lake Rosseau in the Muskoka lakes.

To the Phillips family, Lawren was an anomaly. They always referred to him as "the Artist." This nickname was not meant in a derogatory sense but reflected the Phillipses' perception of him as someone essentially different from themselves. They also overlooked his Presbyterian-Baptist background. The Anglican Church of the Redeemer, site of the Harris–Phillips wedding, was the preferred place of worship for many members of Toronto high society. Upon their return from their honeymoon, the couple lived on Balmoral Avenue.

In a photograph from this time, Trixie looks a bit uncertainly, shyly, at the viewer. Like her husband, Trixie had been born to a life of privilege. Unlike Lawren, though, she had no interest in the world of art. To everyone who knew her, she was a conventional woman of her time, and a person used to everything that money could purchase. In 1910, Harris himself had a very conformist side, even though he was well aware that many artists lived turbulent, hand-to-mouth existences.

He was also—and would remain much of the time—a reserved person. He was comradely, incredibly charming, and pleasant. He could assume public roles easily, but he always held something back. He was never cold, but he often looked at the world from a distance, a character trait that finds its way into some of his best paintings.

Trixie and Lawren shared similar attitudes towards sexuality, which they perceived as a necessary aspect of human life but not a central one. As for many people of their generation, sexual activity in marriage produced children but had no further utility. Throughout his life, Harris remained aloof from any discussions of the body; for example, he did not like pictures displaying the nude. He always retained a remote stance in the face of what he considered outlandish, self-aggrandizing personal behaviour; in this regard he upheld his Baptist ancestry. At the time of his marriage, Harris thought he could somehow blend the life of the socialite with the life of the artist.

Trixie Phillips.

On the very morning he wed, Harris gave his mother in marriage to the wealthy American widower Edward V. Raynolds, her long-time suitor. That marriage was cut short by Raynolds's death five days later in New York City—the second time Annie had lost a spouse in that city.

Annie had remained an independent thinker. Her brother-in-law, Elmore, was pastor of the Walmer Road Baptist Church; one of her sisters was married to William Wallace, the minister at the Bloor Street Presbyterian Church. Rather than seeking solace in either of these congregations, however, Annie became a Christian Scientist, inspired in part by the fact that the Church's founder,

Mary Baker Eddy, was a woman. More significantly, during her husband's protracted illness, Eddy had lost confidence in traditional medicine. For Annie, these words of Eddy's rang true:

> It is plain that God does not employ drugs or hygiene, nor provide them for human use; else Jesus would have recommended and employed them in his healing ... The tender word and Christian encouragement of an invalid, pitiful patience with his fears and the removal of them, are better than hecatombs of gushing theories, stereotyped borrowed speeches, and the doling of arguments, which are but so many parodies on legitimate Christian Science, aflame with divine Love.

Such a move on Annie's part was a rejection of the religious doctrines she had known since childhood, but more importantly, it signified that she was determined to make her own destiny. In this regard, Lawren was similarly inclined.

Her new beliefs completely engaged Annie. The headquarters of her newly adopted church were at 196 St. George Street, a short walk from her home. She helped fellow members of her congregation by "thinking" about them—and praying for them. She sang in church, where she also played the piano and the organ. She was a lay reader and, for a time, in charge of the Sunday school. She was generous with her wealth, helping the poor and, from time to time, her friends. In the few spare hours at her disposal, she painted original flower designs onto pieces of china, which were bestowed on relatives and friends on their birthdays.

Three children were born to Lawren and Trixie in the first decade of their marriage: Lawren Phillips on October 10, 1910; Margaret Anne (Peggie) on December 12, 1913; and Howard Kilborne (Howie) in 1919. Her children would remember Trixie as a devoted parent, but she also wanted them to conform to her expectations as a woman whose life was ruled by the social class into which she had been born. As a parent, she wanted conformity; she never encouraged individuality. If Lawren's own mother had a marked stubborn, rebellious streak, such inclinations were entirely absent in his wife.

(left)
Lawren P. Harris
(Lornie), four
years old, Trixie
and Margaret
Knox (Peggie),
one year old.
Photograph taken
November 1914.

(right)
Lawren P. and
Peggie Harris with
Nanny Stevenson.

From 1908 to 1910, Harris tried to refocus his work in two directions. Very much in the manner of Skarbina and, especially, Liebermann, he made cityscapes that attempted to show urban social conditions in a realistic light. He also participated in sketching trips to look at the landscape of Canada. In 1908 he sketched in the Laurentians with Hamilton-born Fergus Kyle (*c.* 1846–1941). The following spring he went with J.W. Beatty (1869–1941) to Haliburton, Ontario. That autumn he was at Lake Memphremagog in Quebec's Eastern Townships, again with Beatty. Harris's practice was to sketch a subject on wood or fibreboard panels measuring about 21.5 by 25.6 centimetres or to make a similarly sized sketch in oils; later, in the studio, some of these sketches would be worked into full-size canvases.*

The working of the view in *Autumn Trees*, likely done in the Laurentians, is vigorous and straightforward. Like many early twentieth-century German painters, Harris is working in the

---

* Harris always favoured working in oils as opposed to watercolours. In a letter to the artist Carl Schaefer of August 15, 1936, he explained why: "Each medium has its own virtue but oils seem capable of a deeper, a profounder and a more exhaustive expression . . . oils call out deeper resources." LAC.

Lawren Harris.
Laurentian Farm.
Circa 1908.

Heimatkünstler tradition, whereby a painter chose a particular region to explore. The barn in *Laurentian Farm* seems unduly ordinary at first glance, but the painter forces the viewer to analyze its character. Is it a simple building or does it have a hint of a personality?

Harris's next major painting trip was in January and February 1909 to lumber camps in northern Minnesota. Harris went there with Norman Duncan on the same terms as in the Middle East: Duncan wrote, Harris illustrated. This place, he later told a friend, "was one of the most primitive of its kind on the continent. He saw life as it is in the raw with women, bar-rooms and shanties. The lumberjacks went to sleep with a shot of dope in their whisky and piled like cordwood in the shed after their pay had been extracted from their pockets."

This journey allowed Harris to see northern winter landscapes in their full vigour and austerity. Overall, Lawren felt that this "experience finished off his education."[5] At that time, Harris remained naive about the underclass. *The Return from Town* (1911) may have come directly from his experience in Minnesota.

Lawren Harris.
Little House.
Circa 1911.

"In this picture," he wrote, "I have sought to contrast a party of tipsy lumbermen returning, intoxicated and hilarious, to their lumber camp, as against the still dignity, the high solemnity of the forest through which they are passing. I have attempted to bring out the dignity of nature as against the—less worthy qualities in human nature."[6] For Harris, art always retained a strong didactic purpose.

Lawren Harris.
House in Toronto.
Circa 1908.

The impact of returning to Canada may have been "terrific," but it was also traumatic. He had been immersed in Europe. "He spoke, thought and even dreamed in German." He became aware that he now saw Canada with new eyes; he was "transported too into a whole new experience."[7] He likely destroyed many of his early Canadian landscapes because he did not feel they lived up to his expectations. At the outset of his career, Harris was much more assured in his urban views than in his landscapes. There are a number of urban scenes from 1909–10 with which he was pleased.

Very much following the leads he had been given in Germany, Harris began to look closely at downtrodden Toronto neighbourhoods. These are strong, poignant images. The facades in *Houses, Richmond Street* (1911) are placed in the picture area to confront the viewer directly. No overt political point *seems* to be being made, but these habitations have a solemn, austere beauty that transcends their environment. These views are restful, tranquil and inviting. In this canvas, the trees seem joined to the houses. Nature can place man at a distance, but it will, under certain circumstances, blend into human existence. The back view

Lawren Harris.
*Top of the Hill,
Spadina Avenue.*
1909–11.

of *Little House* reveals a structure that seems extremely vulnerable, exposed mercilessly from behind.

Top of the Hill, Spadina Avenue (1909–1911), done in deliberately drab colours—brown and grey—shows the slum habitations of the very poor. The composition is a strong one. In the right foreground, the rectangular building shown in three-quarters view is echoed in the small building, the back of which is seen in the receding plane on the left. The ground between the two houses is a wasteland of upturned earth.

The direct social commentary of this image (as opposed to the more subdued reflections in *Old Houses* and *Houses*) is reinforced by the title, because most of the Spadina hilltop was occupied by the homes of the fabulously rich. Also, Harris goes out of his way to show the outbuilding and almost fortress-like structure of the building in the foreground. He is inscribing a glaring, sobering reality: there, at the top of Spadina Avenue, are the grandiose, splendiferous mansions of the rich, and there are also the shabby dwellings of the poor.

Harris's new, ironical eye may have been inspired in part by "The Homes of Working Men" by Augustus Bridle (1868–1952), published in the *Canadian Magazine* in November 1903. In November 1909 Harris had joined the Arts and Letters Club of Toronto, of which Bridle was a founder. This 1903 article, accompanied by photographs, categorized the various kinds of row housing in Toronto. One photo shows, for example, "The Tough-Cast, Two-Story House, Emblematic of the Second Lowest Grade."

Bridle, an illegitimate child and orphan born in East Stour, Dorsetshire, became a ward of the National Children's Home in London and was sent to Hamilton, Ontario, when he was ten years old. He evidently worked with a shoemaker in Merlin, Ontario, before moving to a farm in 1882. He obtained a teacher's certificate in 1887 and taught in several places, but by 1903 he had become a newspaperman. By 1908, he was associate editor of the weekly *Canadian Courier*.

That year, he, together with the artist Charles Jefferys, was one of the moving forces behind the formation of the Arts and Letters Club, an organization that sought "absolute escape" from a "consumingly commercial" urban existence. This group began with eight men who lunched together and called themselves the Slanderbund.

Harris joined the club "because it afforded the meeting and stimulus of workers in all the arts—this was most marked in its early days in Court House quarters, Adelaide St. East." The group was devoted to championing all the arts—literature, architecture, music, painting, sculpture and theatre—in a Toronto they found wanting in appreciation of the finer things in life. At first mainly a luncheon club, it sought to be a "comradely haven for kindred souls." The permanent headquarters in 1909 was at 36½ King Street East, above the Betty Brown Restaurant. However, the group was soon evicted, and when Harris joined, it was on the second floor of 57 Adelaide Street East, the courthouse of the County of York.

As Harris was later to discover, the club had two distinct constituencies: one Modernist and forward looking, the other decidedly reactionary. As a whole, the members saw themselves as an Anglo-Saxon elite that welcomed poets including the English-man Rupert Brooke and politicians such as Sir Wilfrid Laurier. Bridle may have been taken aback by Harris's wealth, but he recognized in him an "exuberantly democratic radical."[8] Harris entered fully into the club's activities. He drew the cover illus-tration for the first issue of *The Lamps*, the club's magazine, and wrote reviews of exhibitions. He played the violin in the club's orchestra and designed theatre sets for Roy Mitchell (1884–1944), another early member.

One year older than Harris, Mitchell had been born in Fort Gratiot, Michigan, to Canadian parents. The family returned to Canada when Mitchell was two and had settled in Toronto by 1889, where he attended the University of Toronto. Even before he graduated in 1906, he had developed a strong interest in mys-ticism and comparative religion. He joined the Toronto Theo-sophical Society three years after graduating.

Mitchell had a strong bohemian streak and an equally strong interest in theatre. He may have worked as a journalist, but his mind and time were completely taken up with putting on plays, something he fostered at the Arts and Letters Club. His first production, on December 10, 1910, was *Enoch Arden*, which he called a "Tennyson–Strauss melodrama."

Mitchell would have made Harris aware of his basic philoso-phy:

All art deals with relations. A painting, for example, is never of something, but of the relation of the parts of something; as of tree-fibre to tree-fibre, of muscle to muscle, of figure to earth and earth to figure, of cloud to sky or sky to sea or of bending tree to bending tree, bound together by their obedi-ence to the same wind, itself invisible. The overword of an art is "together."[9]

Mitchell also insisted:

With motion for our central fact and the realization firmly
in mind that the visible forms of it are only the external manifestations of an interior and far more potent motion, our theatre can put less stress on mimicry and can begin definitely to
create.[10]

Mitchell's theosophy is clearly reflected in his insistence on
making a corollary between outer and inner realities. Harris would
come to the strong conviction that what is seen in a landscape
painting must encompass an unseen, inner reality. In Harris's later
willingness to make many of his major paintings look like stage
sets, he may well have been influenced by Mitchell, in that the dra-
maturge taught his artist friend how objects placed in a rectangular
format can be given strong, additional meaning if their "together-
ness" to each other is accentuated and properly lighted.[11]

Another close theatre friend and Arts and Letters member
was Merrill Denison (1893–1975), whose *Brothers in Arms* stirred
Harris. Denison's mother, Flora, a suffragist and theosophist, was
one of the funders of the Walt Whitman Society of Canada. In
1910 she purchased the Bon Echo Inn on Mazinaw Lake, north of
Belleville, Ontario, as "a gathering place for artists, thinkers and
writers, all under the northern lights beside" the great cliffs there.

Trained as an architect in Canada, the United States and
France, Denison returned to Canada as art director of the Hart
House Theatre. *Brothers in Arms* was written at the instigation
of Mitchell and first performed at the Hart House Theatre in
April 1921. This play satirizes the attitudes of two individuals, a
wealthy businessman and a backwoodsman, towards an area that
was based on the country near Bon Echo. Harris called this area
"that tired, sparse strip of land that lies between the healthy farming country and the vast northern woods, a country of silent, drab
sawmills, rotting lumber camps, stones, stumps, scrub growth
and lonely rampikes." He praised Denison as the first Canadian
dramatist willing to tackle "authentic, indigenous" issues.

In encounters at the Arts and Letters Club, Harris may have
found a refuge from the workaday world of Toronto. In 1910, he

began discussing theosophy in earnest with Roy Mitchell. These talks must have reminded him of his chats on similar subjects with Paul Thiem three years earlier. At first, Harris was cautious about this newfangled metaphysical doctrine, but, like his mother, he had a marked propensity for religious unorthodoxy. He would not formally join the Toronto Theosophical Society until 1923, but he was immersed in its doctrines well before that.

Theosophy was written about extensively by its founder, Helena Blavatsky (1831–91), a charismatic and unconventional woman of mixed Russian and German descent. Her two major works are *Isis Unveiled* (1877) and *The Secret Doctrine* (1888), often considered her magnum opus. With Henry Steel Olcott (1832–1907) and William Quan Judge (1851–96), she founded the Theosophical Society in 1875 in New York City with the motto: "There is no Religion higher than Truth." In 1878, the Society moved to Bombay and eventually settled in Adyar, a suburb of Madras.

Theosophy had three declared objectives: to form a nucleus of the Universal Brotherhood of Humanity, without regard to race, creed, sex, caste or colour; to encourage the study of comparative religion, philosophy and science; and to investigate the unexplained laws of Nature and the powers latent in man.

Theosophy claimed that the "truth" had been bestowed on mankind from the outset of its existence but that "materialism" had succeeded in separating humanity from that reality. The "white ray of pure truth" had been refracted into various religions and philosophical systems. Thus, the aim of theosophy was to reconstitute those lost, essential verities.

The physical world, according to this doctrine, is in fact dense spiritual energy. It is the first of seven supersensory planes of cosmic reality, but it is the lowest level of perception and provides only a superficial view of reality. However, there is a "Oneness" to the universe that can eventually be uncovered.

For theosophists, strong connections exist between Nature (as experienced by man) and Divine Nature. The word *theosophy* means "god-wisdom," and that was Blavatsky's point: modern man often cuts off his nature from Divine Nature because he does not realize that he is part of a slowly unfolding divine vision. As a religion, theosophy existed to encourage discussion of this central fact of life, which is shrouded in secrecy because man has lost touch with essential truths.

There is one underlying, unconditional, indivisible reality, which is variously referred as "the Absolute," "the unknown Root" and "the One Reality." In its view of human history, theosophy maintains that there is also the law of periodicity, of flux and reflux. Human beings are subject to this ebb and flow, but there always remains "the One Reality."

There is another major axiom: there exists a fundamental identity of all souls with the Universal Over-Soul; there is an ensuing obligatory pilgrimage of every soul to move into a cycle of incarnation. Theosophy sees anticipations of its doctrines in many earlier philosophical systems: Plato, Plotinus, Cornelius Agrippa, Paracelsus and Robert Fludd, to name a few.

Unlike Christian Science, with its many adherences to traditional Western religious beliefs, theosophy is more a religious philosophy than a religious sect. Theosophy is practised when members gather together to discuss its doctrines and to share their individual attempts at coming to grips with the One Reality underlying all experience.

Harris felt that theosophy was a more successful system of belief than Christian Science: "Physical health *is* an effect of thought but [also] of right emotion, just as much as right thought—and I am not at all convinced that Christian Science has the answer to that." To him, the philosophical basis of theosophy was "finer . . . much broader and more embracing—it answers my *inner* questions with a more satisfying sweep and grandeur that thrills something inside me."[12]

In her widely read and thus influential *Mysticism: A Study of the Nature and Development of Man's Spiritual Consciousness* (1911), Evelyn Underhill claimed: "The greater the artist is, the wider and deeper is the range of his pure sensation: the more sharply he is aware of the torrent of life and loveliness, the rich profusion of possible beauties and shapes. He always wants to press deeper and deeper . . . He is always tending, in fact, to pass over from the artistic to the mystical state." This stirring passage captures precisely the feelings that Harris as a young man wanted to capture in his art. He desired to "press deeper and deeper," and his early flirtation with theosophy opened up a possible way to animate both his art and his life in ways that "thrilled" him.

In order to accomplish what he sought, Harris would have to allow his human nature to be emotionally transformed; in order to enter into the mystical state promised by theosophy, he would have to abandon himself. In particular, he would have to learn the language and grammar of surrender.[*]

In their book *Thought Forms* (1905), Annie Besant and C.W. Leadbetter had provided what could be called a theosophical artist's manual. They argued that everything in existence in the physical world emanates vibrations possessing both colour and form, which are objective truths. They even provided a chart of symbolic colours and referred to actual thought forms painted by artists under the direction of clairvoyants.

Harris never applied theosophical aesthetics slavishly, but he believed for a long time that an artist could harness these insights and, in the process, produce not only work that spoke the Truth but also art that released that Truth in ways closed off to those who were not enlightened. For him, religious enlightenment and Modernist expression could thus be conjoined. He always saw the artist as a visionary compelled to share his insights with others in order to better their lives.

Theosophical texts also maintained that there had been at the beginning of time a single race of human beings, Aryans, who

---

[*] Towards the end of his life, Harris attempted to place in perspective the influence of theosophy on his art. He may have been deeply influenced by that movement, but, his wife Bess told Dennis Reid, he "believes it fair (or true) to say that he did not paint from any such point of view—or to put it another way—he did not teach Theosophy in his work. He also states that his endeavour was to imbibe the *spirit* of the ancient eastern wisdom, and then to imbue his own work and life as he went along with the feeling and thought which to some extent was the outcome of his endeavour." Bess Harris to Dennis Reid, October 25, 1968. ANG.

inhabited the northern parts of the world. Here, the physical and spiritual dimensions were at one. Then a large portion of the Aryans left their homeland, migrated elsewhere and became materialistic. This profound disjunction between the material and the spiritual would be remedied only once a strong wave of spiritual energy from the North penetrated the entire planet and collapsed the barriers between material and spiritual.

This theory of history privileges the North as a source of spiritual enlightenment. At the same time, theosophy promotes universal brotherhood, an aspect that Harris tended to downplay because his new-found religious beliefs were allied to his ideas about nationalism. For him, Canada's North was a uniquely sublime place to be exploited in art.*

In 1910, there remained a deep divide in Harris. He was conscious of having taken steps—however tentative—towards using Canada as a setting for his art. His first landscapes were not promising; his first urban scenes suggested some of the directions he wanted to explore. In addition to his desire to find an appropriate Modernistic form of expression was his new-found interest in theosophy. He wanted his canvases to be alive with spiritual meaning.

He was living on Balmoral Avenue, very close to wealthy Rosedale, while at the same time spending a great deal of time in the neighbourhoods of the poor, which he saw as the raw material for his art. As a well-to-do resident of Toronto, he was welcome at the best homes, including Spadina, but he was creating paintings of urban misery such as *Top of the Hill, Spadina Avenue*. Very much his own man, Harris was capable of inhabiting both worlds.

---

* Larisey makes a number of significant observations on this issue: "The word 'race,' since the Hitler era, all but disappeared from expressions of nationalism and from writing about art and culture. But Harris, writing in the 1920s when the notion of race was widespread, showed himself a child of his time." In particular, he "would also have been familiar with the concept of a Canadian race expressed in the popular traditions of Canadian nationalism dating from the time of Confederation . . . The concept of race was also important to the theosophists, who believed that humanity as a whole was evolving towards a higher type of race." (60–61)

5
NEW
ADVENTURES

(1911–1914)

Lawren was getting to know himself better. He had glimpsed intimations of immortality in theosophy. He was gradually set-tling into life in Toronto. He had an infant son, Lornie, with whom he was quite taken. He realized more and more how his inheritance had allowed him considerable leisure to dedicate himself to his art, the passion that consumed his existence.

Early on in his marriage, Lawren had learned to compart-mentalize his daily existence. At home, he was very much the traditional husband and father. However, he spent most of his days and nights sketching and painting, or meeting with other artists and like-minded individuals. Trixie had no interest in discussing art with Lawren, but he did not see this as an impedi-ment to their relationship. As much as possible, he yearned to lead an ordinary domestic existence.

In order to survive as a Canadian artist, he was going to have to access his Harris side—the entrepreneur side. His grandfa-ther and father were courtly men, but they had had cunning eyes when it came to commerce. Blessed with a similar shrewd, businesslike aspect of his character, perhaps, he told himself, he should turn it in the direction of art politics?

W HEN *Houses, Wellington Street* was shown in the Ontario Society of Artists exhibition in 1911, Bridle wrote in the *Canadian Courier*, "L.S. Harris has the only convincing street scene in the show, and it is masterpiece enough to make up for the hugely interesting defects in his two backwoods things, both of which betray a strong potentiality in one of the youngest painters."[1] The notice must have pleased Harris, although of course his real desire was to paint "back-woods things." Harris would explore urban views for more than a decade. This proclivity was inspired by his time as a student in Berlin, but he would have been well aware, among many other possible influences, of Rembrandt's paintings of urban dwellings, especially cottages, Van Gogh's *Yellow House, Arles*, Cézanne's *Hangman's House*, Utrillo's signature street scenes of Paris, and the American painter Childe Hassam's city scenes.[2]

Harris's early commitment to "backwoods things" can be glimpsed in his first published writing in the first issue of *The Lamps*, the journal of the Arts and Letters Club, a short review of an exhibition by Arthur Heming (1870–1940), a painter and novelist known as the "Chronicler of the North":

> A most pleasing thing about these pictures . . . is that the sub-jects which inspired them are truly of this country, and the knowledge upon which they are based must have required not alone a keen observation but a number of years of study in the North. The incident of the northland, the cold crispness of its snows, the suggestion of mystery and bigness . . . is done in a perfectly simple and masterly way.[3]

Harris is praising Heming for capturing the "mystery" of the North, an aspect of his own work that was still badly lagging.

The concept of the North that Harris identified with was born of a desire to find a form of Canadian sublime. That is why more mundane subjects such as settled landscapes did not appeal. The idea of "wilderness" also had an obvious exotic appeal. Arthur Lismer put it this way: In the harsh, primitive landscape of Canada resided the "design, or form, of our country." The character of the landscape "partakes of our own character, its virility and emphatic form is reflected in the appearance, speech, action, and thought of our people."4

In the late nineteenth century, Americans became obsessed with their wilderness, particularly with spending time in the wilderness and with creating "wilderness parks" that preserved what was being seen as increasingly endangered, primitive territories. The search for what was distinctly Canadian as opposed to American preoccupied the Canadian government, which, in part, wanted the North settled to discourage land claims from other countries. The government also became interested in the notion of entrenching special wilderness areas in Canada.

James Oliver Curwood (1878–1927), an American, was employed to write about the Canadian North. In 1919, he and Ernest Shipman (1871–1931) made the film *Back to God's Country*, which portrayed the North as unsullied by modern life. The Manitoba-born Vilhjalmur Stefansson's book *The Friendly Arctic* became enormously popular. The American Robert Flaherty's 1922 documentary *Nanook of the North: A Study of Life and Love in the Arctic* only added to this mystique.*

---

* The notion of the North elaborated here has sparked a number of controversies in recent Canadian art scholarship. Why, for example, didn't Harris (and his associates) take into account the Aboriginal nations? The answer to this question is relatively straightforward: Harris was attempting to define his own version of Canada in his landscape art. In Germany he had seen how German artists attempted to define themselves within the German landscape tradition. It did not occur to him that he should take into account the peoples of the First Nations in defining what he conceived Canada to be because the issue of inclusivity was not one he was sensitive to.

Moreover, if Harris had attempted to widen the base of what he considered to be Canadian art by including the peoples of the First Nations, he might well have been accused of appropriation.

Unlike most artists of his generation, Harris had a vision of Canada that not only embraced the notion of wilderness but also recognized the plight of the urban poor. His definition of Canada was, therefore, extremely catholic at the same time as it was restricted.

Harris's view of Canada, the North, nationalism and art can be found in a passage such as this: "This emphasis of the north in the Canadian character that is born of the spirit of the north and reflects it, has profoundly affected its art, and its art in turn, clarifies and enhances the quality of Canadian consciousness."5*

In November 1911, from the first to the fourteenth of that month, some sketches by J.E.H. (Jim) MacDonald were shown in the clubroom of the Arts and Letters Club. The artist C.W. Jefferys (1869–1951), one of the founders of the club, was deeply impressed: "In these sketches, there is a refreshing absence of Europe, or anything else, save Canada and J.E.H. MacDonald and what they have to say; and so deep and compelling has been the native inspiration, that it has, to a very great extent, found through him, a method of expression in paint as native and original as itself."6 When he saw the exhibition, Harris realized that MacDonald, like Heming, had found a formula with which to capture the northern Canadian landscape: "I was more affected by these sketches than by any paintings I had seen in Europe."7 An immediate bond was established between the two men, because they were both struggling with the same quandary: How does one inject spiritual values into landscape paintings?

In 1887, at the age of thirteen, MacDonald had emigrated with his English mother and Canadian father from Durham, England, to Hamilton, Ontario, where he studied at the art school. Two years later, he and his family moved to Toronto, where he took courses in commercial art and became an active member of the Toronto Art Students' League. From 1895 to 1911, he worked for the Toronto Lithography Company and then at the design studio Grip Limited. At the age of twenty-six, he married Joan Lavis, a student at McMaster University (then in Toronto, at

---

Much of the criticism directed against Harris is misguided in that his proclivities only reflected what he saw. Perhaps he should have seen more and been more sensitive to the Native peoples? That point is worth debating, but much of the criticism, while invigorating and stimulating, nevertheless remains anachronistic.

what is now the Royal Conservatory of Music building); their son, Thoreau, was born in 1901. In 1911, Jim exhibited at the annual spring show of the Ontario Society of Artists, showed a series of oil sketches at the Arts and Letters Club and quit his job. He was now painting full-time. The following year he moved his family to Thornhill.

MacDonald looked like a frail, shy redhead, but he was a man of strong intellectual skills. Whenever he had a free moment, even on a sketching trip, he would grab a book and soon be absorbed by it. In turn, he could be excessively shy and exuberantly opinionated. Like Harris, he was an ideas man. MacDonald was twelve years senior to Harris, who saw his fellow artist as an older brother who could guide and, sometimes, admonish him. Without doubt, MacDonald was the artist from the future Group of Seven to whom Harris was closest.

Harris and MacDonald soon discovered their mutual devotion to the American Transcendentalists. In MacDonald's case, his admiration extended to naming his son after one of the principal leaders of that movement, Henry David Thoreau (1817–62). Harris probably learned from MacDonald of Richard Maurice Bucke (1837–1902), who practised psychiatry in London, Ontario, from 1877 until his death.

Like MacDonald, Bucke had been born in England; his parents immigrated with him to Ontario when he was but one year old. At the age of sixteen, Bucke began a wandering existence. He fought Shoshone in the American West, and nearly froze to death in the mountains of California, where he was the sole survivor of a mining party; he returned to Canada by way of the Isthmus of Panama in 1858. After studying medicine at McGill, he began work as the superintendent of mental asylums, in which field he was a progressive. He believed in occupational therapy and organized sports, and insisted on treating his patients in humane ways. His most important publication was issued the year before he died: *Cosmic Consciousness*.

According to Bucke, there were three stages in the development of consciousness: that of animals, that of most people, and that of cosmic consciousness, in which "the universe is so built and ordered that without any peradventure all things work together for the good of each and all, that the foundation principle of the world is what we call love and that the happiness of every one is in the long run absolutely certain."[8]

MacDonald no doubt informed Harris that Bucke, like Emerson, rightly saw Walt Whitman (1819–92) as the inheritor of the Transcendental movement. Even as early as 1911, both men would have taken comfort in a passage such as this from *Leaves of Grass*:

> The earth never tires;
> The earth is made silent, incomprehensible at first—Nature
>   is rude and incomprehensible at first;
> Be not discouraged—keep on—there are divine things, well
>   envelop'd
> I swear to you there are divine things more beautiful than
>   words can tell.[9]

Of course, the two Canadians were trying to extract "divine things" in sketches and paintings out of elements of the landscape of their native country. The two began sketching together that winter and went on a sketching trip to Mattawa and Temiskaming in the spring of the following year.

They also worked side by side along the industrial waterfronts of Toronto and Hamilton in the winter of 1911–12, especially

Lawren Harris.
Mattawa.
Circa 1912.

at the gasworks at the foot of Bathurst Street in Toronto. Both men saw the industrial wasteland that confronted them in similar ways, but MacDonald's *Tracks and Traffic* is slightly more anecdotal than Harris's *The Gas Works* and *The Eaton Manufacturing Building*. Harris bestows luminous yellows to the top of the Eaton building, giving that structure's facade an almost ethereal quality, in contrast to the urban desolation that occupies the picture's lower half. The colours in the other canvas are dingy browns and greys; a giant ball of red smoke has escaped from the ominous-looking structure that occupies the top centre of the canvas; the buildings in the foreground are the dingy, pollution-infested dwellings of the workers.

Much more than MacDonald, Harris, as in *Top of the Hill*, is providing social commentary. He is suggesting that the demands

Lawren Harris.
The Gas Works.
1911–12.

of industry are stripping the urban landscape of the vital ingredient essential to their existence: the physical well-being of the
workers who maintain the system. In such instances, Harris is
echoing concerns expressed by the Berlin Secession.

MacDonald's *By the River, Early Spring* and Harris's *The Drive*
were shown at the Ontario Society of Artists exhibition in the
spring of 1912. MacDonald stated that his aim in his painting
"was to convey a sense of the awakened strength and motion of
nature after the comparative quiescence of winter . . . The general colour is sombre, suggesting soft and dull weather, but there
is a hint of veiled blue in the sky."[10]

In contrast to MacDonald, Harris's image is from an extremely
low point of view across a valley and up a hillside. Snow, rendered
in broad and lengthy brush strokes, envelops the lumberjacks
moving the logs downriver at the top and bottom. The sun shines
dramatically upon the workers, but of greater compositional
interest is the frame of the water—straight on top and crescent
shaped at the bottom. This picture—his largest and certainly his
most distinctive Canadian landscape painting up to that time—
was purchased by the National Gallery of Canada. It was Harris's
first major sale.

Lawren Harris.
The Drive. 1912.

Fully aware of the financial gap that separated him from most other artists, Harris wanted to find a way to be of practical assistance to his confederates. His first opportunity came in an off-hand way.

James MacCallum (1860–1943), twenty-five years older than Harris, was born in Richmond Hill, north of Toronto, the son of a Methodist minister. When James was ten, his father was posted to Collingwood, and the boy came to know many parts of Georgian Bay and also Muskoka. He attended Victoria College at the University of Toronto and later earned his doctorate in medicine at the same university in 1886. He then went to England, where he studied ophthalmology for two years. Upon returning to Canada, he practised both ophthalmology and ear, nose and throat medicine. He was also deeply knowledgeable about pharmacology, and

James MacCallum.

taught all three subjects at the University of Toronto, in addition to maintaining a private practice. He was affiliated with the Toronto General Hospital and the Hospital for Sick Children. He was also an influential member of the Medical Council of Canada and the Council of the College of Physicians and Surgeons of Ontario. In his life outside medicine, MacCallum was regarded by many as overly caustic; in fact, his detestation of "stuffed shirts" was so extreme that it was often regarded as eccentric. He was an excellent runner, canoer and sailor.

In the summer of 1911, when MacCallum was building a cottage at Go Home Bay, Lawren and Trixie were renting a cottage there from Dr. D.E. Staunton Wishart in the Madawaska Club's enclave.[11] Harris and MacCallum likely met at that time and discussed some shared feelings about Canadian art. Later, in November, Harris suggested that MacCallum visit the MacDonald exhibition at the Arts and Letters Club.

From these early meetings, Harris and MacCallum deliberated on the possibility of constructing a building in which artists could live, meet, socialize and work. Eden Smith (1858–1949) was selected as the architect, but the result, the Studio Building—three-storeyed, with north-facing windows and eighteen-foot-high ceilings accompanied by clean, sharp lines—was not in its exterior in the Arts and Crafts style (pitched roof, tall chimneys) for which this architect was famous. Instead, Harris and MacCallum must have insisted that the building have a lean, minimalist exterior appearance. The interior was a different matter. There were six double-height studios (two to a floor), each with a cottage-like living room with fireplace. The walls were covered in canvas, and a wrought-iron staircase led up to a small loft.

From the outset, the building, completed in 1914 and located on Severn Street in the Rosedale Ravine, was operated on a nonprofit basis (rents were pegged to cover only the expense of maintaining the building). Harris and MacCallum jointly sponsored the building, but Harris was the sole purchaser and the mortgagee. Later, the two agreed to the terms of their joint ownership: three-thirteenths were MacCallum's, the remainder Harris's.[12] It was intended that there would eventually be a gallery and a theatre. Harris and MacCallum were hoping to establish a community of artists who could work side by side.*

The oldest tenant was Curtis Williamson, nicknamed "the Canadian Rembrandt" and known primarily as a portraitist. In 1907, he had been a founding member of the Canadian Art Club. His painterly style had been developed after ten years in France and the Netherlands. In the Arts and Letters Club's *Year-*

---

* In the English-speaking world, the Arts and Crafts Movement, which lasted roughly from 1860 to 1910, emphasized the idea of artists working together as craftsmen; the resulting work was seen as being in direct opposition to the machine-made productions of industry. Harris and MacCallum were obviously intent on establishing a similar kind of regimen in Canada.

The Studio
Building.

book of Canadian Art in 1913, Harris labelled his work as "full of
strength and half-subdued fire. It is eloquent of ability and an
almost arrogant mastery of technique." Another resident was J.W.
Beatty, with whom Harris had earlier gone on two sketching trips.
Another, Arthur Heming (1870–1940), was famed as a painter and
writer entranced with "the back of beyond" that constituted Canada's farthest northern reaches.*

Always the optimist, Harris had assumed that the Studio Building would help artists to produce "favourable" results. However,
Jackson observed that Heming

> settled down to make pencil portraits of beautiful women.
> Curtis Williamson had been painting low-toned old master-
> ish pictures. He moved from his dark little studio . . . , shut
> out most of the light in his big new studio and continued

---

* Harris occupied Studio 2 from 1914 to 1916 and then Studio 3 from 1917 to
1934; A.Y. Jackson was in Studio 1; MacDonald was in Studio 6 from 1914 to 1916
and then in Studio 2 until 1930. (In 1913 and perhaps earlier, Harris maintained
a studio at 2 Bloor Street West above the Bank of Commerce at Yonge and Bloor
Streets.) Subsequent residents included Yulia Biriukova, Lawren P. Harris, Charles
Comfort and Harold Town.

painting as he had always done. J.W. Beatty, stirred at first by the enthusiasms of his younger confreres, soon lost all sympathy with their modern ideas.[13]

Having worked with MacCallum to establish a building to minister to artists—the first in Canada—Harris decided he had to do something more on behalf of that endangered, although sometimes difficult-to-assist, species, the Canadian artist. He wrote to the *Globe* on June 4, 1914, in response to an article about the Federal Art Commission and the National Gallery. Taking no prisoners, he spoke his mind on what he considered the fundamental flaw in the National Gallery's collecting policies: "We have no assurance whatever that the dearly beloved art commission is not going to continue spending fifteen or twenty times as much on foreign art as on Canadian. We are already too well supplied with European pictures." According to Harris, the gallery was simply out of touch; it had no interest in the future of Canadian art. It had become the residence of "second-rate foreign pictures." Canadian art was headed for oblivion unless the National Gallery "cuts itself loose from Barbizon and Holland and the Royal Academy of England and becomes somewhat more than a mere echo of the art of other countries."[14] This is an extraordinary document in that a European-trained and -influenced young Canadian was cutting himself loose from some of the very traditions in which he had been trained. Yet he felt something radical had to be done if Canada was to develop its own tradition in art.

Only someone with unquestioned patrician authority could have written this angry letter; MacDonald, for instance, would never have authored such a document. There is a strong possibility that the letter was a ploy, a plot hatched between Harris and Sir Edmund Walker (1848–1924), the president of the Canadian Bank of Commerce and a fellow member of the Arts and Letters Club.

Like his fellow layman James MacCallum, Walker held the strong conviction that a nation's art should be the cornerstone of its existence. He was an ardent collector: his home, Long Garth, at 99 St. George Street was a treasure trove of prints, embroideries, carpets and bronzes. He helped form the Toronto Guild of Civic Art and served as its first president in 1897. He was directly involved in the formation of the Art Museum of Toronto (later the Art Gallery of Toronto and, after that, the Art Gallery of Ontario); he convinced the Goldwin Smiths to leave their elegant, perfectly symmetrical red-brick mansion, the Grange (*c.* 1820), to the new museum.[15] In 1914 he was chairman of the Advisory Arts Council and of the Board of the National Gallery, in which position he adamantly sought to have Canadian art purchased. Since fellow council members frequently challenged Walker efforts at the National Gallery, Harris and Walker may have hatched a publicity stunt whereby Harris penned the letter and then Walker made a dramatic, pre-arranged appearance at the Studio Building to promise official help for Canadian art.

This conspiracy scenario suggests itself because there is a whiff of something odd about the Harris–Walker exchange. In 1910, Walker had used his influence to have Eric Brown (1877–1939), a young Englishman from Nottingham, appointed curator of the National Gallery (he became director in 1913). Only two years later, the gallery moved into the recently built Victoria Memorial Museum. From the outset, Brown was a fearless defender of Canadian art. In 1912, he made his thoughts crystal clear: "There is no doubt that Canada has growing along with her material prosperity a strong and virile art which only needs to be fostered and encouraged in order to become a great factor in her growth as a nation. No country can be a great nation until it has a great art."[16] However, Brown added an important caveat: "This encouragement of our national art in its broadest and best sense is not achieved by the exclusive purchase of Canadian works of art . . . we must have in addition to our own Canadian pictures the best examples we can afford of the world's artistic achievements, by which we may judge the merit and progress of our own efforts."[17] This was a considerable rub. Harris felt strongly that he had to lobby on behalf of the Canadian side of things for fear that the gallery would ultimately be inundated with European imports.

Brown and Harris immediately formed a strong compact, inspired in part by the fact that they were both religious men who pursued their beliefs in unorthodox ways. Like Annie Raynolds, Brown was a devout Christian Scientist, whereas Harris's fascination with theosophy was an ongoing part of his development as an artist.

The sense of shared intimacy can be glimpsed in a later, undated letter from the 1920s to Brown wherein Harris mentions that he had heard that "Dr. Insulin Banting" (a facetious reference to Frederick Banting, 1891–1941, one of the discoverers of insulin) "paints a bit and is considerably interested in pictures." Harris then asks for Brown's assistance in manipulating Banting. In this missive, the reader catches a glimpse of a very determined person, one willing to do anything in his power to get what he wants on behalf of Canadian art:

It would be a great pity if he went the way of most incipient connoisseurs and became a prey to dealers. That is almost certain to happen unless he can be interested in what is being done here.

Here is a creative individual—a thorough going Canadian whose interest would benefit everyone—Such individuals should know what is going on in their own land and be friendly to all truly creative endeavour.

I know that he has a keen interest in things Canadian but that he is being dragged by his intimates towards the usual nice, comfortable, conforming, valueless ways of our self-satisfied, dull, pseudo-aristocratic bourgeoisie! Heaven help us all!

Why could not you as director of the National Gallery of Canada write the fellow offering your services etc. and give him a survey of art all over this poor pill and point out the significance (if any) of what is being done here and now in Canada?

We don't want to sell the fellow anything.

We want him around.

If we could get the interest of a *few* such individuals, appreciation would progress very quickly.[18]*

Harris wanted Canadian intellectuals to be aware of the existence of a Modernist Canadian art. In 1913, he was also fully aware of the fury that had been unleashed in the United States by the International Exhibition of Modern Art organized by the Association of American Painters and Sculptors that opened in New York City's 69th Regiment Armory on February 17 and ran to March 15. This event became a legendary watershed in American art, introducing as it did to astonished New Yorkers a wide assortment of Post-Impressionist, Cubist and Futurist works by three hundred European and American artists. For many visitors, the pieces on display were simply outrageous. According to one journalist, Marcel Duchamp's *Nude Descending a Staircase* looked like an explosion in a shingle factory.

Harris was not set upon introducing Cubist or Futurist principles into Canadian art; he simply wanted to rid the art of his country of a tendency to rely too heavily on English pastoralism, French Impressionism and Dutch provincialism. It may be that in 1913, at a turning point in his career, Harris was not aware of precisely

---

* Apart from institutional sales and an inner circle of friends and acquaintances who purchased his work, many of Harris's paintings remained unsold during his lifetime. He had a significant number in storage at the Studio Building in Toronto and, later, in Vancouver. A large number of canvases were stored in the fifties and sixties at the Art Gallery of Ontario. During a lunch with Harris at the Benvenuto Hotel in Toronto in the sixties, Paul Duval noticed a large number of canvases hanging in that establishment. "These had been placed there by Dick van Valkenburg, the director of the Eaton's College Street Department Store, Fine Art Gallery with the hope of finding buyers for Lawren's work. Eaton's was then Harris's main sales outlet in Toronto and his major works were never priced at more than two thousand dollars. There were very few serious collectors interested in buying Harris's paintings in the sixties" (*Where the Universe Sings*, 20). Duval purchased a significant number of paintings directly from Harris and at Eaton's. The Laing Galleries in Toronto were also eager to handle Harris. The best general account of the collecting of work by Harris and other members of the Group of Seven can be found in Hill, 223–38.

what he wanted to do. But even if he wasn't fully conscious of the process on which they were embarking, he and MacDonald were looking for appropriate ways to make symbolist landscapes from Canadian material. When he went to Buffalo late in 1913 to an exhibition that received much less publicity than the Armory one, he was deeply shaken.

> MacDonald and I had discussed the possibility of an expression which would embody the varied moods, character and spirit of this country. We heard there was an exhibition of modern Scandinavian paintings at the Albright Gallery in Buffalo—and took the train to Buffalo to see it. This turned out to be one of the most exciting and rewarding experiences either of us had. Here were a large number of paintings which corroborated our ideas. Here were paintings of northern lands created in the spirit of those lands and through the hearts and minds of those who knew and loved them. Here was an art bold, vigorous and uncompromising, embodying direct first hand experience of the great North. As a result of that experience our enthusiasm increased, and our conviction was reinforced.
>
> From that time on we knew we were at the beginning of an all-engrossing adventure. That adventure, as it turned out, was to include the exploration of the whole country for its creative and expressive possibilities in painting.[19]

Jim MacDonald, slightly more matter-of-factly, described his response:

> Now Harris and I were fortunate in this exhibition. We were full of associated ideas. Not that we had ever been to Scandinavia, but we had feelings of height and breadth and depth and colour and sunshine and solemnity and new wonder about our own country, and we were pleased to find a correspondence with these feelings of ours, not only in the general attitude of the Scandinavian artists, but also in the natural aspects of their countries. Except in minor points, the pic-

tures might all have been Canadian, and we felt "This is what we want to do in Canada." [The Scandinavian artists] seemed to be a lot of men not trying to *express themselves* so much as trying to express something that took hold of *themselves*. The painters began with *nature* rather than with *art*.[20]

Well before setting out for Buffalo, Harris may have had high expectations for what he would see. While living in Germany, he had seen landscapes that had been infused, very much in the manner he was now contemplating, with symbolical meaning that transported the viewer to a realm of existence beyond simple views of trees, mountains, rivers and valleys.

The exhibition of contemporary Scandinavian art at the Albright Gallery from January 4 to 26, 1913, contained 165 works, only 70 of which were landscapes. MacDonald's annotated copy of the catalogue indicates that he and Harris were most taken with *Ripples* by the Swedish artist Gustav Fjaestad (1865–1948) and *Mountains, Winter Landscape* by the Norwegian Hârâld Sohlberg (1869–1935).

Gustav Fjaestad.
Winter Moonlight.
1895.

MacDonald's glowing words may hold the key to what happened to him and Harris: they saw the possibility of creating a distinctly Canadian landscape because their country shared many geographical features with Scandinavia. They wanted to express themselves as Canadians; they believed that if the geography of Canada was warmly embraced, a native art tradition would follow.

In the short biography of Fjaestad that he wrote for the Albright catalogue, Christian Brinton claimed that the Swedish artist viewed his native landscape "with something of an arbitrarily chosen viewpoint . . . bringing out the decorative elements . . . In all this work he has unquestionably said new and personal things concerning the treasury of beauty, left unregarded for centuries, to be found in the fantastic and varied shades and shapes the snow can assume."[21] The word "decorative" is an important one since as an adjective it can imply superficiality: a "decorative" painting might be one that fails to probe beyond mere appearance. Brinton obviously used the word in a much more positive (symbolical) manner. In a similar way, Eric Brown, the first director of the National Gallery, who purchased *Snow II* in 1917, described his reaction to the picture:

> Lawren Harris leans more toward decoration than any other [of the Studio Building group] . . . he finds in the snow laden spruces and stark pines the patterns for his compositions which do not evade a sufficient truth and add to it a satisfying surety of space and balance. Lawren Harris is a seeker, and the problems he attacks change from year to year, and his buoyant and fetterless art admirably typifies the new spirit of Canadian landscape painting.[22]*

---

* In a letter to Katherine Dreier, undated but from 1926 (MS copy: Yale), Harris provided a biographical sketch. There, he made this claim: "For a number of years the work of these painters [the Group of Seven] was realistic, then it became strictly decorative. In the last six years it has gone through a process of summarization to a definite plastic statement of ideas that over the years ha[s] come to artistic clarity." This overview is more indicative of Harris's career than it is of his fellow artists. Moreover, Harris is emphasizing the fact that the "decorative" was an important step in his development as an artist.

Lawren Harris.
Snow II. 1915.

Between 1914 and 1918, in at least a dozen canvases, Harris was obsessed with replicating what he had learned from Fjaestad. He located in the Swede's winter scenes a kind of visual paradigm that allowed him his first distinct glimpse into a way of creating a Canadian landscape tradition. The resulting images are worked on sharply focused receding planes, with photograph-like illusionism, tranquil hues of pink, mauve and pale blue, and curving, flowing lines from art nouveau, as well as precise, controlled brush strokes. It is as if, in beholding Fjaestad's winter scenes, Harris witnessed what were for him the "essential" qualities of snow and how the vision of the Swedish artist could be utilized for his own purposes. MacDonald also tested himself in comparison to Fjaestad in a canvas such as *Snowbound* (1915), but he soon abandoned that stylistic preoccupation.

In contrast, Harris's experiments with snow lasted four years. In 1918 he finally abandoned this approach because he had discovered other means of re-creating what was unique about the

J.E.H. MacDonald.
Snowbound. 1915.

Canadian landscape; in so doing, he uncovered more satisfactory ways of infusing symbolism into his work. During this experimental phase, Harris, who was competing with the Swede as if in a wrestling match, may have copied from and parodied him, but nevertheless he managed to make paintings that are the equal of his sources. Imitation can be the sincerest form of flattery, and this is true in this particular borrowing of one artist from another. Moreover, in the process of imitating Fjaestad, Harris fine-tuned his ability to obtain finely turned, flat passages in his paintings, a skill that would stand him in good stead.

The remarkable experience in Buffalo shared by MacDonald and Harris had been undergone twenty years earlier by C.W. Jefferys, the English-born painter-illustrator. He had felt a "first potent stimulus" in the formation of a distinct Canadian art at the World's Columbian Exhibition in Chicago in 1893. For the first time

> on the continent pictures by contemporary Scandinavian painters [were shown]. Here we saw the works of artists dealing with themes and problems of the landscape of countries similar in topography, climate and atmosphere to our own:

snow, pine trees, rocks, inland lakes, autumn colour, clear air, sharply defined forms. [Some of these artists] were painting subjects that might have been found in Canada. Our eyes were opened. We realized that on all our painting, admirable as it was, lay the blight of misty Holland, mellow England, the veiled sunlight of France, countries where most of our painters were born or had been trained.

To us younger painters these Scandinavian painters were a revelation. They encouraged us, they gave us confidence to tackle our problems without reference to the standards of other and quite different countries and to try to find an adequate way of expressing the character of our surroundings.[23]

Harris knew Jefferys at the Arts and Letters Club, and may well have anticipated what he would see in Buffalo if he discussed the 1893 exhibition with him. Moreover, Jefferys could have reminded both Harris and MacDonald that the search for a distinctly Canadian way to render Canada *remained* an intriguing puzzle, one that had not yet been solved.

Earlier, in the 1880s and 1890s, the Canadian Pacific Railway (CPR) had offered free passes to landscape painters. This allowed many artists and photographers to roam the entire country, although the most significant destination was the Rocky Mountains. The CPR obviously hoped that those allowed to travel free would produce publicity materials.

Then there was the Toronto Art Students' League, founded in 1886, which was not only a school but a setting where members met to draw, discuss, comment on each other's work and create projects. As Jefferys recalled, "We felt [in the verse of the pre-Confederation poets an interpretation] of Canada that was familiar to us and that we were trying to depict."[24]

Like the American Transcendentalists, this Canadian group deepened their "consciousness of a quality peculiar to North America" that they "deemed essential" to artistic expression. "We became Northern minded. Some of us were radical enough to revel in Walt Whitman." Many years later, Jim MacDonald remembered the "Canadian evenings" with their singing of canoe songs and the "visiting evenings we used to have at different artists' studios, to make half-hour compositions on Canadian subjects. There was a great stirring of *Canadian* ideals."[25]

From 1893 to 1904, the League published an annual illustrated calendar. Jefferys reflected, "During its existence this publication produced numerous excellent drawings, depicting the characteristic features of Canada, and the life of its people, past and present. It gave an opportunity for the early efforts of several of the younger artists." One of those artists had been MacDonald—the League was obviously the place where he had learned about *Leaves of Grass*—and so Harris most certainly knew of these early efforts to produce uniquely Canadian works of art. The problems he was confronting, Harris must have realized, were perennial. Was any breakthrough possible?

Early in 1913, the Montreal-based painter A.Y. Jackson received a letter from MacDonald: another young artist, Lawren Harris, wanted to buy Jackson's painting from 1910, *Edge of the Maple Wood*, if he hadn't sold it. "If I still possessed it! I still possessed everything I had ever painted," the artist wryly recalled decades later.[26]

Harris, three years younger than Jackson, had been startled when he saw his contemporary's canvas at the Ontario Society of Artists exhibition: "It stood out from all the other paintings as an authentic, new expression. It was clear, fresh and full of light, luminous with the sunlight of early Canadian spring . . . that painting is significant because it marked the first time that any Canadian painting had contained such startling verity."[27] In 1913, Harris was struggling to find himself as a Canadian artist, but he reached out immediately to someone he perceived as having advanced further than himself. Harris's natural impulse was to be generous, to connect with others.

Jackson was deeply stirred by Harris's purchase:

MacDonald tells me you are a real enthusiast, a good live artist; one who can practise and preach and wallop . . . It really looks as though the sacred fires [are] going to burst into flame

in Toronto by the faithful efforts of yourself and MacDonald
and the modest millionaire [MacCallum]. We once had some
smoldering fires in Montreal which might have blazed up if
they hadn't fanned them with bricks and wet blankets.

A few months later, in May or June 1913, the two met in Berlin, Ontario, where Jackson was visiting relatives. Later, Jackson
wrote:

[Harris] was, I found, a
young man, well educated,
well travelled, and well to
do . . . To Lawren Harris
art was almost a mission.
He believed that a country
that ignored the arts left no
record of itself worth pre-
serving. He deplored our
neglect of the artist in Canada and believed that we, a
young and vigorous people,
who had pioneered in so
many ways, should put the
same spirit of adventure into

Private
A.Y. Jackson.
Circa 1915.

our cultivation of the arts . . . He believed that art in Canada
should assume a more aggressive role, and he had exalted
ideas about the place of the artist in the community.

Jackson's evaluation of his new friend could, if anything, be stated
even more emphatically. Canadian art was not for him "almost a
mission"; rather, it had become the living, breathing reality of his
cosmic consciousness.

Jackson, touched by the purchase, later ruminated further
on what had occurred: "I began my association with the artists
responsible for changing the course of Canadian art for many
years to come." Jackson's claim is a crucial one. There had been
many landscape artists in Canada before Harris, Jackson and their

confederates. However, these young men had the sense that the direction in which Canadian art was drifting was a singularly uneventful recipe that mixed and matched English-inspired models and sometimes added French-inspired Impressionism in for good measure. They wanted to accomplish something new. Why drift, when you could attempt something fresh and exciting?

6

CAMARADERIE

(1913–1916)

If I am by nature shy, no one knows, Lawren wistfully told him-self. Some days he saw himself as a bit of a windbag, but if he did not speak up, who would? Since returning from Germany, he had become obsessed not only with his own career but with that dubious entity, Canadian art. His personal destiny was somehow intertwined with the culture of his native land. This conjoining remained mysterious. He certainly could not separate the two threads from each other.

A S A YOUNGSTER, outwardly gruff but warm-hearted Montreal-born Alexander Young Jackson had worked as an office boy for a lithograph company, where he took his first tentative steps towards becoming an artist. He was one of six children abandoned by their father. In the evenings, the teenager took art classes at Montreal's Monument-National. In 1905, at the age of twenty-three, he worked his way to Europe on a cattle boat, returned the same way, and then headed to Chicago, where he joined a commercial art firm and took courses at the Art Institute of Chicago. He saved his money and in 1907 vis-ited France to study Impressionism. He enrolled at the Académie Julian.

In further pursuit of his own version of Impressionism, he also travelled to Italy and the Netherlands. Upon returning to Canada, he painted in Sweetsburg, Quebec. He held a joint exhibition in 1913 with Randolph Hewton at the Art Association of Montreal gallery. Discouraged by his inability to make a living, he was on the verge of moving to the United States. Then Mac-Donald's letter arrived.

On the same day he met MacDonald for lunch at the Arts and Letters Club, Jackson was introduced to Arthur Lismer (1885–1969) and Frederick Varley (1881–1969), also members. In this assemblage of artists, Harris was the odd man out in that he had never been trained or worked as a graphic designer. Franklin (Frank) Carmichael (1890–1945) and Frank (later Franz) Johnston (1888–1949), with whom Jackson and Harris were soon to be associated, were also graphic designers, as was Tom Thomson (1877–1917).

With the exception of Harris and Jackson, all these men had at some point worked for Grip Ltd., the importance of which in the formation of Canadian art remains central. The firm was founded in 1873 by the cartoonist J.W. Bengough (1851–1923) to publish his satirical weekly magazine, *Grip*. In addition, he published chapbooks and did design work for a variety of clients. After Bengough lost control of the company, it became an important design firm, the first in Canada to produce engravings in metal. The bosses had a reputation for being tough, but the artists were actually given free rein in designing layouts for real estate firms, mail-order catalogues, railway posters and a wide variety of advertisements.

One employee recalled the art room: "At one end of the room sat Jimmy MacDonald, as he was then familiarly known. His desk was covered with sketches, notebooks, paints and brushes, all in utter confusion. It was said that, when he left Grip, he found on his desk material which had been missing for years."[1]

MacDonald claimed there was little of the "analytical mind" at Grip: "There was a lot of fun in general and a healthy humility about art." This observation extended most of all to Tom Thomson: "He didn't consciously analyze. He worked from the inside

J.E.H. MacDonald
(foreground)
at Grip.

feeling, and he let that govern *him*, even sometimes when he produced something that he didn't think he intended."[2]

By August 1912, when Varley joined the firm, Grip was in disarray. The year before, MacDonald had left. Albert H. Robson, the head of the art department, was about to follow. He would join Rous and Mann, Grip's main rival, taking with him Tom Thomson, Frank Johnston and Frank Carmichael. Varley too later moved to Rous and Mann.

The impact of Grip on Canadian art derives from the fact that the artists who worked there incorporated the strong design principles from their working lives into their own sketches and paintings. Advertising art demanded strong, eye-catching images, and these artists began to conjoin their art school training to their design work. This process resulted in extremely balanced designs, often with unusually bright—what would soon be labelled derisively "hot mush"—colours. Design artists at this time were highly indebted to the sensuous curves of art nouveau, and many of the Grip artists began to incorporate such spatial decoration into their artworks. The distinctive Modernist look of the Grip artists is due in large part to their mastery of strongly conceived and articulated design elements blended with bold, sometimes aggressive colour palettes. From his training in Germany, Harris knew how to build carefully articulated compositions. Glaring colours in the works of his friends he deeply admired. However, he himself was bashful in this regard.

The name "Grip" has strong literary associations. Charles Dickens had a pet raven called Grip, and he even used this bird in *Barnaby Rudge* (1840–41). When Edgar Allan Poe reviewed the novel in 1842, he offered this observation: "The raven, too, intensely amusing as it is, might have been made, more than we now see it, a portion of the conception of the fantastic Barnaby, its croaking might have been *prophetically* heard in the course of the drama." Poe invented his celebrated prophetic raven a few years later.

There was, moreover, an even more significant literary-artistic inheritance at Grip. G.A. Howell, the first secretary of the Arts and Crafts Society of Canada, was managing director of the design firm in 1908 (before that, he had been a director and secretary-treasurer). The ethos of Grip was thus influenced both directly and indirectly by the English Arts and Crafts Movement led by William Morris and John Ruskin, who linked careful and precise handcrafting to nationalistic ideals. Morris in particular insisted that the artist-designer had a quasi-messianic mission to reform, and thus better, his society.*

---

* In about 1900, MacDonald seriously considered joining the Roycrofters, the Arts and Crafts community in East Aurora, New York. (The Roycroft Press was

These artists were familiar with all the European modernisms. Some, such as Harris and Jackson, had been trained in them. For propaganda purposes, they tended to deny all such knowledge or influences. Their language is suffused with quasi-religious, quasi-mystical jargon vis-à-vis Canada. For example, J.E.H. MacDonald defined the role of the Canadian artist in this way: "The painter will look around him, like the Creator in Genesis, and finding everything good, will strive to communicate that feeling."[3] Although Harris would later become the great defender of his associates in the Group of Seven, his art remained, largely through his training and inclination, different from theirs. They often chose bright, gloriously clashing colours; Harris was never comfortable in this manner of making art, and when he achieved his signature style in landscape painting in the mid-twenties, he worked in a deliberately restricted palette. What he did learn from the Grip artists was an inclination to infuse his paintings with strong, lean lines in which unnecessary or fussy elements are removed.

Throughout his late twenties and early thirties, Harris remained fixated on the project of establishing some sort of quasi-mystical-based national art in Canada, and he was not averse to working within a group of similarly inspired individuals. Although not educated as a designer, he had become engrossed with the notion of decoration in making his snow pictures. In 1913, ever ready to pick up any hints that came his way, he realized that he could learn a great deal from his new acquaintances, soon to become friends. Perhaps, he pondered, he had to strengthen his decorative work even more by moving to absolute clarity in the removal of unnecessary details. Fjaestad provided some leads in this direction, hence

---

inspired by William Morris's Kelmscott Press.) Instead of joining this group, in 1903 he followed three colleagues in the Toronto Art Students' League to London, where they had founded the Carlton Studio in Fleet Street. This firm designed for the book trade, and their work was very much in the Kelmscott and Roycroft manner. MacDonald worked there until 1907, when he and his wife and son returned to Canada.

Harris's emulation of him. Harris's designer friends provided further clues.

In their personalities, Harris's new compatriots were extremely different from one another. Varley, who had trained at the excellent Sheffield School of Art in England, could be explosive; his bursts of rage were completely unpredictable. Lismer, also trained at Sheffield, was altogether more sedate. Franklin Carmichael, the office boy at Grip, was significantly younger than the others and tended to keep silent in their presence. Johnston, who worked in tempera rather than oil, had trained at the Philadelphia Academy of Fine Art and then worked in New York before returning to Toronto.

Years later, Lismer, remembering how these diverse artists came together, described the problems confronting them: "We felt locality but not mood. We felt topography but not colour. The fact was we could neither draw nor paint. We were adven-

Tom Thomson.
The Pool. 1915–16.

turous, but it never got into pictures."4 This is certainly how Harris felt in 1913: he had the willingness but lacked the know-how.

In looking at a canvas such as Tom Thomson's *The Pool* (1915), Harris would have seen how readily the other artist incorporated decorative techniques in his work. Harris depicted snow in blue and a series of associated colours (mauve, pink, yellow), but in

Tom Thomson.

his painting Thomson places the water in the background and then assembles his decorative elements in a riot of reds, oranges and yellows. His work in a decorative vein is much more visceral than Harris's.

In contrast to Harris, Tom Thomson possessed both willingness and know-how. There is the possibility that Thomson studied painting with William Cruikshank (1848–1922), but if he did, it was likely for only a short period of time. He was that genuine rarity: an artist whose keen eye sees directly into a landscape and possesses the capability of transforming it into an astounding piece of art. As a person, he was cordial, untamed, melancholic, mercurial, difficult, moody and exuberant.

Since Harris was out of town at the time, he had not attended the momentous luncheon at which Jackson made his first appearance at the Arts and Letters Club, but, as we have seen, he met him shortly afterwards at the home of Jackson's aunt in Berlin, Ontario.

Shortly thereafter, Jackson visited some cousins on Georgian Bay. At the age of thirty-one, he was uncertain about his future. That autumn he stayed in a shack on Portage Island in Freddy Channel. Meanwhile, MacCallum was preparing to shut up his cottage on Go Home Bay when he received a letter from Harris:

There is a Montreal artist named Jackson sketching somewhere around your part of Georgian Bay, one of the younger
crowd from Montreal who feels the same about the country
as we do . . . We want to get him to come to Toronto and work
in the new studio building, but he's hard up and talks about
going to New York. If you see him, have a talk with him about
it.[5]

When MacCallum located Jackson, the younger man was in
the middle of patching up the many cracks in the shack with birch
bark and moss. MacCallum asked to see Jackson's work, of which
he instantly approved. When the young man told the doctor that
he was about to leave for the States, MacCallum, in his typically
owlish way, upbraided him: "Art in Canada is never going to get
anywhere if you young fellows all go off to the States." Then he
made an offer that was hard to refuse: if Jackson would return to
Toronto, move into the Studio Building and take one young artist under his wing, MacCallum would guarantee all his expenses
for one year.[6] Jackson was beside himself with surprise—and joy.

That December, in an effort to further encourage Jackson,
Harris and MacCallum arranged to have some of his recent
Georgian Bay sketches displayed at the Arts and Letters Club.
The idea was that this would prove the young artist with an entree
into the Toronto art scene. However, there were many members of the club who looked at art from a very different perspective from these young men. One such was H.F. Gadsby who,
in an article that bore the headline "The Hot Mush School,"
attacked the work on display. The headline referred to the fact
that since "all the pictures look pretty much alike, the net result
[was] more like a gargle or glob of porridge than a work of art."[7]
MacDonald shot back a rebuttal: Gadsby's attack on progressive-
minded art had "got my goat, my horse, my ass and everything
which is mine . . . Let us support our distinctly native art, if only
for the sake of experiment."[8] Like Harris, MacDonald realized
that all publicity of their shared endeavours worked to their benefit. (Harris's early landscape work is not as garishly coloured as
that of his associates, but he too would be accused of this crime.

Later, he would use his propensity to employ a cooler palette to his advantage.)

The efforts of this slowly coalescing circle could also be gently satirized, as in Peter Donovan's wry words from a piece in *Saturday Night* in 1916:

> When your up-to-the-moment artist decides to wreak his soul on the canvas, he puts on a pair of Strathcona boots, rolls up his blanket, and [takes enough] beans to last a month, takes a rifle and a paddle, and hikes for the northern woods. He can't work this side of the Height of Land. The only rivers worth painting, from his point of view, are those which run down to Hudson's Bay. He can't work in peace unless he has a bear trying to steal his bacon or a moose breathing down his neck. That's why the coming Canadian artist is such a husky beggar . . . Old style painters used to be sparing of colour— probably on account of the expense. But these modern chaps bring joy to hearts of dealers in artists' supplies. They seem to mix their paint on a big flat rock and throw it on with a scoop- shovel. It's a great way to get unpremeditated effects.[9]

Before the Studio Building was ready, Jackson used Harris's studio over the bank. The artist whom Jackson had promised to take under his wing was Tom Thomson, to whom he taught theory and technique and lent books on Impressionism. In the Studio Building, the two occupied Studio 1. None of the units had cooking facilities and so, after moving there, the two took 25-cent meals at a bar on nearby Yonge Street or visited the more homey, slightly more expensive The Busy Bee. The two were so poor that they could afford only the occasional film at a nearby cinema on a Saturday evening.

Soon afterwards, Thomson was destitute. He moved into a shack behind the Studio Building. On sloping ground and sur- rounded by saplings, this place had once been the workshop of a cabinetmaker and then a henhouse. Harris and MacCallum had the modest building reroofed and insulated, had an east window added for light, and furnished it with a bunk and a box stove. This shack, which resembled many of the houses in Harris's urban views, replicated the primitive living conditions in which Thomson thrived in Algonquin Park, the first of the Canadian wilderness parks (established in 1893).

Later, Harris recalled Tom's way of "adapting" to Toronto: "When he was in Toronto, Tom rarely left the shack in the daytime, and then only when it was absolutely necessary. He took his exercise at night. He would put on his snowshoes and tramp the length of the Rosedale ravine and out into country and return before dawn." When in the North, he would sleep in the bottom of his canoe. Attracted by Thomson's enthusiasm to Algonquin Park as a repository of primitive landscape, Jackson, MacDonald, Lismer and Varley all painted there in 1914.

From 1913 until 1918, Harris remained committed to various winter landscapes, but his new friends prodded him in new directions. In 1913, when Jackson was still working in his studio, Harris saw him labouring on a huge Georgian Bay landscape. Slowly the white rock rose in the central foreground and was graced by the tall, scraggy spruce tree. Above the rock and the tree was a majestic cloudy sky. When MacDonald saw this piece, he suggested calling it Mount Ararat after the high ground where Noah's ark came to rest. The suggestion is that Jackson's imagination is so archetypal as to have captured the world after the flood. The forms—trees, rock, clouds, sky—are elemental. The canvas uses a lot of "dragging," whereby wet paint is placed over previously painted portions.

Harris, as he witnessed the evolution of Jackson's painting, was seized with a corresponding boldness. He took one of his earlier Laurentian paintings (*Near St. Jovite*) and made it larger and changed the proportions; the earlier painting was horizontal, the new one square. The colours are brighter in the new canvas (*Laurentian Landscapes*). Jackson, realizing the influence he had exerted, remarked: "There were lively interchanges of opinion [in Harris's studio]. There was the stimulus of comparison and frank discussion on aims and ideals and technical problems that resulted in various experiments. One of Harris's efforts to get vibrant colours was to drag his brush quickly through three or four colours and slap it on the canvas. Among ourselves it was known as Tomato Soup."[10]

Within what became the Group of Seven, Harris's closest ties were to MacDonald and Jackson. From Jackson, he received technical inspiration, although the two of them were drawn in contrasting directions. In 1932, Harris explained it this way: "A.Y.J. has never sought to influence me in the slightest—has never been anything but encouraging and his criticism has ever been in Terms of design, rhythm etc. and never once as far as I can remember been otherwise than helpful—and because we see differently he has had no more effect on my work or thought or mood than I have had on his." Nevertheless, Lawren realized, Jackson had an instinctive understanding of what he was trying to accomplish. All in all, he was "sound, generous, very real and deeply true."[11]

Sometimes inspiration came in a different way. In April 1916, Harris, his cousin Chester, MacCallum and Tom Thomson travelled to the Cauchon Lakes area in the northeastern district of Algonquin Park. Harris had a vivid recollection of an incident "one afternoon . . . when a dramatic thunderstorm came up. There was a wild rush of wind across the lake and all nature was tossed into a turmoil. Tom and I were in an abandoned lumber shack. When the storm broke, Tom looked out, grabbed his sketch box, ran out into the gale, squatted behind a big stump and commenced to paint in a fury."[12] James MacCallum described what occurred in this way: "It was blowing very hard and Harris was painting further up the shore. The wind blew down the tree [shown in *The West Wind*] and Harris at first thought Thomson was killed but he soon sprang up, waved his hand to him and went on painting."[13] In this instance, Harris was not so much interested in what Thomson was painting as much as he was moved by the artist's intensity, by his ability to surrender to the unexpected moment. "Here," he recalled, "was symbolized . . . the function of artist in life: he must accept in deep singleness of purpose the manifestations of life in

Lawren Harris.
Algonquin Park.
Circa 1917.

man and in great nature, and transform these into controlled, ordered and vital expressions of meaning."[14]

Algonquin Park displays just how much Jackson and Thomson were beginning to influence Harris. The colours—especially the reds, yellows and burnt oranges—are rendered in what is essentially a new way. This sketch certainly does not have the fineness of decoration that had been the artist's preoccupation for the past few years. Instead, the foreground rocks, the lake, the trees, the foliage and the sky are painted in a vigorous, swirling way that is

suggestive of the kind of art Jackson practised and Thomson per-
fected. Such an approach did not sit easy with Harris.

Harris recognized Thomson's natural talent, but he was well
aware that Jackson was the person who enriched it: "His painting
had been tight and sombre, almost a grey monotone in colour.
Jackson's sparkling, vibrant, rich colour opened his eyes, as it did
the eyes of the rest of us, and Tom saw the Canadian landscape
as he had never seen it before. It amounted to a revelation. From
then on nothing could hold him."[15] Harris's German-trained eye
tended towards sombre colour tones; his later iconic landscape
pictures employ a very restricted colour palette. In this way he
would make a virtue of necessity.

Algonquin Park and Georgian Bay never elicited Harris's eye
as it did Thomson's or Jackson's. At this time another location
favoured by Harris was Kempenfelt Bay, the nine-mile bay that
leads into Barrie, Ontario, sixty miles north of Toronto. This
place, which connects to Lake Simcoe, was known for ice fish-
ing and as the residence of Kempenfelt Kelly, a Loch Ness–style
monster. Harris and his mother owned vacation property there,
and he, Trixie and their children often holidayed there at their
summer home, Woodend, in Allandale, on Lake Simcoe.[16]

In 1914, Harris was attempting, in various ways, to move forward as a Canadian painter. He had established camaraderie with
some fellow artists. The spirit of this group of very dissimilar
individuals was captured by Frederick Varley, writing of a trip to
Algonquin Park in 1914:

> There's a small party of us here, the young school, just 5 or 6
> of us and we are all working to one big end. We are endeav-
> ouring to knock out of us all the preconceived ideas, empty-
> ing ourselves of everything except that nature is here in all
> its greatness, and we are here to gather it and understand it
> if only we will be clean enough, healthy enough, and humble
> enough to go to it willing to be taught, and receive it *not* as we
> think it should be, *but as it is*, and then to put down vigorously
> and truthfully that which we have culled.[17]

For Harris, the way to become a Canadian artist was to cull in the right way, to place oneself unreservedly in the present moment.

That culling had been going on at a somewhat leisurely pace. Then everything was shattered with the outbreak of war in 1914. Howard, Lawren's brother, who had graduated from University College at the University of Toronto in 1909, attended Osgoode Hall (the Upper Canada Law Society) and been called to the bar in September 1912, resigned his job as a bond trader, sailed for England in the spring of 1915, obtained a commission in the Eleventh Battalion (the Third Essex Regiment) and joined the imperial army.[18]

(left)
Howard Harris
in uniform.

(right)
Lawren Harris
in uniform.

In the spring of 1916, as Howard was getting ready to cross the Channel into France, Harris enlisted as a private in the Canadian Officers Training Course. On May 5 he was given his "Infantry Certificate" and a week later was appointed lieutenant with the Tenth Royal Grenadiers Regiment. He was taken on as a "supernumerary" officer, that is, as someone who would not be sent overseas. Ten days later he was declared medically fit. (According to his daughter, Peggie Knox, Harris was turned down for active duty.)

In Ontario, tensions about the war hit boiling point after the sinking of the *Lusitania* on May 7, 1915, with the loss of many lives of people from that province. Electric signs advertising German beer were removed; Toronto civic employees of German origin were dismissed. Berlin, Ontario, changed its name to Waterloo, in large part because its residents, many of them German in origin, wanted to proclaim their solidarity with their fellow Canadians. At the Canadian National Exhibition in the autumn of 1916, the dachshund entered "was a minority of one. This long elongated native of sausage-land was discovered in a pitiful state of depression and low morale. While all the other fellows were being patted and petted, this forlorn alien enemy looked around it with a woebegone expression and actually whined and shed tears when a charitable onlooker stroked it."[19]

On a more serious note, a German-born professor who was dedicating himself to recruiting speeches on behalf of the Canadian army was lambasted by a Member of Parliament: "He may be a spy; I do not know; if he is not, he is a deserter from his own country and no man for us to mix up with. The British cause does not need such advocacy. His German accent is so strong and so objectionable that his English is not understandable. He is the typical German soldier from every point of view and I do not think Anglo-Saxon people have any use for such persons."[20] The German-born painter Gustav Hahn (1866–1962) was asked to resign from the OSA; he and his family were impecunious as a result. In Ontario, feelings may have run high against the Germans, but there was a great deal of anger among enlisted men concerning the living conditions on base.

That July, Harris began work as a musketry instruction officer at Camp Borden, on the outskirts of Barrie. Harris was among thirty thousand recruits living at this large training base consisting largely of dirt roads and filthy huts. This place, filled with blowing sand, was quickly nicknamed Camp Horror. So awful were the living conditions that at the opening ceremony in July 1916 the recruits yelled at the Minister of Militia and Defence: "Take us out of this rotten hole!"[21]

Harris spent some time in Toronto at Hart House, now an army headquarters. The next month he was reassigned to Camp Borden, where he assisted in the training of recruits by constructing, much in the manner of a carnival sideshow, realistic targets of German soldiers on which he painted faces that popped up here and there for a second then disappeared. When Annie went overseas to run a convalescent hospital in England funded by Massey-Harris, Lawren, Trixie and their children moved to 123 St. George Street to look after her home. (In 1917, after Annie returned home and shortly after the death of Trixie's mother, Lawren, Trixie and their children, who had taken possession in about 1915 of a house on Clarendon Avenue designed for them by Eden Smith, moved to 63 Queen's Park Crescent, the Phillipses' grand house. They remained there until 1926.)

In December 1914, Jackson returned to Montreal, where in June 1915 he enlisted as a private in the Sixtieth Battalion. The following year he was wounded in the hip and shoulder at Maple Copse and transferred to England.

The war had devastating economic consequences for free-lance commercial work. The Lismers moved in with the Mac-Donalds in the summer of 1915 in order to work the Thornhill farm for cash crops. Subsequently, Lismer moved to Halifax to assume the directorship of the Victoria School of Art and Design. That place closed after the Halifax explosion in December 1917; it became a storage space for coffins. The budget of the National Gallery was slashed from $100,000 in 1914 to $8,000 in 1918. Recognizing that the country's artists were suffering badly, the gallery allocated all its meagre spending allowance to Canadian works of art.

Just as Harris had been trying to get hold of the idea of Canada as a locale in which to paint, the world he and his fellow artists knew came apart. By 1914, Harris had effectively cut himself off from Germany, and yet it must have been unsettling to know that the country in which he had trained was now enemy territory. The Arts and Letters Club's Augustus Bridle proclaimed: "Modern art as exemplified most successfully in Germany was but one outcropping of the conditions which brought about the war."[22]

In an interview in the *Toronto Daily Star*, the artist and journalist Carl Ahrens (1862–1936), commenting on the OSA's sixteenth annual show, attacked artists such as Harris, Lismer, MacDonald and Thomson as being part of a European gestalt that had led to war: "The so-called new art has no excuse, and bespeaks only of a hermaphroditic condition of mind and an absolute lack of the knowledge of drawing, colour, and design. I feel that these young persons who are indulging in these pastimes would gain a much higher standing before men if they gave their now misspent efforts to the destruction of the Hun."[23] The adjective "hermaphroditic" in the parlance of the time would have been a synonym for homosexual; he was accusing the Group members of not being sufficiently masculine to take on the complexities of Canadian landscape painting. He was also accusing them of being afraid to fight for their country.

Not surprisingly, Hector Charlesworth, a friend of Ahrens, weighed in with his own distinct brand of castigation. This time, he set his sights on MacDonald, two of whose paintings he famously dubbed "Hungarian Goulash" and "Drunkard's Stomach." He also accused him of hurling "his paint pots in the face of the public."[24]

Not only did Harris have to deal with the grim facts of war, but he was being labelled as an active participant in the moral degeneracy that had supposedly brought the war into existence.

7

PARADISE LOST, PARADISE REGAINED

(1917–1919)

Just as Lawren was feeling that he had finally placed himself on the right path towards achieving his goals as an artist, war intervened. What kind of blackness was going to invade Western civilization? He had fond memories of Germany and the Germans. He did not wish those sentiments to be eradicated. He had turned a corner in his spiritual and artistic existence, but now he was afraid of being stymied once again.

His new artist-comrades bucked him up. He had a keen sense of a shared purpose. He had used his money well in paying for the construction of the Studio Building, which was a kind of headquarters for a new kind of artistic existence in Canada. He was no longer alone.

ON MARCH 24, 1917, fellow Arts and Letters Club member Hector Charlesworth (1872–1945), the critic for *Saturday Night* who would become the most outspoken opponent of advanced art, called *Decorative Landscape*, Harris's contribution to the OSA exhibition, a "garish poster."[1] This canvas, similar in technique to the *Winter* images that had been preoccupying the artist since 1913, differs from them in that the viewer's point of view has been moved back considerably and a great deal of emphasis given to the pink and pale blue of the rock formation in the foreground. Over this element hover blue trees and a radiantly golden sky. In this instance, by applying the adjective "decorative," Harris was signalling that the landscape was meant to be fanciful and somewhat surreal. In any event, he was trying to push his experiments with winter landscapes a bit further, and was rebuffed for doing so by the critic from *Saturday Night*.

Lawren Harris.
Decorative
Landscape. 1917.

A year later, when Harris submitted eight winter canvases to the OSA, the reviewer in the *Weekly Sun* found the pictures strong but puzzling: "When I stepped through the arch of entrance into the blaze of colour, involuntarily I took a deep breath . . . But certainly the colours [in *Snow VI*] are exaggerated. As to the sky, I have seen it in delicate tints of apple green, but never have I seen it entirely and uniformly green."[2] However, Lewis W. Clemens's praise in the *Toronto Sunday World* was unstinting: "The most important leader of this [contemporary] movement is Mr. Lawren Harris, whose work possesses strength in colour composition and tone. Anyone who is at all interested in the art of Canada, should not under any circumstances, miss seeing this exhibition for . . . there has never been offered before in Canada a consistent show of this new work." In contrast to the other reviewer, he found that the "light on the snow of a pine tree in shadow, as contrasted against snow in sunlight, is an example of the fidelity to nature in which Mr. Harris is working."[3]

Clemens's praise fell on partially deaf ears that autumn because two events had ravaged Harris, leaving him despondent. The first was the death of Tom Thomson, who drowned at Canoe Lake in July 1917. Thomson was an expert woodsman, someone known to be especially adept at using a canoe. In *Paddle and Palette: The Story of Tom Thomson* (1935), Blodwen Davies asked questions that have never been answered:

> Who met Tom Thomson on that stretch of grey lake, screened from all eyes, that July noon?
> Who was it struck him a blow across the right temple—and was it done with the thin edge of a paddle blade?—that sent the blood spurting from his ear?
> Who watched him crumple up and topple over the side of the canoe and sink slowly out of sight without a struggle?[4]

Tom Thomson unlikely died in the sort of freak accident that can befall even an expert woodsman, and before his death there was already an aura about this artist. His reputation as an untutored genius was just beginning to take off, and his sudden death in his thirty-ninth year demanded some sort of explanation beyond the mundane. In addition, he had the reputation of being an ornery person on occasion and a womanizer. Had an angry husband done away with him? Or had he quarrelled with another expert outdoorsman?

Harris had no doubt that Thomson was a "natural" in the way he was not: "Thomson knew the north country as none of us did, and he made us partners in his devotion to it. His last summer saw him produce his finest work. He was just moving into the full tide of his power when he was lost to us. Tom was an adept woodsman and canoeman."[5] People often visited Tom, who would freely give away a sketch when it was admired. He had to be protected by his friends from such spontaneous acts of generosity.

The following sentences by Harris can as easily be applied to him as to Thomson: "He was at the same time sensitive and given to despondency. He would often sit in the twilight, leaning over from his chair, facing his painting, after working at high pitch all day, and flick bits of wooden matches on the thick wet paint where they stuck. He had a poor opinion of his own work, but an exaggeratedly good opinion of the work of the rest of us."[6]

To Harris and his confederates, the death of Thomson was devastating. A man in the prime of life, the perfect man—"tall, lithe, and very graceful"—had vanished, been snatched away forever. Moreover, there was the suspicion of foul play. However one looked at it, the event was shrouded in mystery.

Harris, like many of his associates, believed that Thomson had been murdered, and he may even have wondered if the profession of artist was, at bottom, an immoral one. Tom had conducted his life in a way that was seen as unconventional and unseemly by many. Harris, who had the propensity to feel guilty, could have been led to wonder if he was part of a community that attempted to transgress traditional moral codes. Harris's increasing interest in theosophy was designed to protect him from such concerns; his life was supposed to be connected to the harmony of existence.

Moreover, there was the glaring fact that Thomson had by 1917 completed a substantial body of first-rate work. Then he was taken. There might have been for Harris the unconscious fear that he too might labour to reach the heights gained by Thomson only to have his life removed.

Or, Harris may have speculated that the true gift of art was given only to those the gods quickly destroy. He could have thought that he was somehow cursed: he would never attain the heights he envisioned for himself. Perhaps he had been passed over, did not really possess the talent he thought he did. In the midst of the misery of world war, such speculations would have been especially frightening.

After Thomson's death, late in 1917, Harris negotiated permission for himself and other officers to take a trip to New York City that lasted from December 30 until January 7, 1918. This excursion may have been some sort of attempt to renew himself away from Toronto. Then, on February 22, 1918, thirty-one-year-old Howard Harris, a decorated veteran of both the Somme and Passchendaele, was killed while inspecting a German trench near Bapaume.*

Harris and his brother moved in the same social circles in Toronto, and the two brothers obviously saw each other often. Lawren was completely devastated. He began to suffer from a sleep disorder in which he experienced "troublous, somewhat terrified tossings and turnings and apprehensive opening of the eyes."[7] He was the "victim of moods . . . I can't or don't rather, keep on one track." He felt that he had "built everything . . . on sand."[8]

Annie was in England when the news of Howard's death reached her other son. Harris could take comfort from his two young children, to whom he was deeply attached, but he and Trixie were not emotionally close. He suffered a nervous breakdown, and on May 1 was medically discharged from the army.

As the war progressed, the news coming out of France of the loss of many Canadian lives had had a cumulative effect on the home front, where depression was rife. The nervous exhaustion that overwhelmed Harris was a bitter refrain of the suffering he had endured as a child of nine. For over twenty years, Harris had

---

* He had served on the Somme and Ypres–Passchendaele fronts. He was promoted to captain in February 1917 and in May was awarded the Military Cross for successfully directing an attack on the German trench near Albert.

lived in the shadow of his father's sudden passing, but he had not been engulfed by it; he had carried on. Now he could no longer do this. He had lost the ability to face life with a stiff upper lip.[9]

Later that May Harris left Toronto, accompanied by James MacCallum, on a sketching trip that he hoped would speed his recovery. The two travelled to Manitoulin Island, which Harris found disappointing. So, from there, they crossed to the mainland, heading west to Sault Ste. Marie. There, they transferred to the Algoma Central Railway, spent some time at a lumber camp and then went on to Michipicoten Harbour on the eastern end of Lake Superior.

Harris was deeply impressed, and his reaction to the landscape he beheld can be discerned in Fred Housser's words (based on what Harris told him): "The Algoma country is charted on a grand scale, slashed by ravines and canyons through which run rivers, streams, and springs, broadening into lakes, churning lightly over shoaly places or dropping with roll and mist for hundreds of feet. Granite rocks rise to noble heights—their sides and tops solidly covered with hardwood, spruce and pine."[10] A bit more prosaically, Harris told Jim MacDonald that it was possible, entering "this paradise," to "forget entirely to give your health or state of mind even a passing thought." In fact, it was a place that fed the senses. You could abandon yourself to "drinking its gorgeousness with your eyes." There were also the "sweet, woodsy sounds" and "crisp, clean air" to fill the lungs.

So revitalized was Harris that he organized another trip there that autumn. He was thrilled, as he told MacDonald, that the Algoma Central Railway would provide a boxcar: "Well, James, Me boy, down on your knees and give great gobs of thanks to Allah! We have a car awaiting us on the Algoma Central!"[11] This time the group was larger: on September 10, 1918, Harris, Jim MacDonald, Frank Johnston, James MacCallum and Harris's dog, Prince, left Toronto for Algoma. This was the first of the boxcar trips. The artists lived in CPR boxcar 10557, which was fitted with bunks, a stove, a water tap and sink, a kitchen bench and shelves, bracket lamps, lanterns and foodstuffs. Excursions were often made on a three-wheel handcar suitable for two to take short trips up and down the tracks.

MacDonald, who had suffered a stroke the year before, stayed close to the boxcar so that he could rest when necessary. His response to the country he beheld was, if anything, more rhapsodic than Harris's:

> I will not attempt to describe this country for you as I haven't a great flow of language at present. Perhaps that will come as usual when I get back and talk as usual after a trip. But the country is certainly all that Lawren and the Dr. said about it. It is a land after Dante's heart. The canyon is like a winding way to the lower regions and last night, when the train went through just after dark, with the fireman stoking up, the light of the fire shining on the smoke clouds, it was easy to imagine his Satanic majesty taking a drive through his domain. I had walked a little distance up the canyon and the effect was eerie enough to make me speed up for home. The great perpendicular rocks seemed to overhang as though they might fall any minute, and the dark Agawa moving through it all had an uncanny snakiness. On a fine day, such as this, the canyon seems to lead *upwards*, and has all the attributes of an imagined Paradise.[12]

This expedition was so successful that in mid-September 1919 Harris, MacDonald and Johnston undertook a month-long boxcar trip to the same region. This time they were accompanied by A.Y. Jackson.

The Algoma landscapes are remarkably different from anything in Harris's previous work. For one thing, the paint is applied in a much heavier, thicker, more vigorous fashion. Gone is the fastidiousness of the winter canvases. The structural strengths of the latter have been replaced by a more penetrating organic unity in which extremely diffuse colours and objects are forced together. The decorative has been replaced by a firmer insistence on underlying structure: the differing aspects of nature are recognized but then conjoined.

In the Algoma region, Harris's eyes feasted on a much wilder landscape than he had witnessed before. In part, this explains the remarkable change that occurred in his art. However, it does not sufficiently account for it. Here was a man who had suffered two tremendous losses and who was attempting to rebuild and refortify himself. Harris had obviously begun to see the world differently, and that alteration can be witnessed in the new canvases.

Moreover, Harris made a significant adjustment: he started to venture even more in the direction of Tom Thomson's inclinations as an artist. He had done this before when he had been influenced by both Jackson and Thomson. The new Harris pictures use a colour palette even closer to Thomson's; the paint is applied in a manner reminiscent of the dead artist.

In the process of mourning him, Harris internalized Thomson's creative strengths. Harris may not have entered into this consciously, but it is the greatest tribute he could have paid to his dead comrade. Consciously, Harris may have been well aware that he had to separate himself in some way from the elegant winter pictures in order to enter a potentially more chaotic terrain, one in which he would be pursuing new leads and thus become more vulnerable. Though the new path might be difficult to discern, he would find his way forward artistically if he followed it. This he resolved to do.

Falls, Agawa River (1918), *Algoma Woodland* (1919) and *Autumn, Algoma* (1920) are deliberately less finished-looking landscapes than those of the previous six years. In *Waterfall, Algoma* in particular, he combines decorative richness with a rough, vigorous handling of brush strokes. They have what Harris later called, speaking of Algoma, "a rich wildness."

In that region, he and his friends "found there were cloud formations and rhythms peculiar to different parts of the country and to different seasons of the year. We found that, at times, there were skies over the great Lake Superior which, in their singing expansiveness and sublimity, existed nowhere else in Canada."[13] In those stirring words can be discerned a person who is in the process of recovering from the emotional storms that had engulfed him after the deaths of Tom Thomson and Howard Harris.

Lawren Harris.
Waterfall, Algoma.
1918.

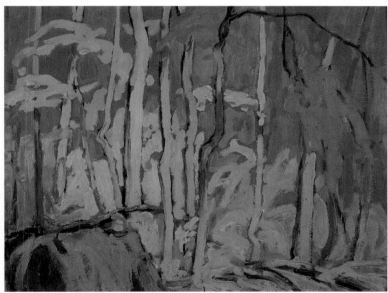

Lawren Harris.
Algoma Woods II.
Circa 1918.

8

ASCENDING

(1918–1921)

---

*Lawren was recuperating. He was not quite sure how he had sur-
vived the deaths of Tom and Howard. With his brother, he had
shared many happy and sad moments. They had sometimes fought
bitterly as youngsters, but deep, unspoken bonds united them.*

*From time to time, he had to put aside any envious feelings
he had about Thomson, the truest artist he had ever known. The
fellow simply breathed art. In what seemed an effortless way,
he came up with astounding pictures. He was so much a creature of the wilderness, an expert in its ways. He was destined to
become the greatest Canadian painter of all time, but then, in an
instant, he was gone, leaving a huge hole in his wake.*

*Am I a genuine artist? Lawren was forced to ask himself.
He had a great many ideas about art, but did he possess the eye of
someone like Thomson, who intuitively created art? These were
unsettling questions to ask oneself on a daily basis.*

HARRIS attempted to convince MacDonald to accompany him to Algoma in the autumn of 1918. Mac-
Donald was also physically and psychically overcome
by Thomson's death. During a move from Thornhill to a house
nearer Toronto, he suffered a stroke in November 1917. He was

bedridden for many weeks. Harris advised his friend that it might be advantageous "to refrain . . . [from] tying one's self into knots." It was better, in his opinion, to acknowledge that one was "plumb at the bottom of the ladder that leads to all infinity and blessedness," and be "grateful that even if one cannot see at all distinctly," one could "anticipate the time when one is ready to start climbing."[1]

Harris was using theosophical terms to describe how he was dealing with the devastation of the losses of his friend and his brother. Although reduced to standing at the bottom of the ladder of eternity, he anticipated that he would be able to climb upwards. The Algoma canvases demonstrate Harris's capacity to restore, and thus heal, himself.

He spent much of the summer of 1918 at Woodend and kept busy cutting down trees, pumping water, fitting the house with screen doors and reassembling the dock. He also commenced work on a 120-yard-long urban landscape for U.S. Army recruits to use in target practice. This contained "a ruined village, trenches, shell holes, wire, and general junk."[2] In general, he told Jim MacDonald, attending to the "usual business" of country life "strengthens the old body, more or less dulls" the emotions and induces "a profound slumber." He seemed to have developed an immunity from the terrors that had previously engulfed him.[3]

In his personal life, things were not quite so well integrated. As a father, he was a wonderful companion. Peggie Knox recalled an ideal parent:

> He didn't talk down to his children; he was invariably supportive and fun to be with. He rarely said "No," so we had full scope to try just about anything. It was, "go ahead, but watch it." Our projects often didn't work out—many ended in disaster—and when we disappointed him with our failures we felt worse than if he'd been angry. At summer camps, when he wasn't painting all day, he was full of ideas for things we could all learn to do. He made kites (with faces painted on them), and we flew them. He carved reed flutes that could play tunes, made swings from trees, painted pictures on the

other side of jigsaw puzzles. Sometimes he'd get everyone cleaning up the beach or woods around the camp, replanting ferns and wildflowers, making it all look more attractive. He did sleight of hand tricks, juggling, acrobatics, and any number of other things children love to see and do.4*

When, as young teenagers during the Depression, Lornie and Peggie wanted to find jobs, he told them no. "You should be providing work." He set the two up at his studio above the Bank of Commerce at Yonge and Bloor Streets, where, with funds provided by their father, they paid poor (street) people to sit for them.5

Unfortunately, Lawren's parental behaviour contrasted sharply with Trixie's. Where he was indulgent, she was harsh; where he told the children to give their imaginations free rein, she pulled them back. The differences in parenting styles underscore the emotional distance between the two grown-ups.

The children's most vivid memories of Trixie centred on her habit of isolating a disobedient child and then forcing the other two into opposition against the miscreant. The two eldest children also resented the fact that Howie was their mother's favourite. He was nine years younger than Lornie, six years younger than Peggie. He long remained Trixie's "baby," and she often accused the other two of bullying or teasing him. A favourite child is often segregated from his siblings, and this is exactly what happened in Howie's case. He was never quite able to cast off the stigma of being the youngest child and, in the opinion of his father, he never really grew up.

---

* On a scrap of paper, at about the time she wrote the above paragraph, Peggie Knox drew up a list of her father's "main attributes":

  Great enthusiasm, drive & courage
  Keeping up momentum of work
  Kindness & understanding
  Tolerance—sense of humor
  Keen on health & fitness
  Interested in every new idea
  taught us outdoor skills & sports

In the early 1920s, the couple pasted over their differences. An early canvas, *Woodland Snow, Family Outing*, may in fact represent carefree, happy moments spent together.

Lawren Harris.
Woodland Snow,
Family Outing.
Circa 1918–21.

Harris's sense of humour remained intact. In filling out a printed questionnaire on May 11, 1920 ("INFORMATION FORM for the purpose of Making a Record of Canadian Artists and Their Work"), he observed that he "grew a moustache 2nd year of [the] world war. Improved appearance. First gray hair, June 1916." In reply to whether he had any "honours conferred in connection with art," he replied: "sold one picture once to a citizen. Citizen still alive."[6]

If aspects of Harris's personal life remained stagnant, his art was moving in new directions, as can be seen in the Algoma landscapes. There was a parallel development in Harris's urban landscapes, but the transformation here works differently. The artist's great anguish about the misery and degradation of the war is now inserted into the facades of the buildings he paints, almost as if these canvases are his own form of war art.

Harris's early urban views may be reminiscent of artists such as Vlaminck or Utrillo, while the use of highly saturated reds and yellows may well derive from School of Paris sources or the colour schemes of Group of Seven members. (He would have been aware of the Montreal and Quebec City cityscapes of Morrice; his future collaborator Arthur Lismer undertook urban views in the 1910s.) Nevertheless, he was working in the Secessionist tradition, with its strong undertones of social commentary.

(Although Harris painted many houses in the Toronto inner city over a considerable period of time, from 1909 to the early twenties, he sometimes painted houses in rural settings—for instance, *Untitled (Lake Simcoe Summer)*, 1918, and *Red House, Barrie, circa* 1918–20. In these instances, the emphasis is on experimenting with various methods of representation; no social commentary is being exerted.)

Outskirts of Toronto (1918) employs a far deeper depiction of space than any of the previous urban pictures, such as *Hurdy-Gurdy*

Lawren Harris.
Red House, Barrie.
Circa 1918–20.

(1913). The area shown is Earlscourt, a squatter, semi-slum settlement from the early twentieth century that was annexed by Toronto in 1910. The early residents of this area were from Britain; its name is an ironic reference to Earls Court in London, and this part of Toronto had one of the highest enlistment rates in the entire British Empire. This canvas is bathed in a pale, almost nauseous, yellow; the brush strokes are patchy, incredibly disorganized. Harris's depressive feelings from 1918 are mirrored here.

Lawren Harris.
Hurdy-Gurdy.
Circa 1919–20.

In contrast to *Outskirts, Old Houses, Toronto, Winter* (1919) and *A House in the Slums* (1920) are much brighter canvases, using a far richer array of pigments than found in Harris's earlier depictions of similar subjects. However, the houses themselves are penetrated by a kind of blight or mange that is eating them away. In *Old Houses*, the mustard-yellow paint above the red door looks as if it is about to detach itself and fall to the ground; in *Slums*, the house's murky orange front has mainly disappeared, leaving behind a yellow-cream exterior. The earlier pictures could be said to depict the handsome stolidity of workers' homes; these new canvases are about things falling apart, almost as if Harris had chosen to incorporate some conventions of symbolical landscape into urban views.

In its layering, *Shacks* (1919) displays another innovation in Harris's work. The undulating waves of snow in the foreground are kept in bounds by the fence; behind the snow and the fence are two buildings in relatively subdued colours on the right, while at the far left there is one in bright red; between these houses is a view of the neighbourhood in the background. The word "shack" may have had a particular connotation for Harris because Bridle, in an article published in 1919, had argued that such poorly constructed buildings were harbingers of "hope": the residents had usually constructed these dwellings themselves and as a result a strong sense of community had emerged.

Lawren Harris.
Old Houses, Toronto, Winter. 1919.

Lawren Harris.
Shacks. 1919.

The houses, buildings and shacks painted by Harris come from various sections of Toronto. Some are on the outskirts of the city; some are in those parts of the inner city where immigrants from England, Scotland and Ireland settled; some—especially from 1919—depict the Ward. This district, as described in an anonymous article from 1915, was considered dangerous:

> The district that lies between College and Queen Streets, Yonge Street and University Avenue is generally regarded by the respectable citizens of Toronto as a strange and fearful place into which it is unwise to enter even in daylight, which after dark—no sane person would dream of running such a risk! The danger that lurks in these crowded streets is not always clearly formulated in the minds of those who fear it, perhaps it is the dagger of an Italian desperado of which they dream—perhaps the bearded faces of the "Sheenies" [Jews] are sufficient in themselves to inspire terror—but at any rate the fear remains and probably it could best be analyzed as Fear of the Unknown.

In 1918, a report by the Bureau of Municipal Research entitled "What is 'The Ward' Going to Do with Toronto?" was, if anything, even more outspoken about this neighbourhood as a place of degradation:

> Properly speaking, "the Ward" is a condition, an attitude of mind toward life, a standard of living—not merely a geographical location.
>
> In rough-cast houses, plaster has fallen off, and there is, more or less, an absence of paint or whitewash. Fences about the houses have partly collapsed and no effort is made to repair them or to remove them altogether. Sidewalks leading to the houses and doorsteps are in a broken condition, and the doors themselves in a state of ill-repair. Wooden shutters sag from one hinge or have many slats missing . . . Rags and unused clothing lie scattered about, mingled with broken pieces of furniture, tin cans, broken stove pipe, and other junk, without any danger of being disturbed by the residents.

Children in Price's Lane. *Circa* 1912.

The streets of the Ward were cluttered with refuse; the air smelled of waste; the roofs were leaky. Demand to rent in this area was high (the cost was between ten and twelve dollars a month). Harris once called the Ward "the sordid fringe of his native Toronto."[7]

Lawren Harris.
January Thaw,
Edge of Town.
1921.

Bridle, aware of the deprivations endured by the residents of the Ward, nevertheless characterized it as "the most cosmopolitan part of Toronto, on cross streets and side streets are the rows of blinking little modern shops, the phonograph blaring at the corner; everywhere the shuffling, gabbling crowds, and the flaring little shops—fronted with people."[8] That sense of life must have been a strong draw for Harris, who never found such vivacity among his own social set.

There is a tinge of irony in the title of *January Thaw, Edge of Town* (1921). A thaw could signify that winter is coming to an end; here, it appears that a spring thaw might do damage to the houses, especially the one in the left foreground. The title might also hint that there is never any real thaw—significant change—in the lives of the people who live in this slum.

The pronounced differences between the earlier urban scenes and the new ones astonished the critic for the *Telegram* when he reviewed the OSA exhibition in March 1919 in a piece entitled "Noisy Chaos of Colour":

> People who know nothing of Art will remember the charming studies of scenes in the Ward which this artist had produced in the past years—quiet old houses with a charm of colour and a reality that held the unversed, the mere outsider, cub reporters and all the rest spellbound. This year Mr. Harris has pressed the very brightest tubes upon his palette, and has let his brush, knife, trowel, shovel or whatever tool he has used run away with itself. The pictures shout from the walls, and quite disturb the equanimity of the show.[9]

Canvases that were "charming" have been replaced by those that are disturbing.

The same sort of process can be glimpsed in a different way in *Return from Church* (1919). Here the relatively bright colours of the houses are juxtaposed against the dark clothing of the churchgoers in a way that suggests those who attend Christian services are often cut off from any knowledge of the social conditions in which some of their fellow residents of Toronto exist.

In the urban landscapes done after 1918, Harris is inserting more straightforwardly than before a critique of the underlying discrepancies between rich and poor. In such a context, all men may be equal, but they are not treated equally.

A completely different spirit reigns in *Billboard* (1921), originally called *Jazz*, which shows two workers in front of an enormous sign that they are presumably putting in place. However, the image on the panel is a vibrant, Modernistic, abstract one that would never have been a suitable piece of public advertising. The picture has a fanciful quality in its juxtaposition of urban squalor

with Modernism, as if to suggest that Harris himself was trying to find an appropriate contemporary vocabulary in which
to encapsulate his art. Later, when he was struggling to become
an abstract artist, he must have thought back to this whimsical,
exuberant piece in which he first displayed a propensity to abandon the conventions of traditional realism.

Lawren Harris.
Billboard (Jazz).
1920.

The theme of the gulf between rich and poor is treated even more
dramatically in two urban views (*Black Court, Halifax* and *Elevator Court, Halifax*) done after a trip to Nova Scotia and Newfoundland in the early spring of 1921. If this sketching trip was
supposed to reinvigorate his landscape art, that purpose was not
fulfilled, since there exist no significant canvases or sketches corresponding with such an aim. Instead, Harris was deeply moved
by the slums of Halifax. Perhaps he was shocked to find that city
blighted like Toronto by grim poverty, but it is entirely possible
that his inner demons were somehow unleashed in a new way by
looking at a different urban landscape.

At the time of the American Revolution, many Loyalists brought their African-American slaves with them to Canada, while formerly enslaved black Americans also made their way to the colonies of British North America, settling predominantly in Nova Scotia. This latter group was largely made up of tradespeople and labourers. As well, there were black Loyalists, many of whom were free people of colour who had never been slaves but relied on British promises of equality. They too had left the United States after the Revolution and settled in Nova Scotia. During the American Civil War, that colony was a frequent destination on the Underground Railway.

Black Court is set in a slum housing area between the downtown and Africville, the black section of Halifax. The town never received proper roads, health services, water, street lamps or electricity. Simple things that all towns routinely obtained, they did not. The lack of these services had serious health implications for the lives of the inhabitants. Contamination of the wells was a serious and ongoing issue, so even the little water they did acquire needed to be boiled before use. As the city of Halifax expanded, Africville became a preferred site for all types of undesirable industries and facilities—a prison in 1853, a slaughterhouse, even a depository for fecal waste.

This canvas looks very much like a stage set, with the building occupying the left foreground area receding sharply to meet another building; between the second building and one parallel to it, there is an opening that gives a restricted view of the sea. The sky is rendered in menacing, undulating lines. However, the viewer's attention is focused on the area in front of the buildings, in which three children seem trapped. The land in front of the tenements rolls down in layers of mud.

Elevator Court is much more deliberately stylized than any of the previous city pictures, and its various passages are clearly demarcated into zones: the elevator court and the stack next to it in the middle picture area; the blue and black earth in the foreground; the blue and beige-white sky; the building on the far right. All of these structures have straight, sharp angles, a geometric regularity

Lawren Harris.
Black Court,
Halifax. 1921.

Lawren Harris.
Elevator Court,
Halifax. 1921.

not seen in Harris's previous work. These changes signal that he was on the verge of finding a startling way forward as an artist.

These canvases are not mere exercises in form; there is a quiet anger here. To express his disdain at the prevailing power structure that created vast wealth for a few at the expense of the many, Harris used new Modernistic means to encapsulate his derision for those who hold the poor in an iron grip and ensure that their lives become even more wretched. In *Black Court*, despair is evident, whereas in *Elevator Court* the dark, dingy colours suggest the trimming that has taken place to force the members of the underclass into their subservient places.

9

CONFEDERATES

(1919–1922)

Lawren had become something of an exhibitionist. He spoke loudly, brashly and sometimes abrasively in defending the concept of modern Canadian art. In his heart of hearts, he was not quite so certain as he sounded in his various pronouncements. He wondered where exactly he was heading as an artist.

Jim MacDonald was just as successful a decorative painter as he was. Lawren could say the same about some of Jackson's pictures, and he remained convinced of Thomson's genius, which seemed to have emanated from his soul in one mighty burst of cosmic energy.

ART POLITICS was an activity to which Harris was increasingly drawn, sometimes in a wilful, self-destructive way. Harris, Johnston and the portraitist E. Wyly Grier were chosen to act as the selection committee for the OSA's 1919 exhibition. The trio ignited a tempest in a teapot when they rejected a pair of paintings by Elizabeth Annie McGillivray Knowles (1866–1928). The lady in question, a specialist in barnyard subjects, was a member of the Royal Canadian Academy, as well as the National Association of Women Painters and Sculptors in the United States. One of her paintings had been acquired by the

National Gallery in Ottawa. Her uncle was a specialist in Rocky Mountain paintings and her husband a prominent artist. The couple hosted a salon at their home at Spadina and Bloor.

Harris was well aware that the exclusion of McGillivray Knowles would cause a controversy, and that was exactly what happened. In an interview with the *Toronto Star*, he added fuel to the fire that had been created by suggesting that the best way to avoid disputes was for the OSA to hold two separate exhibitions, one for artists like McGillivray Knowles that "the older men consider meritorious," the other for "what pleases the younger men," a group of artists including himself who were likely to "produce something really significant."[1]

Harris found great comfort in being part of a group of men with a common purpose. At this stage, women were excluded from his coterie; this was the (unfortunate) norm at the time. In Harris's case, a group provided him with a great deal of psychic comfort because it gave him a sense of existing in an assemblage into which his father, his brother and certainly Tom Thomson would have fitted.

The 1919 OSA exhibition featured eight canvases by Harris, which garnered some favourable reviews, although, as we have seen, the reviewer from the *Toronto Telegram* felt his canvases disturbed "the equanimity of the show."[2] Three weeks afterwards, Harris, MacDonald and Johnston mounted "Algoma Sketches" at the Art Gallery of Toronto, from April 26 to May 19. Along the central hall were placed "Algomaxims" such as: "If you never saw anything like that in nature do not despair," "The more you know the less you condemn" and "The great purpose of landscape art is to make us at home in our own country."[3] The reviewer in the *Mail and Empire* compared the paintings to the work of the Confederation poets, and added that they deserved enthusiastic support: "In their work the spirit of young Canada has found itself."[4] None of the paintings sold.

By the end of the summer of 1919, A.Y. Jackson, returned from the war, was back in residence in the Studio Building; Lismer had been appointed vice-principal of the Ontario College of Art; and Varley too had returned to Toronto.

In the autumn, Harris arranged once again for the Algoma Central Railway to make a boxcar available for a month. Mac-Donald, Jackson, Johnston and Harris left Toronto on September 15 for Sault Ste. Marie. They went south from Canton to Hubert and finally Batchewana. The accommodations, as before, were sparse: built-in bunks, a table and four chairs, an iron stove, a sink, a water tank and storage shelves. The artists decorated the car with a small fir tree and a moose skull, under which they inscribed the motto *Ars Longa Vita Brevis* (Art is long, Life is short). Once again, the railway company supplied them with a handcar. The artists also brought a red canoe with them.

The four paddled the dark waters of the Agawa River, gliding in their canoe "through the yellow floating leaves, and breaking the still reflections of crimson and gold and green with waving streamers of sky colour."[5] They often worked in pairs, one group using the handcar, the other the canoe. At night, they critiqued each other's works and read the "two Henrys": Henry David Thoreau and O. Henry (famous for his short stories with surprise endings).

Jackson fondly recalled the cold nights, "but in the boxcar, with the fire in the stove, we were snug and warm. Discussions and arguments would last until late in the night, ranging from Madame Blavatsky and Mary Baker Eddy."[6] Outside was the aurora, the murmurs of rapids and the silence of the night. Harris initiated many of the discussions, often concerning mystics and metaphysics.

With considerable elation, Harris later recalled that trip:

This was a time for criticism, encouragement, and discussion, for accounts of our discoveries about painting, for our thoughts about the character of the country, and our descriptions of effects in nature which differed in each section of the country. We found, for instance, that there was a rich wildness and clarity of colours in the Algoma woods which made the colour in southern Ontario seem grey and subdued. We found there were cloud formations and rhythms peculiar to different parts of the country and to different seasons of the year.[7]

The fall colours were astonishing, as MacDonald noted: "Birch woods, that were dense yellow in the morning, were often grey by night. But the wild cherry trees still hung as though the high fifes and violins were to finish the great concert of colour."[8] The hills that had been crimson and scarlet eventually became purplish

Arthur Lismer.
Lawren Harris.
1920.

grey. However, as Jackson accurately recalled, this landscape was too voluptuous for Harris's taste. At this time Harris, in his own practice, looked askance at sensuous use of colours. Despite his best efforts, Lawren's Baptist ancestry still influenced his work.

After returning from this trip in mid-November, Harris, Mac-Donald and Johnston applied to the Art Gallery of Toronto for permission to stage another exhibition, one more encompassing than the Algoma exhibition; ten artists would be included.

Early in 1920, Jackson suggested to Harris that this show include three Quebec artists: Randolph Hewton, Albert Robinson and Robert Pilot. At a meeting in March 1920 at Harris's home at 63 Queen's Park Crescent were MacDonald, Lismer, Varley, Johnston and Carmichael (Jackson was snowshoeing around Georgian Bay). That evening, Lismer sketched a sprawling Harris puffing at a cigarette and perched on an ottoman. Looking very much the leader of the assembly, he would have led this strategy discussion.

The idea of a group designation was at the forefront of the agenda. Harris must have been immensely pleased since he would have been aware that in 1897 Fjaestad had become a member of the Rackenmålarna, a colony of artists. Realizing that bands of artists often gave themselves names based on the number of members (the Group of Eleven in Berlin, the Belgian Les XX), the Canadians must have quickly decided to call themselves the "Group of Seven." In theosophy, the number seven is especially fortuitous.

In the celebrated photograph of the Group of Seven (Carmichael is absent) with Barker Fairley, their differing personalities are readily evident. On the extreme right, Jackson looks a bit grumpily but waggishly at the photographer, as if anxious that his privacy not be disrupted; Varley sits straight up and stares at the photographer; Harris, cigarette in mouth, looks down casually—easily the most elegant-looking of the company; Fairley, pipe in mouth, stares as if in the midst of contemplating a point in aesthetics; Johnston appears markedly reserved, even disgruntled; a slightly sprawled Lismer looks quizzically into space, as if thinking how he might draw the scene; MacDonald, left hand on chin, smiles genially.

Arthur Goss, photographer. Group of Seven at the Arts and Letters Club. 1920.

A visitor to the first Group of Seven exhibition, which ran from May 7 to 17, 1920, would have seen 121 catalogued works (54 canvases and 44 oil sketches by the Seven, 16 temperas by Johnston, 5 canvases and 2 pastels from the Montreal artists). The foreword to the catalogue recapitulated many sentiments Harris, Jackson and MacDonald held dear:

> No country can ever hope to rise beyond a vulgar mediocrity where there is not an unbounded confidence in what its humanity can do . . . the artists here represented make no pretence of being the only ones in Canada doing significant work. But they do most emphatically hold that their work is significant and of real value to the country.

There was also a "word as you view the pictures":

> The artists invite adverse criticism. Indifference is the greatest evil they have to contend with. But they would ask you—do you read books that contain only what you already know? If not, they argue, then you should hardly want to see pictures that show you what you can already see for yourselves.

Harris's own belief system is strongly articulated here: he always welcomed criticism of any kind; indifference was anathema to him. Yet this statement also implies that any genuine Modernist art actively seeking to show things in a new way might court serious negative responses.

The Group's mandate was especially catholic. MacDonald exhibited the largest number of early works, one from 1914 and three from 1916, including *The Tangled Garden*; both Jackson and Lismer had Nova Scotia subjects; and Harris, Johnston and MacDonald had Algoma ones. Carmichael showed four decorative landscapes from rural areas surrounding Toronto and his home at Lansing. Jackson's *Terre Sauvage* (called *The Northland*) and *Spring in Liéven*, Lismer's *Halifax Harbour* and *Camouflage*, and Varley's *The Sunken Road* were also on display. There were three portraits by Varley, including one of Vincent Massey, Harris's friend. Johnston was the most prolific presence: eighteen works.

Harris may have been the leader of the group, but his entries in this exhibition were not as innovative as those of Jackson,

A.Y. Jackson.
Terre Sauvage.
1913.

J.E.H. MacDonald.
The Tangled Garden.
1916.

Varley, Lismer and, especially, MacDonald. There were five urban views, some Algoma and decorative landscapes, and four portraits.

Margaret Fairbairn in the *Daily Star* drew attention to Varley's portraits, Carmichael's landscapes and the "Japanesy" effect of Jackson's Nova Scotia landscapes.[9] Bridle in the *Canadian Courier* was, as expected, generous in his praise:

> They are not decadent, but creative. They go direct to nature. Their aim in art is greater vitality—and they have got it . . . Seven men go the record limit interpreting north-country landscapes in colours that make the rainbow look like the wrong side out. Symbolism mixes with Jazz, Realism with old-fashioned Beauty, Individualism with Collectivism. Is this Radical Eruption the Canadian Art of the Future? Nobody knows. But it is the work of men who act on the belief that Canada has a colour scheme and subject interest entirely her own.

However, Bridle, commenting on Harris's urban views, observed that he "has no eye for the details of squalor. His snow-capped roofs and his pied and painted rough-cast walls are all clear."[10]

Startling is Harris's decision to enter four portraits into the exhibition: *Eden Smith* (the architect of the Studio Building), *Bess Housser* (the wife of Harris's friend from St. Andrew's, Fred Housser), *Mrs. Leslie Wilson*, and possibly *Mrs. Oscar Taylor*.

Bess Housser, the daughter of Charles and Hannah Larkin, was born in Brandon, Manitoba, in 1890 but received her early education at Havergal College in Toronto. She married Fred Housser in 1914. At the time of their marriage he was a clerk at the Central Loan and Savings Bank, but in the 1920s he became the financial editor of the *Daily Star*. In 1921, the couple lived at 456 Kingston Road in Pickering, about twenty miles from Toronto; in about 1927 they moved to 10 Glengowan Road, "on a hill-top in a beautiful new house"[11] in the Lawrence Park area.

Bess was a mainly self-taught artist, although she studied briefly with Fred Varley. Like her husband and Harris, she wrote on art, contributing many articles to the *Canadian Bookman* between 1923 and 1926.[12] In 1922, Fred and Bess Housser became members of the

Bess Larkin (later Housser and Harris).

Toronto Theosophical Society, but in 1920 they were probably already contemplating that step. When Harris painted her portrait, however, Bess was, like Annie Raynolds, a Christian Scientist, and he nicknamed the painting *The Christian Scientist*.[13]

In her portrait, Bess Housser looks steadfastly at the viewer; her countenance is suffused with quiet confidence; she seems just about to smile. This woman emerges out of the shadows. She has a strong corporeal appearance, but at the very same time she has an otherworldly aura. This is probably exactly what Harris intended.

The face is that of a person deeply attracted to and obviously in tune with theosophist principles; as such, it can be read as a tribute by the artist to his own religious beliefs. The portrait can also be seen as evidence of Lawren's attraction to the woman who would become his second wife a number of years later. The spiritual bond—the essential element in their relationship—can be witnessed here.

At about the same time, Harris painted Mrs. Oscar Taylor (given name Lucille). She and her husband owned a parcel of land at York Mills, where the Arts and Letters Club had their wartime farm adjacent to MacDonald's home. Mrs. Taylor, with a slightly

Lawren Harris.
Bess Housser. 1920.

Lawren Harris.
Mrs. Oscar Taylor.
1920.

worried look on her face, stares ahead. Like Bess, Mrs. Taylor was a Christian Scientist. So was Mrs. Wilson. Her given name was Mabel, and she was a good friend of Trixie Harris. All three women, in their different ways, are models of religious propriety.

For years, Harris had struggled to establish himself as a landscape artist, but at the Group of Seven's first show—an event he masterminded—he chose to make his mark with portraits. Why Harris did so is not easy to understand, but he may have wanted to signal that in whatever genre he worked, interiority was his primary concern.

There is also the distinct possibility that Harris in 1920 was well aware that his reach far exceeded his grasp. He had the concept of what he wanted to achieve in landscape painting, but the means of attainment eluded him. If this is the case, he deliberately held himself back at the Group's first exhibition.

The strongest presence in the exhibition rooms at the Art Gallery of Toronto in May 1920 was Tom Thomson, now five years dead. All of the Seven were poignantly aware that there was an eighth man who could justifiably claim to be the greatest of the lot. Harris, especially, would have been haunted by his sense of the presence of his dead friend.

Eric Brown continued to be an assiduous ally. In May 1920 he offered the "best exhibition of modern Canadian painting ever seen"[14] to various American museums. The show opened in Massachusetts at the Worcester Art Museum in November and travelled to Boston, Rochester, Toledo, Indianapolis, Detroit, Cleveland, Buffalo, Columbus and Minneapolis; it closed at Muskegon, Michigan, in January 1922. This exhibition of the Group of Seven was a reduced version of the one in Toronto. Since Varley's work in the latter had all been commissioned works, they were not available to travel, so four canvases by Tom Thomson were added. In this posthumous way, Thomson at last became one of the Seven.

MacDonald had major trepidations about this venture: "I should judge, by comparing our own show with a fine collection of American pictures recently shown here, that we Canadians are developing a rather cold austerity of character, which may be uninviting, however noble."[15] His fears were in part justified when a Boston critic linked this exhibition to the one in Buffalo in 1913 that had inspired both MacDonald and Harris:

> The work of these landscape men of "Our Lady of the Snow" has been plausibly compared with that of the present-day Scandinavians. The comparison deems not to be altogether inapt, as one recalls the heavy-handed, strong-hued canvases of the Scandinavian exhibition at the museum six or seven years ago. Most of us in Boston did not like the exhibition, and we said so.[16]

Such smug self-satisfaction was absent from the Buffalo notices, such as this one: the Group of Seven "strives to paint Canada, Canada as it is—the wilds with the tangle of underbrush, the streams, the lakes, and islands with their lonely wind-bent pines, and the hard, sharp distances."[17]

Harris's *A Side Street* was sold to the Detroit Institute of Arts, but it was the only canvas sold on this tour. Another exhibition, this one of sketches, simultaneously travelled to Fort William, Brandon, Moose Jaw, Calgary and Edmonton. Of course, these landscapes did not show views with which many Westerners could identify. In Edmonton, one commentator suggested the painters were misusing "the talent the Lord gave them" by making "His handiwork . . . hideous."[18] The *Moose Jaw Evening Times* was much more sensitive to what the group was trying to accomplish, and categorized Harris as the "recognized" leader of the Group and MacDonald "the poet-colourist." Jackson was lauded for venturing into dangerous places, but this writer reserved his highest praise for Thomson "as the most unique, spontaneous and remarkable of them all." He was the group's "martyr, its great genius, its founder, its champion, its dominating influence."[19]

In March 1920, the library of the town of Sarnia, Ontario, which had begun to hold annual exhibitions of Canadian art and acquire some of the works shown, staged a Group exhibition. Norman Gurd, the nephew of Richard Maurice Bucke, was one of the members of the organizing committee and the moving force behind the choice of works by members of the Group. The *Canadian Forum* lauded this initiative:

> The importance of what is happening in Sarnia is hard to exaggerate for those who care for things of the Canadian mind . . . We seem to have the painters and yet they have remained unknown hitherto to the country at large. Sarnia is the breach in the line. If it is followed, as it can hardly fail to be, by other small cities the credit of solving the problem of Canadian art for Canadians will go to the small cities, and not to the big ones. Sarnia has been the first city to show that civic pride can be enlisted in this admirable cause.[20]

For Harris, muted support came from another source. In 1921, a year after the first Group exhibition, Barker Fairley, the Yorkshire-born professor of German at the University of Toronto, made this comment on Harris's urban views:

It is human nature and human society that contradicts itself
and this we think is Mr. Harris's great and peculiar field.
Irony is never far to seek in a modern city and Mr. Harris has
a unique gift for seizing on it . . . One recalls his sensitiveness
to the beauty of the city as well as to its ugliness [and] one
cannot but think that he will go furthest in this field and find
it suited to his strangely compounded temperament. Perhaps
as time goes on he will shift the emphasis somewhat from the
buildings people inhabit to the people themselves.[21]

Harris did have a "strangely compounded temperament";
he was a man of contradictory impulses. He could speak out
strongly, sometimes vehemently, on the place of art in human
destiny, but his personal voice in letters is discreet to the point of
evasiveness. He never spoke directly of personal matters unless
he could insert those issues into matters relating to theosophy or
aesthetics. Only a decade later would he open up, and then only
to the one Canadian artist he considered his equal in exploring
art's spiritual dimensions: Emily Carr.

An important early friend was Doris Mills (1894–1989), who
remained a devoted admirer of Harris. Although never a prominent artist, she was inspired by the Group. Early on, she catalogued Harris's work and devised a scheme whereby Canadian
works of art could be rented, thus increasing the market for
a large number of artists. Bess Housser was one of her closest
friends.

Lucille Taylor introduced Doris, then a Christian Scientist,
to Harris in about 1921–22. Before that, in 1919, Lucille, Doris
and Bess Housser "decided to start a little circulating gallery of
pictures."[22] They asked Harris if they could rent three of his canvases for a year and circulate them. He readily agreed. Doris later
recalled: "*The Star* was very, very amused at this and had quite a big
write-up. Laughing at us, just roaring at us for doing this . . . For
one thing, they thought the Group of Seven were simply absolutely terrible, and the idea of people renting these pictures . . . and
circulating them, just amazed them."[23]

Fairley, who was a close friend of Varley and a frequent booster of his work, had a clear understanding of Harris's character; he would also have known that Harris welcomed criticism, even though it might be severe. In this spirit, perhaps, the professor penned his review of *Contrasts*, Harris's 1922 volume of verse:

> Mr. Harris has been betrayed by the appalling laxity of the *vers libre* habit, now rife on this continent, into publishing an extremely bad book of verses.
>
> In his writing, Mr. Harris seems to be preoccupied to an almost monotonous extent with vague, transcendental reflections on life and humanity. He shows no interest in or feeling for Nature and no interest in particularized individual human life. His mind runs to humanity in the abstract and the aggregate. For this shadowy Leviathan he entertains a mixture of affection and irony which seems to be personal to him . . . It helps to explain the coldness and lack of intimacy in his landscapes and his preference among city subjects for houses and streets with no people in them. The shack brings him closer to humanity in the abstract than the human individual does, and yet holds him in the visual world which he wishes to paint.[24]

By any reckoning, this is a harsh notice. There was most certainly a side of Harris that disdained "particularized individual human life," and this "coldness and lack of intimacy" pervades the poems.

Fairley understood that the visual was Harris's métier, and he attempted to judge the urban views accordingly. He also was well aware that Harris was taking a huge risk by revealing himself in verse, but he was unsympathetic to the book's glaring faults wherein Harris tried—and failed—to find an appropriate speaking voice.

Contrasts is divided into five sections: "Descriptive" is intended as an overview of the steadily deteriorating conditions of modern urban existence; "Emotional" dissects modern man's inability to feel; and then "People" attempts to provide verbal portraits; "Definitions" aims to encapsulate various key concepts, such as

Suffering, Isolation and The Irrepressible; and finally there is the "Spiritual," the solution avoided by most contemporary urban dwellers, although the point is made that the reluctance to embrace this realm is largely due to the ennui in which modern man exists. There is a transcendent spiritual reality, but most people remain enmeshed in materialism.

The free verse of the sixty-nine poems is obviously influenced by Walt Whitman but much more directly by T.S. Eliot's *Prufrock and Other Observations* (1917). In fact, as a whole, *Contrasts* expresses a similar sense of despair over the modern condition as seen in Eliot's *The Waste Land*, published the same year (1922). Emerson's brand of Transcendental thought is perhaps the most direct literary inspiration for the collection, particularly the American's distinction between "finite" and "infinite": "For it is only the finite that has wrought and suffered; the infinite lies stretched in smiling repose."[25]

The opening poem, "A Note of Colour," attempts to place the observations that are to follow in context:

> In a part of the city that is ever shrouded in sooty smoke and
>   amid
> huge, hard buildings, hides a gloomy house of broken grey,
> rough-cast, like a sickly den in a callous soul.
> Streams of wires run by it wailing in the murky wind.
> Two half dead chestnut trees, black and broken, stand wearily
> before it, subdued by a bare rigid telephone pole.[26]

In a direct imitation of the Baudelaire-influenced speaking voice in *Prufrock*, the speaker in one poem suggests that

> . . . you and I, friend, take off our disguise and rest awhile—
> Let us unmask—
> We need no longer assert our little selves—
> no longer insult one another.[27]

In "This Fog," the speaker suggests that if the fog

. . . would lift but for a moment,
This fog we live in and are lost in, close-hugging us in pain
This seething fog, weighted with prejudices, dense with the
  close-packed particles of selfishness, crowding vision
  into blindness,
We would see some strange sights, some wonderful sights—so
many welcoming voices; such music![28]

As an examination of the socio-economic plight of contemporary man, *Contrasts* fails. The point of view is never clearly established; the poems utilize images in too broad a manner. However,
as an indicator of Harris's confusion and ongoing sense of depression in 1922, this book of verse is invaluable.

Only in his visual images did Harris find a way to display his
interior landscape. He was always reluctant to expose his feelings
in letters; in conversation, he was also reticent. He remained a
humble man who did not like to burden others; he also never
learned how to utter his most intimate feelings. He was both a
deeply intellectual and an emotional person, but he was hardly
ever willing to exhibit those feelings in words. He may have overtly
rejected his Baptist heritage, but it clung to him as an invisible
shield: one was self-effacing in deportment, reticent in words.

The Group's second exhibition was held at the Art Gallery of
Toronto from May 7 to 29, 1921. They were now a group of six
since Frank Johnston had resigned. He had had an extremely
successful show of two hundred temperas at Eaton's, and he may
have feared that his new-found success might be compromised
by association with the Group. In any event, the Group's second
show was significantly smaller than the first, comprising forty-
eight canvases and forty-one oil sketches. If the first exhibition
had been in the nature of a retrospective, the present show contained recent work only.

In the foreword to the catalogue, the nationalistic ideals of
the Group were again put forward strongly: "A word as to Canada. These pictures have all been executed in Canada during the
past year. They express Canadian experience, and appeal to that

experience in the onlooker. These are still pioneer days for artists and after the fashion of pioneers we believe whole-heartedly in the land." Once again, the Group maintained it was a Modernistic, pioneering entity.

Fairley was overcritical of Harris's *Island, MacCallum Lake*: "It expresses to the intelligence the weirdness of the North Country, but it does not evoke the feeling of nature nor even place one out-of-doors. The point of view seems to have been dictated by the intellect and directed towards the curious and the occult."[29] Bridle, usually a strong supporter, expressed his astonishment at Harris's "frankly neurotic studies of colour and form, phantom trees that never grew, distorted nightmares of deadwood and much else."[30]

Lawren Harris.
Island, MacCallum Lake. 1921.

Neither critic discerned that Harris was valiantly trying to posit a new form of expression in the shaping of the "phantom" trees that almost seem to possess some human characteristics. Nor did they give him credit for the breakthrough represented by *Jazz*, one of the artist's monumental achievements. As for the other canvases by Harris, they do not signal major changes in direction. Up to 1921, Harris may have been the de facto leader of the Group, but he was certainly not its strongest artist.

Bridle, in responding to the Group's third exhibition, again at the Art Gallery of Toronto, from May 5 to 29, 1922, was mildly critical of the homogeneity he beheld:

> In their search for what lies beyond, the group are becoming rather more alike. Two years ago I could easily spot any of the painters by their pictures. Now there are times when I wonder at first glance which is a Jackson or a Lismer, at odd times a Harris and now and then a MacDonald. Even Carmichael is toning down or keying up, or whatever it may be, to catch the spirit of the group. Varley alone seems to hold out, although most of Harris's are known by their subjects, often by the technique, nearly always by the unmistakable lustre of the light.[31]

A wide variety of Harris canvases were on display: *Spring in the Outskirts*; *Early Summer Afternoon, Barrie*; *Rock, Algoma*; *Algoma Country*; *Evening, Kempenfelt Bay, Lake Simcoe*, an Algonquin Park picture, a winter study of houses, *Elevator Court* and *Black Court*, an extremely angular Modernist design. Despite the ample number of canvases, however, Harris felt that somehow he was not yet tapping something vitally important. He remained both confused and disappointed. At the time, he did not seem fully to recognize the importance of *Above Lake Superior*, which was also on display.

10

BREAKTHROUGH

(1921–1922)

For too many years, Lawren told himself, he had been overly concerned with the decorative. Fairley was right about Contrasts: *it was too diffuse—"vague and transcendental," as he rightly claimed. Life was filled with difficult hurdles. Lawren made this claim in his verse, but he failed to articulate it.*

In his art, he was also divided. He showed the dwellings of the poor, often embroidering the exteriors of their homes with the marks of decay and disintegration. His landscapes, by contrast, were not really him. Some vital ingredient was missing. Even though he had become aware that he had a great many feelings pent up inside him, he was unable to articulate them in his sketches or paintings.

Then, at Lake Superior, the gauze was suddenly removed from his eyes. He could see clearly in this woebegone, charred landscape what he had long wanted to witness and desired to paint. Here was a land that had been devastated by fire—a true wasteland—and yet managed to keep itself alive. It had resurrected itself from death, and for him it was a place of hope. He had, at long last, found the perfect vehicle for his talents. This was a moment of pure ecstasy.

A S A WOULD-BE MODERNIST ARTIST, thirty-six-year-old Harris had hoped to locate the perfect objective correlative, a subject to which he would be so perfectly attuned that it would unleash all the potential that had been lingering in his soul. This is exactly what happened in 1921.

When Harris, Jackson and Lismer travelled to Sand Lake, in the Algoma region, that autumn, Harris was soon dissatisfied with the landscape. Then, in search of something new and perhaps significantly different, Harris and Jackson journeyed for the first time to the north shore of Lake Superior.

Jackson later recalled that Lawren "liked to have a system for everything."[1] On this occasion, he devised a methodology for swimming whereby the two men would stand as far away as possible from the beach then run at full force towards it, waving their arms and yelling loudly. "This procedure," Jackson wryly observed, "was supposed to distract our attention from the cold water."[2]

Jackson liked to sleep in; Harris was up before dawn, making a great deal of noise clanging pots and pans as he prepared breakfast. Then he would insist Jackson get up, even though the weather might be awful.

"What's the use of getting up? It's raining."

"It is clearing in the west," was Harris's invariable reply. When it began to clear after days of constant rain, Harris would inform his friend: "I told you it was clearing."[3]

Harris was obsessed with Roman Meal (this cereal was supposed to emulate the Roman centurion's daily intake of whole wheat, whole rye, bran and flaxseed) and claimed it made him impervious to wet and cold. He insisted Jackson have a full bowl each morning.

On one of the Lake Superior trips, Harris took along ten pounds of Bermuda onions. As Harris recalled for the column "My Most Memorable Meal" in *Maclean's*, Jackson one evening sliced a large mess of these onions, buttered the skillet, covered the bottom with water, dumped in the onions and half boiled and fried them. This entree was delicious, and was followed by a pannikin of stewed apricots and several cups of tea.

Lawren Harris.
*Above Lake
Superior.
Circa 1922.*

At nine we crawled into our bedrolls and were soon asleep. Sometime during the night I suffered the most gosh-awful nightmare. I was being choked, smothered and bedeviled by dreadful shapeless beings. I groaned and whimpered. Jackson, though the soundest sleeper this side of the grave, was wakened by the horrible racket and whistled in an attempt to waken me. This didn't penetrate. He finally leaned over from his bedroll and poked me awake. I was saved.

In much more elevated fashion, Jackson related what happened halfway through the first expedition to Lake Superior:

The Algoma country was too opulent for Harris; he wanted something bare and stark, so at the conclusion of one of our sketching trips he and I went to the north shore of Lake Superior, a country much of which had been burnt years before. New growth was slowly appearing. The CPR main line follows the north shore of Lake Superior from Heron Bay westward to Port Arthur. I know of no more impressive scenery in

Canada for the landscape painter. There is a sublime order to
it, the long curves of the beaches, the sweeping ranges of hills,
and headlands that push out into the lake. Inland there are intimate little lakes, stretches of muskeg, outcrops of rock; there
is little soil for agriculture. In the autumn the whole country
glows with colour; the huckleberry and the pincherry turn
crimson, the mountain ash is loaded with red berries, the pop-
lar and the birch turn yellow and the tarmac greenish gold.[4]

During the 1918 Algoma trip, MacDonald had witnessed the
largest freshwater lake in the world from the Canyon area: "I have
never seen anything so impressive as the half-revealed extensive-
ness of the lake."[5] Harris was also deeply touched by the primor-
dial splendour on which his eyes now feasted: "At times, there
were skies over the great Lake Superior which, in their singing
expansiveness and sublimity, existed nowhere else in Canada."[6]

Harris's first Lake Superior images were obviously inspired by
an actual terrain, but this does not mean they do not have other
sources. For example, Harris owned nineteen black-and-white
photographs* of work by his American contemporary Rockwell
Kent (1882–1971).[7] Harris was apparently well aware of Kent's
work in the early twenties and in fact may have met him briefly
in the Rockies in the mid-twenties.[8] In any event, when Harris's
friend Doris Mills visited Kent's studio in about 1924, she told
him that she discerned many similarities between his work and
Harris's. In Kent's *Tierra del Fuego* (1922—and so obviously not
seen by Harris in 1921), a highly stylized, sculptured dead tree
rises in the foreground, its branches juxtaposed against the water,

---

* "In the scenery of Fox Island [Alaska], Kent felt evidence of the inner power of
nature. Using such natural forms as trees, the sea, the sun, and the northern light,
he composed pictures that . . . projected an iconography both personal and Christian . . . [These paintings] use the burned remains of once-luxuriant trees. These
realistically rendered images are suggestive of crucifixion, martyrdom, and guilt,
and perhaps, too of nature's power to destroy as well as to create . . ." In one image,
however, "Kent chose to emphasize the warmth and redemption of light from the
sun." Richard V. West, "Rockwell Kent: Before the Odyssey," in Constance Martin, *Distant Shores: The Odyssey of Rockwell Kent* (Berkeley: Chameleon Book and
University of California Press, 2000), 27.

mountain and sky. The starkness of *Above Lake Superior* may well be directly indebted in part to the photograph Harris owned of Kent's *Indian Summer*.*

Rockwell Kent.
*Indian Summer,
Alaska.* 1919.

---

* Paul Duval offers this information about Harris's later interest (1930) in the Arctic: His concern with such landscapes "had unquestionably been stimulated by his association with the American artist, Rockwell Kent, who had been painting in Alaska and Greenland since before 1917. (Some of Kent's canvases of the 1917–1920 era can easily be mistaken for Harris's paintings of the post-1930 period.) The American was a frequent guest of Lawren Harris during the 1920s and often visited the Studio Building, where many of the Group of Seven had their quarters. During this period, Kent delivered a number of lectures in Toronto at the local Eaton Auditorium, under the auspices of the Art Gallery of Toronto." *Four Decades: The Canadian Group of Painters and Their Contemporaries, 1930–1970* (Toronto: Clarke, Irwin, 1972), 23.

According to Lawren P. Harris in an interview with Peter Larisey on January 31, 1982, his father attended Kent's 1929 lecture "Cold Feet and Warm Hearts in Greenland," advertised by the art gallery as "one of the outstanding events of this season." Kent spent that evening at Harris's home and the two artists talked well into the night. According to Doris Mills Speirs, it was at this time that Kent and Harris became "great friends. And that friendship lasted, right, right straight along . . . for a long time." Interview with Charles Hill, October 15, 1973.

There are other influences. For years, Tom Thomson's *Burnt Land* had been in his collection; there was also an obvious debt to Caspar David Friedrich. In a sense, Harris—as in the case of the Scandinavian exhibition at Buffalo—recognized what he had been imagining in his mind's eye and been seeing in the work of other artists when he beheld the actual Lake Superior landscape. Everything finally came together.

Caspar David Friedrich.
The Solitary Tree.

The reviewer for the *Mail and Empire* of the Group's third exhibition instantly recognized that some form of synthesis had occurred. For him, *Above Lake Superior* was

> one of those paintings in which the work of Mr. Harris makes one think of Rockwell Kent on account of the simplicity of the design and the use of colours. There is a mountain in the background against a bleak sky, and in the foreground gnarled, dead trees with snow. The use of light in this picture, especially on the snow-covered trees, is extraordinarily effective. It is the sort of painting that only a master of the brush like Mr. Harris could achieve. In it you feel the vital north country air. It is one of the finest efforts shown by Lawren Harris in recent years.[9]

Tom Thomson.
Burnt Land. 1915.

Not surprisingly, Hector Charlesworth found the canvas repulsive: *"Above Lake Superior* has the morbid, sinister qualities one finds in the drawings of William Blake, with its uncanny arrangements of stripped dead trees set against a sullen background."[10] The reference to Blake was not meant as a compliment to either artist, but Charlesworth may have been correct to see some Blakean influences at work in that Harris was attempting to conjoin opposing spiritual forces in the same canvas.

Harris would have been well aware of the trope of the solitary tree, particularly in a work of that name by Friedrich from 1822. In such compositions, the placement of the tree at the foreground of the picture area suggests it is part of nature and yet somehow apart; in its isolation, the tree may be self-sufficient, but the suggestion is that it has learned to thrive on its own. It is part of nature and yet distant from it. Very much a part of this convention, Thomson's *Burnt Land* displays dead tree trunks silhouetted against hills and sky. Although long deceased, the trees continue to put up a valiant fight against extinction. Unlike Thomson's roughly textured brush strokes, Harris now worked in an extremely refined way that insisted on removing any semblance of clutter in either the elements of the composition or how they were painted.

The light in *Above Lake Superior* is diffuse and perfectly complements the deep pictorial space that is established. There is great regularity in the simple shape of the mountain and the vertical clouds that drift against the sky. The trees may have died, but they have achieved new life as pieces of sculpture. In fact, two of the five vertical trees are intersected on the left, suggesting some sort of interaction between the standing and fallen forms. Part of the picture's power emanates from the drama being established between the trees, almost as if the viewer is looking at a stage set—a common feature in Harris's work—just as a performance is about to begin. The trees can be said to be characters interacting in some mysterious way with each other. Part of this canvas's power derives from the fact that these relationships are not precisely defined.

Four years later, Fred Housser, who had conducted a kind of unofficial poll, characterized the various responses the picture elicited:

> People either love it or hate it. When Leon Bakst the Russian artist saw it he exclaimed, "It is not painting, it is sculpture." An Oxford Ph.D. described it as "a horror." A little Irish woman spoke of it as "The Place Where the Gods Live." One man said that Harris should have been locked up for painting it. Another referred to it as a picture of "The Top of the World."

In his attempt to come to grips with the meaning of this Harris image, Housser, likely under the artist's influence, spoke of it as capturing the

> North's being. A flowing emotional quality is absent but the emotion of this picture is in the power of its intensity which is directed and subjected to a mood of emotion sublimated beyond fluxiousness and agitation.[11]

Housser's use of the word "sublimate" is significant because he is suggesting that Harris has found a way to project his emotional concerns into a work of art in which dark, confused feelings find an appropriate outlet.

> If we feel its bleakness and hate it, it is our own inner bleakness that hates, the finite part of us that dares not meet that unfathomable thing,—the wilderness.[12]

For Housser and Harris, the Wilderness becomes and remains a key concept. The vast expanses of the North are such a distinctively Canadian subject because that mythical, largely uninhabited, place holds the key to understanding what Canada is and could become. Harris, as we have seen, had very definite ideas about how Canada's identity was tied to the North:

> We in Canada are in different circumstances than the people of the United States. Our population is sparse, the psychic atmosphere comparatively clean, whereas the States fill up and the masses crowd a heavy psychic blanket over nearly all the land. We are in the fringe of the great North and its living whiteness, its loneliness and replenishment, its resignations and release, its call and its answer—its cleansing rhythms. It seems that the top of the continent is a source of spiritual flow that will ever shed clarity into the growing race of America, and we Canadians being closest to this source seem destined to produce an art somewhat different from our Southern fellows—an art more spacious, of a greater living quiet, perhaps of a more certain conviction of eternal values. We were not placed between the Southern teeming of men and the ample replenishing North for nothing.[13]

The North and the Wilderness are, in theosophic terms, repositories of the "mystical experience" that links Harris to Blake: "In a flash . . . peace comes through a vision which makes it plain that 'every moment of life is filled with eternity' and that the ugliness of Time are ways to a realization of untemporal beauty.

The uglinesses of *Above Lake Superior* are beautiful and its lonely austerity, peace."[14] Mystical thought works through paradoxes, and this is what Housser is declaring here.

In this canvas the organization of the pictorial elements emphasizes the spiritual coherence residing behind the seeming incoherence of material reality. As such, this painting reflects one of Harris's central notions: "Art is concerned primarily with relationships. The harmony, the order of art, its organization as a living power that can work within us, depends on its inner relationships. It is the epitome of the cosmic order."[15]

As Jackson presciently stated, the Algoma country was much too opulent for Harris. Jackson, MacDonald and Thomson liked to use a full assemblage of colours in their paintings and were not averse to utilizing a wide range of reds, oranges and yellows. This observation does not hold true for Harris, who was to remain much more comfortable with blues, browns, greens, and greys as can be seen, for example, in *Mount Schäffer*, an oil sketch from 1926. In order for him to express his passion—in a symbolical landscape distinctively his own—he used these colder tones to elicit a sense

Lawren Harris.
Mount Schäffer
(Yoho National
Park). *Circa* 1926.

of those that were absent. *Above Lake Superior* may be a bold picture, but it is an aloof one because it emphasizes a limited palette. It is also a canvas on which the brush strokes are rendered in a deliberately flat manner.

The design elements of the Grip tradition never sat easily on Harris's shoulders. He tried to emulate his confreres (in their choice of colours and vigorous brush strokes), but he became a great landscape artist only when he chose to follow his own instincts rather than those of others.

If a viewer experiences *Above Lake Superior* properly, the canvas proclaims itself: there is a side to human existence in which loneliness and sadness dwell, and yet within each person there is the potential to grasp those negative feelings and transform them into beauty. Within that paradox lies the discovery made by Harris at Lake Superior.

11

LIVING
WHITENESS

(1922–1923)

*Almost unaware, Lawren had discovered a new land, one encom-
passing all the strands he had been slowly gathering together.
Was his humanity about to disappear, to be subsumed into some
grand, extravagant scheme that no one but himself would be
able to comprehend? This was a disturbing thought, but he had
uncovered a way of painting that clarified the confusions beset-
ting him for so long.*

IN THE AUTUMN of 1922, Jackson and Harris returned to the
north shore of Lake Superior; in 1923, Harris, Lismer and
Jackson (accompanied by MacCallum) were in Algoma; that
autumn, Harris and Jackson went again to the north shore.

Harris was travelling in pursuit of symbolical landscapes; he
also spent a great deal of time in Toronto trying to comprehend
the new spiritual direction in which he was heading. Thus, at the
same time that he had arrived at the much sought-after transformation in his art, Harris attempted to understand even more clearly
what such art signified. In a book review of Bucke's *Cosmic Consciousness* and Ouspensky's *Tertium Organum*, he tried to explain

clearly the writings of these two men, but he was also grappling with his own perception of himself as an artist. What exactly does the artist do? What can he hope to accomplish? He was amazed at what Bucke had achieved:

> Think of this book written in the Ontario of forty years ago and written with such a glorious, sweeping gesture. Consider what life in this province was then, the people submerged in the severest orthodoxy, divided and blinded and sustained by sectarian views, comfortably warped by provincialism and remote from all cultural centres. Such occurrences convince one that vision is paramount in life—and that there is a rhythm of majesty swinging around this globe and illuminating all great souls.[1]

This passage can be read as containing autobiographical reflections. Harris was born into an Ontario of "severest orthodoxy" and to an extent felt "blinded" and "warped" by this experience. However, he had now gained access to "the rhythm of majesty" that underlies human experience and, in the process, his life and art had been enhanced.

While reading Bucke and Ouspensky, he also realized just how profound their understanding was of the relationship between the physical and spiritual worlds:

> They can evoke an amazing awareness of all that is profound and high and glorious, they can inspire a soaring, breathtaking wonderment that overrides all quibbling, all littleness, all doubts. Ouspensky concludes that . . . to strive after the wondrous . . . is the beginning of vision . . . If anyone is not satisfied with the usual statement that art is merely an adornment of life, or is concerned with the creation of entirely fictitious, happy and remote worlds . . . let him read *Tertium Organum*. For here at last, we have given us a reasoned, spiritual basis for our conviction that art is the beginning of wisdom into the realm of eternal life.[2]

The excitement in Harris's language is palpable, and comes from his sense of having discovered a secret, the full meaning of which has been long withheld and now stands revealed. In referring to the notion that art can sometimes be seen as a kind of "adornment of life" rather than what it really is—the essence of life itself—it is possible that Harris is wondering if his "decorative" phase had led him nowhere.

George William Russell (1867–1935), who wrote under the pseudonym AE, was another writer to whom Harris was drawn. In 1919 he told Jim MacDonald that AE was "a truly sweet and grand man," who belonged to the "clan of christs." He was one of those rare spirits "who shew us where we're headed for, those dear mystics who live in eternity and let time go hang."[3]

At the instigation of the poet W.B. Yeats, AE became assistant secretary of the Irish Agricultural Organization Society. Later, having become an ardent nationalist, he opposed John Redmond's compromise on Home Rule. From 1908 to 1923, he edited *The Irish Homestead*. AE's first book of verse, *Homeward: Songs by the Way* (1894), established him as a key figure in the Irish Literary Revival or Irish Renaissance. He was also a theosophist.

A writer in the *New York Times* in 1912 characterized AE as a mystic but not one who withdraws from the world.

He is the mystic who stays in the urgent ways of life, keeping the poise of the spirit and creating about him an atmosphere of serenity and peace. In this day when all branches of art vie with each other to startle and waylay, when the staccato note dominates and sensation is rife, when paradox has been exalted to a literary method and to gain a hearing one must shock all sense of established values—a poet like A.E. seems himself the chief paradox in a strident age. But as a whisper will sometimes quiet an uproar, A.E.'s voice and the voices of others like him make themselves heard, and help us to that poise and sanity which we are in danger of losing in this modern Babel.[4]

Like AE, Harris was looking for equilibrium.

In AE, Harris also saw a reflection of himself. Like the Irishman, he was a committed nationalist who wanted his native land to be freed from cultural oppression. He shared with AE a similar religious vision. In fact, Harris told MacDonald that although AE possessed a "remarkable" talent, he had stopped painting because it might give him too much pleasure and so limit his vision. While Harris may have shared a puritanical streak with AE, he certainly did not wish to cease painting.

In 1923, Harris sharpened and refined what he had accomplished in *Above Lake Superior*. He wanted poise and clarity, and those qualities can certainly be seen in *Lake Superior Sketch LI* (1923), *Morning, Lake Superior* (1923) and the various *Pic Island* canvases from 1923–24. In these images, Harris is going even further than before in simplifying his lines, flattening brush strokes, and reducing the elements of his canvases to what are essentially abstract concepts of sky, cloud, water and land. Put another way, the movement is towards reducing these entities into their most basic forms, again using a very restricted colour range.

Lawren Harris.
Pic Island.
Circa 1924.

Ice House, Coldwell, Lake Superior is a canvas of austere grandeur. The blues dominating the other Lake Superior images have been supplemented by the greens of the mountain to the ice house's left and the trees to its right. The house is nestled between these two forms, and the left (front) side of the house, bathed in luminous yellow, seems to be affirming that embrace. In addition, the house's willowy angles synchronize with the undulating, flowing lines of the shore, waves and sky. The two other architectural elements are similarly quiescent. In this image, the man-made house seems on the verge of merging with the trees, mountains and clouds.

Lawren Harris.
Ice House, Coldwell,
Lake Superior.
Circa 1923.

The precocious musician and journalist Marcus Adeney (1900–1998) claimed the painting was

purely mystical . . . and an excellent introduction to Lawren Harris's rarefied atmosphere. Here the shock of contrast between our expectation of sentimental associations and the wisdom of a stark solitude is in no way relieved. At first we seem to encounter death itself. But it is not death in tragic guise; for a tragedy over which we may weep is but another form of sentimental expression. It is death as it would appear to eyes that have passed beyond death. Here is a world in which all things are potential or have been already expressed, a world in which no single form of life triumphs over other forms, in which there are no idle dreams. Here is a vision of a single, shouting reality in which life and death as we know them have appeared to God during countless ages before the various forms of life had evolved, each with its private and shifting scale of values; the world as it was and as it will be, as it must be even today, regarded in the light of eternity. Here the soul of a man may become one with the Everlasting, beyond sentiment, beyond good and evil, beyond victory and defeat, beyond death itself . . . His works should be contemplated in silence and immobility: only thus do they become comprehensible.[5]

If this painting is about death, it seems the ice house has become the repository of some elemental secrets that long to make their truths known. Using the same kind of vocabulary as the young musician, Bridle was sympathetic but puzzled. He labelled the painting "a gabled ghost . . . Space and time to Harris are the mother of colour and form. He might explain this religiously. I might call it transcendentalism; others—bunk. But it is all despairingly beautiful and inhuman."[6]

Was the image one of surpassing beauty or pure bunk? Bridle was not sure of the answer. There can be no question that this painting is arresting. What no contemporary critic seems to have noticed was that Harris, unusual for him, had taken the opportunity to place a house in a landscape painting, thus bringing together two strands in his career usually carefully segregated.

In his urban views, most of Harris's houses had been proud survivors—very bloodied but very unbowed. In this picture, the house has been given a majestic setting in which to live and breathe, and it obviously welcomes such generosity. The artist has finally fused two portions of his career. However, this was a person who was never content to rest on his laurels.

12

MOUNT

HARRISES

(1924–1925)

"When I first saw the mountains, travelled through them, I was most discouraged. Nowhere did they measure up to the advertising folders, or to the conception these had formed in my mind's eye. But, after I became better acquainted with the mountains, camped and tramped among them, I found a power and majesty and a wealth of experience at nature's summit which no travel-folder ever expressed."[1]

A S WAS OFTEN THE CASE with Harris, a sense of triumph followed initial disappointment or hesitancy. Buoyed up by his success at Lake Superior, he decided to try a new location, and spent August and September 1924 with A.Y. Jackson on a sketching trip to the Rockies in and around Jasper Park.

Although they had been painted earlier, it was only in the 1880s, after the Canadian Pacific Railway had been completed, that the Rockies became easily accessible. The CPR encouraged artists to paint in these majestic mountains, often providing free passage in return for watercolours. Sometimes, the CPR even commissioned views. In 1914, for example, A.Y. Jackson and J.W.

Beatty were hired by Canadian Northern Railway. The results—
often reproduced in the form of lithographic posters—could be
used to lure tourists to visit the sublime views. This was an example of a splendid marriage between commerce and art.

In visiting the Rockies, Harris would have been familiar with
the achievements of Ontario-born Lucius R. O'Brien (1832–99)
and the English-born John A. Fraser (1838–98), both of whom
had produced rapturous views of these ranges. In daring to take
on such illustrious predecessors, Harris was well aware that his
efforts would be compared with theirs. In order to rival those
two dead artists, Harris instinctively knew that he would have to
incorporate the stylistic mannerisms he had discovered at Lake
Superior.

Lucius O'Brien.
View of the
Rockies. 1887.

Harris and Jackson were good companions, although Harris's
relentless attention to details sometimes annoyed Jackson, who
liked to think of himself as happy-go-lucky. This could lead to
amusing consequences, as Harris recalled:

> Sometimes we camped in order to sketch in more remote
> mountain country. In September [1923] . . . we made a camp
> high up on the east side of Maligne Lake. We had spent a

week there a month earlier and had then blazed a trail to this site. We started early in the morning to tote our bed rolls, small tent, sketching material, and food for ten days up to this spot. The going was tough and so it was not until late that same evening that we were settled. We pitched the tent just above the timber line on sloping ground, there being no level location. I built up a pile of crossed sticks under the foot of my bed roll so that it was level. Jackson did not bother to do the same: he simply crawled in and went to sleep. Next morning at sunrise I awoke and glanced over to where Jackson was when I last saw him. He was not there; neither was his bed roll . . . I looked out of the tent flap and there he was twenty feet below, pulled up against a rock, buried in his bed roll, still fast asleep.[2]

The two men were so unalike in how they perceived things that they could see the same person in vastly different ways. Jackson provided this character sketch of a park warden named Goodair.

He was far from friendly, and made it quite clear that he did not like intruders among whom, obviously, he numbered us. After supper there was some desultory conversation in the course of which Harris asked Goodair what he did in the wintertime. Goodair replied that he went to Edmonton where he spent most of his time in the library. When Harris asked him what he read, he replied that he was most interested in history, biography, and theosophy. Harris was a theosophist and soon they were deep in a discussion of all the books they had read on the subject. After that evening we would have been welcome to stay a month with Goodair.[3]

Harris's account of the same person is markedly different:

We lived with the park rangers in their log cabins in Jasper Park. Sometimes we camped in order to sketch in more remote mountain country. We first spent ten days with an iron-haired, taciturn ranger named Goodair, whose cabin was high up in the Tonquin valley. We became good friends and corresponded until he was killed by a grizzly bear one evening outside the same cabin.4

Harris, somewhat self-effacingly, does not bother to mention that it was his friendliness—his willingness to ask questions—that brought about the rapprochement with the surly Goodair. Jackson made no effort to engage the warden in conversation, whereas Harris's sociability provided an immediate advantage in their dealings with this gruff fellow.

After stopping with Goodair for a couple of days, Harris, Jackson, their guide and four horses took an eighteen-foot canoe down Maligne Lake and landed on a gravel beach, where they pitched their tent. There were, as Jackson recalled, "flowers all about us, many we had never seen before. On both sides of us, a few hundred yards away, milky glaciers came hurrying over great gravel deltas into the lake." The lake was crystalline—"not a fish, not even a minnow, not a weed growing in the water." Towering above them on all sides "were giant crumbling mountains like the ruins of a gigantic Nineveh. One big pile of remains just opposite the tent looked like six mouldy old sphynxes sitting in a row."

Another day they climbed up beyond the timber line and walked into the snow. They stopped for lunch five hundred feet from the top. Then rain poured down, but they resolutely pushed on. The rain stopped. "The sun came out, and from the top of the ridge in the sunshine they looked down over a cubist's paradise of red, orange and grey rock and sharp cliffs running in long diagonals, and glaciers sprawling down the treeless valleys; a land as remote as the far side of the moon."5 Startled and delighted, the two retrieved their sketch boxes and got down to work, until a cloud swept down upon them, followed by sleet and a fierce wind.

In the Rockies, Harris's trip to Buffalo in 1913 provided an unexpected dividend. When he sketched Maligne Lake (the longest naturally occurring lake in the Rockies), he remembered a painting he had seen in Buffalo a decade earlier: *Lake Thun* by the Swiss artist Ferdinand Hodler (1853–1918). The compositions are very similar, although Harris removed the view of the shore in his rendition. In contrast to Hodler, he also simplified and geometricized the mountain, lake water and sky so that the resulting painting is reminiscent of a Harris Lake Superior landscape.

Harris's painting possesses strong verticals and horizontals, forces the viewer's eye to the dead centre of the composition, and reflects the mountains and sky in the water of the lake. The energy in this image radiates a sense of tranquility because all its passages are so perfectly balanced. The long, hard-won battle that had resulted in *Above Lake Superior* had provided a rich vein of ore for Harris to mine.

Lawren Harris. *Maligne Lake.* 1924.

At the fourth Group of Seven exhibition, which ran from January 9 to February 2, 1925, Harris displayed two Algonquin Park subjects, three Lake Superior pieces and five Jasper Park paintings, including *Maligne Lake.* More than any other member of the Group, his works were startling in their consistency of purpose.

In the *Toronto Star*, Salem Bland praised the entire show: "I felt as if the Canadian soul were unveiling to me something secret and high and beautiful which I had never guessed—a strength and

Ferdinand Hodler.
Lake Thun. 1904.

self-reliance and a mysticism I had not suspected. I saw as I had
never seen before the part the wilderness was to play in mould-
ing the Canadian spirit."[6]

Bridle in the *Star Weekly*, overcome by Harris's entries, provided a detailed analysis of them.

> The painters are certainly evolving. They have been succes-
> sively, and generally successfully, house-haunted, tree-mad,
> lake-lunatic, river-ridden, birch-bedlamed, aspen-addled,
> and rock cracked. This year they are mountain mad . . . One
> might say that the whole show is an expanse of lakes and foot-
> hills between one Mount Harris and another Mount Harris.
> At one end of the gallery stand his "Pobotkan Mountains,
> Jasper Park," at the other end twin mountains, in the same
> gallery and the same park. He has put these piles of granite
> into a powerful metal press and squeezed out of them every
> common ocular property of mountains, leaving only their
> cold austere sublimity. He does not give you a mountain, but

the platonic idea of a mountain, a mathematical infinite series of mountain impressions, something gigantically geometric, and impressively pyramidal, if not veridical, a real brainstorm among mountains.7

In claiming that Harris gave the viewer of the Jasper Park paintings a "platonic idea of a mountain," the commentator was responding to what he perceived as a deliberate move to geometrical forms; he realized that this transformation gestured in the direction of abstraction. Taken with all the Harris paintings he saw, the reviewer nevertheless pointed out that the paintings were highly intellectual, perhaps too rarefied, in their conceptualizations.

His fancy is bred in the head and not the heart, and the average man who wants his mountains as pretty as Christmas cards or frosted wedding cakes will complain that Mr. Harris is too mental and temperamental. In his latest phase he is not a house decorator with an appeal to young brides, but an Einstein who demands an audience of post-graduates in mathematics. He has gone in not for reform, but for pure form . . . [Harris] has flung not a pot of paint, but whole mountains in the faces of the critics, and any audacities the rest of the seven may venture upon seem in comparison quite playful and almost conventional.

Politely and dexterously, Bridle is warning that the pictures may be a bit on the cold side, but he is also making the point that Harris has outdistanced his confreres in the Group.

Not surprisingly, Barker Fairley had major reservations about where Harris was heading:

The success of the evening was really a personal success for himself. Yet he never painted so rigidly as now. From an aesthetic standpoint, one canvas . . . says almost as much as ten. There is the same mood and the same handling in every one of them. It is a spacious mood somewhere between the sumptuous and the austere; the handling is thorough in its kind, and sometimes it is masterly. Yet I fear . . . Harris has taken a wrong turn. Have these violently stereoscopic effects which he is getting any real place in the painter's art? Do they not belong to the art of the theatre . . . Harris might achieve fame in either, but not by confusing the two.[8]

Although Fairley was unsympathetic to canvases that aspired to exist in any kind of Platonic realm, he was correct in his judgment that the paintings were determinedly theatrical.

In the past, Harris had asked Eric Brown to cultivate Frederick Banting's friendship with the hope that the scientist, an amateur painter, would favour the new Canadian landscape painting and promote it. Brown did not take the initiative, but Banting was so disturbed by one of Harris's Lake Superior paintings that

he went to the art gallery six times to see it. It made him angry. Then he tried to analyse his own feelings. Why should some paint on a canvas so disturb him? So he came round to the studio to see Harris and hear his reasons for painting the picture. He was willing to believe that artists did research work too. He began to see a kinship between scientists and artists.[9]

The encounter was arranged by MacCallum. When Banting cross-questioned Harris on why he had painted the picture, Harris assured him he was trying to be "creative the way Banting had been as a scientist, by transforming old realities into new."[10] Subsequently, Banting called on Jackson at the Studio Building and purchased one of his sketches.

One source of Banting's irritation with Harris was a comment made by a critic for the *Star Weekly*, who, on viewing Banting's first small public showing of his paintings, at the Hart House Sketching Club in January 1925, remarked that Harris had evidently influenced the scientist.[11]

The mid-1920s were for Harris a time of cautious optimism. The ever-resourceful Brown had arranged a second American tour,

Modern Canadian Paintings, which opened in Minneapolis in November 1923 and then visited Kansas City, Omaha, Milwaukee, Providence and Worcester; its final stop was the Brooklyn Museum in August 1924. Each of the six Group members had six canvases (W.J. Wood, 1877–1954, was the seventh for this tour). Harris acted as coordinating secretary. Members of Montreal's Beaver Hall Group were also invited contributors.

Restrained were the reviews, although Helen Appleton Read in the *Brooklyn Daily Eagle* made some astute observations. She discerned Russian and Scandinavian influences at work; she recognized the absence of the "Cézanne–Picasso–Matisse tradition," but for her that was not a bad thing because those artists practised a "special form of art which obsesses the young American artist to, in many cases, the utter obliteration of his personality."[12]

Brown's biggest coup on behalf of the Group was to secure them a prominent place in the 1924 British Empire Exhibition at Wembley. The Royal Canadian Academy of the Arts usually took charge of all showings of Canadian art abroad, but Brown seized the initiative because he did not wish the staid taste of that group to influence what was perceived as Canadian art's debut in a major international exhibition. Aided and abetted by Edmund Walker, he appointed a jury to select the show. Charlesworth, well aware of Brown and Walker's intentions, was furious: "If the walls of the Canadian section are to be covered with crude cartoons of the Canadian wilds, devoid of perspective, atmospheric feeling, and sense of texture, it is going to be a bad advertisement for this country."[13]

The jury chose 270 works by 108 artists. The Group, including Tom Thomson, was represented by merely twenty paintings, including Harris's *Shacks* and *Grey Day in Town*. In the catalogue, Brown wrote in language reminiscent of Harris: "The Canadian fine arts are stirring, too, for which we may be devoutly thankful, for if they were not, they would be either dead or degenerate."[14]

The English press's attention was fixed on the more modern painters. The writer for *The Times* was clear in his praise: "It is here [Canada], of all the Dominions, that the note is what we understand by 'modern'—very emphatic, a little crude, leaving plenty of room for refinement without loss of character. To anybody who conceives of a picture as a decorative construction in paint, the landscapes by [these Canadians] . . . cannot fail to give satisfaction."[15] Back home, Charlesworth was consistent in his unmeasured condemnation of the positive reviews in England: "Britishers, above all people, object to have preconceived opinions upset, and there is nothing in these pictures to disturb the popular belief we have all encountered among uninformed Englishmen, that Canadians are crude and commonplace in taste and ideals."[16]

There was one sad note to the Wembley show. A month before the opening, on the eve of his departure for England, Sir Edmund Walker caught pneumonia and died, on March 27, 1924, at the age of seventy-five. Harris's obituary for Walker was unstinting in its recognition of all he had done for the arts in Canada: "He was the first and only man of position to detect that in the modern movement in Canadian art the country had found the beginnings of a distinctive, significant, and bold expression. He announced the fact publicly and did all in his power to encourage and assist the artists and to further the public's understanding of the movement." He added, very significantly: "It isn't enough to achieve material well-being. It is ever a crying necessity to evoke spiritual well-being from within ourselves."[17]

Harris's urban views of Toronto began as a continuation of similar studies he had done in Berlin. They are not, as we have seen, simply street scenes that should be viewed as conventional pieces following art school practices; most of them are carefully selected images of the impoverished lives of many immigrant groups to Canada (English, Scots, Irish, east European). As such, they are works of social criticism in which an attack is being mounted on the rigid discrepancies between rich and poor in Toronto.

The two 1921 canvases from Nova Scotia, more harrowing than their Toronto equivalents, are obviously major indictments of social injustice. Four years later, in April 1925, Harris wrote about the lives of such slum inhabitants in Nova Scotia during the 1925 miners' strike that lasted five months and culminated in a bloody battle at Waterford Lake, where one coal miner was killed by company police on June 11, 1925.

> The real life of the place presents the most unfavorable phases of our vaunted civilization, and these [are] accentuated because utterly devoid of all glamour and romance. Here we see the hard bare facts underlying the industrial machine and it's not a pretty sight . . . These people strain every nerve for a way out, look everywhere for a ray of hope, search all men for a solution, where perhaps there is none. They constantly face starvation, they face the sight of wives and children suffering from squalor and privation and hunger, they face utter dejection, complete loss of faith in mankind.[18]

These sharp jabs come from an article Harris wrote for the *Toronto Daily Star*.

Harris had gone to Glace Bay, where he drew a map of his visit in a notebook, and then wrote passionately about what he had witnessed. His piece was focused on the Reverend Dr. McAvoy, a former employee of the Massey-Harris foundry in Brantford, who, having lost an arm in a farm accident, had become a Baptist minister. In 1925, he was doing his best to provide the bare necessities of life for strikers' families during their bitter conflict with the British Empire Steel Corporation. In his article, Harris described not only McAvoy's long-standing commitment to the workers but also his determination not to allow any religious convictions of the miners to interfere with their determination to defeat their oppressors.*

---

* Harris's thoughts on capitalism are frankly set out in "Theosophy and Art," LA: "In this industrial civilization—the closer to the heart of the industrial centres— the blacker and more sordid, ugly, hard, and callous becomes life . . . Out from the industrial centres toward nature uncontaminated air is sweeter—majesty and purity live in nature . . . Humans become hourly slaves with crippled children, dwarfed, starved, ragged souls—bodies clothed in dirty rags, under rotted roofs, in sordid surroundings.

"The successful businessman works to maintain the status quo—thinks his civilisation is good . . . The artist [knows] that his civilisation is nothing less than a mean shambles."

Lawren Harris.
Glace Bay Parson.
1925.

GLACE BAY - PARSON -

If Harris's earlier urban images are not sufficient evidence, his actions in 1925 demonstrate clearly his sentiments on matters of social justice. He may have been drawn to return to Nova Scotia in 1925 in part because of McAvoy's links to Massey-Harris, but he was also going because he had a sense of unfinished business. As he was coming into his own as a landscape painter, perhaps he wanted to put the finishing touches to the agenda he had set for himself in his urban views.

Harris called the homes of the miners "huddles of box-like houses," and this is exactly what he depicts in *Miners' Houses,*

Glace Bay (*c.* 1925–26), to which the reviewer in the *Toronto Star* responded in an emotion-filled outpouring:

> It might be properly called "Dies Irae," and looks like a scene from Dante's Inferno. Two rows of thin, starved houses stand like sepulchral monuments along the Appian Way, or like crucifixes on the skyline of a place of skulls. The street between these rows of cottage cadavers is like a stream of lava.
>
> The greenish-indigo sky is cleft with a shaft of vengeful light as if signifying the impending wrath of Heaven. It is a powerful satire on industrial peonage.[19]

The religious imagery in this review is apt, because the canvas itself looks as if it is influenced by German expressionism crossed with a sense of religious wonder. The bleakness of the houses and the mounds upon which they sit is relieved by the shaft of light on the left. The world of the miners is one of black oppression, but the picture seems to offer a glimmer of supernatural assistance.

Lawren Harris.
*Miners' Houses,
Glace Bay.
Circa* 1925.

Harris's response to the miners' strike of 1925 has a corollary in his portrait of the Reverend Salem Bland (1859–1950), which was first shown at the Canadian National Exhibition in 1925. The son of a Methodist minister, Bland's early career was centred on temperance reform and the observance of the Sabbath. At about the age of forty, he changed direction and began to make public statements on social issues. He emphasized that a good Christian was someone who in his daily life was a good neighbour and a friend to the oppressed. In 1906, he was dismissed from his post at Wesley College in Winnipeg in large part because he was so outspoken on such issues. In 1919, he became pastor of the Broadway Tabernacle in Toronto, where he became embroiled in a dispute with his board of management on the issue of freedom of expression.

Thoreau MacDonald, Jim's son, claimed, "Lawren had great respect for [Bland] & thought of him as a type of spiritual leader."[20] The circumstances surrounding Harris's decision to paint Bland are not known, but it seems likely that Bland's review of the Group's fourth exhibition may have precipitated an encounter. The two men would soon have discovered that they had similar views about the miners' strike.

Seated in an armchair in his clerical garb, his hands resting loosely in front of him, Bland's head confronts the viewer, but the sitter's eyes are tilted slightly upwards, as if he is thinking of otherworldly matters. His strong, square jaw accentuates his inner strength of character. In a piece in the *Canadian Bookman*, Gordon Mills described the response to this portrait by various members of the audience at the CNE reception. Some shrugged in irritation, some gazed reverently; some thought they were looking at a modern-day Enoch, a fitting companion for God; others thought the picture a "touchstone" of "pure spiritual symbolism."

Mills, Doris's husband, was very partial to what Harris was trying to accomplish. Mills also pointed out that this portrait captured many of the qualities seen in the artist's landscapes: "In it, as in so many of his landscapes, one feels that he passes altogether beyond the ordinary realm of paint into one of pure spiritual symbolism. His canvas is not so much representation or portraiture as the expression of inner mysticism."[21]

There can be little doubt that the "pure spiritual symbolism" of the Bland portrait should be read autobiographically. Harris identified with the minister's social gospel. He had earlier painted portraits of three women who were devout Christian Scientists and thus linked to his mother's religious convictions and, more loosely, to his own. Here, in a forceful depiction of an unorthodox man of God whose life was dedicated to meaningful intervention in support of the poor and outcast, Harris's own inner anguish found release, as it had in *Miners' Houses*.

Lawren Harris.
Dr. Salem Bland.
1925.

After 1925, there is little evidence of social activism on Harris's part. He was preoccupied with his landscape paintings, and he was encountering many difficulties in his personal life. Moreover, and most importantly, Harris's theosophist convictions and his accelerating interest in non-representational painting meant that his critiques of society moved into an altogether different sphere. He did not evade representing the living conditions of the underclass; he simply decided to voice his concerns by addressing the essential conditions of humanity in another form of artistic discourse, one liberated from the here and now.

13

JOYFUL VISION, INNER SORROW

(1926)

Lawren and Bess were spending a lot of time together. Perhaps Fred thought too much time? He never said anything, never remonstrated, but he must have noticed that his friend and his wife were completely taken with each other. "Not in that *way," Lawren reassured himself. He would never practise such deceit!*

Bess and I share a love that is beyond the body, Lawren comforted himself. It was—and would remain—chaste. Yet he worried constantly: was this a form of adultery they were allowing themselves?

THE FIFTH Group exhibition, from May 8 to 31, 1926, was a triumph for Harris. In addition to eight Lake Superior sketches, he had fifteen canvases on display, including *Miners' Houses, Glace Bay* and *Dr. Salem Bland*. A.J. Casson, Carmichael's close friend and assistant at the design firm Rous and Mann, was now the seventh member of the Group. Among the non-members included in the exhibition were Thoreau MacDonald and Bess Housser.

In the *Mail and Empire*, Fred Jacob proclaimed: "Undoubtedly, Lawren Harris is the man who will cause the greatest gnashing of teeth in the present exhibition. He marches steadily ahead with his process of simplification, so that his pictures are more and more hard sheets of colour."[1] In the *Star*, Bridle was similarly ecstatic: "The school of seven . . . have reached new heights, mostly mountain heights . . . The air breathes an exhilarating pictorial ozone which will give heart failure to those who are not accustomed to climb higher in the scale of Canadian landscape grandeurs than the suburban prettiness of the Don and Humber valleys or the level loveliness of the Niagara peninsula."[2] In the *Star Weekly*, he also waxed enthusiastically: "I have never seen so much colour, paint, light, texture, technique with so little normal life." However, he reserved his warmest words for Harris:

> His mountains rise like great teeth of cosmic lime out of calm lake pedestals . . . He achieves a remarkable structural synthesis and present[s] landscape purged of its grossness of detail in quintessential symbolism . . . In most of these Harris bids farewell to mankind and goes into a world sometimes as obviously simple as the fourth dimension to a man on the twentieth plane. What does he mean? Who knows? What matters?[3]

Having managed a few words of dim praise when writing of the Group's previous exhibition, Charlesworth was back on the attack: "The numeral 'Seven,' whatever it meant once, is of course merely cabalistic in meaning today like the phrase 'Ku Klux Klan.' In fact the extravagances of the group suggest a certain affinity with the KuKluxers. The latter excuse their vagaries by calling themselves 100 per cent American, and the Septimists proclaim themselves 100 per cent Canadian."[4] Not minding that he was mixing oranges with apples to cast a slur, Charlesworth expressed his disdain for the Group's increasing success.

Notwithstanding the critic for *Saturday Night*, many were beginning to understand Harris on his own terms. Two months after the exhibition closed, Harris published "The Revelation of

Art in Canada," in which he enunciates the relationship between Harris the Man and Harris the Artist:

> You cannot sever the philosophy of the artist from his work. You belittle the man in his work when you accept his skill, his sensitivity in patterning, in building forms, his finesse in accenting, his suavity in technique, but reject his philosophy, his background . . . Without the philosophy, or in other words, the man in the work of any great artist, you have nothing . . . Indeed the occurrence of a living art in every age, with every people . . . is a tremendous factor in the evolution of the soul. It is a sign that the human can achieve an attitude of child-like wonder, exuberant devotion, a simplicity and directness that goes straight through all erudite deviousness, all cynical, all sorting and labeling and telling of heads, all smugness and satisfaction, to the exacting light of spiritual realms.[5]

In this credo, Harris is explaining as precisely as he can how he wants his art to be interpreted. His is an art devoted to "spiritual realms."

In the Rockies and at Lake Superior in 1926, Harris discovered further clues in his search for spiritual enlightenment and for pictorial equivalents.

Such concerns were his top priority when, in July 1926, Harris and his family stayed at Lake O'Hara Cabin Camp in the Rockies. On such trips, his daughter recalled, he "went off on sketching and climbing treks for a week or so at a time, leaving us at one of the bungalow camps to ride the trails up in the mountains."[6] That summer he also travelled to Banff National Park near Lake Louise.

Mountain Forms was the purest abstract form that Harris had yet achieved when he showed it in the Group exhibition of 1926, and it foreshadows his later experimentations in non-realistic painting. A deliberately non-representational depiction of a mountain, it is a visual exposition of religious ideas such as Madame Blavatsky's notion of the triangle, which she claims "played a prominent part in the religious symbolism of every great nation; for everywhere it represented the three great principles—spirit, force and matter; or the active (male), passive (female), and the dual or correlative principle which partakes of both and binds the two together."7

Such Harris paintings can also be read in conjunction with some of Kandinsky's pronouncements in *Concerning the Spiritual in Art*:

> The life of the spirit may be graphically represented as a large acute-angled triangle, divided horizontally into unequal parts, with the narrowest segment uppermost . . . The whole triangle moves slowly . . . forward and upward . . . At the apex of the highest segment often stands one man. His joyful vision is the measure of his inner sorrow. Even those who are nearest him in sympathy do not understand. Angrily they abuse him as a charlatan or madman . . . There are artists in each segment of the triangle. He who can see beyond the limits of his own segment is a prophet and helps the advance.

Despite his successes in his art, there can be no doubt that Harris felt emotionally isolated in 1926. While he may have been growing more and more aware of how he was integrating certain aspects of his life with his art, he remained distant from his wife. In some ways a creature of his time, he could not *directly* share his sense of being lost with others.

That autumn, Harris and Jackson travelled to the Coldwell Peninsula of Lake Superior. It was on this trip, presumably, that Harris came upon the "Grand Trunk." As Jackson made clear, this was an improvised landscape: "I was with him when he found the stump, which was almost lost in the bush; from its position we could not see Lake Superior at all. Harris isolated the trunk and created a nobler background for it."[8]

The Grand Trunk or, as Harris called an earlier oil sketch, the Old Tree Stump, can be read in a variety of ways; the painting is now known as *North Shore, Lake Superior*. The stump can be the primeval North of Canada bathed in cosmic sunlight; it can represent the search of any lonely human soul for connection to some grand scheme beyond the self. The sculptural form, the

Lawren Harris.
North Shore, Lake Superior. 1926.

husk of a dead tree, reaches upwards and touches sublimity. When *North Shore, Lake Superior* was entered in the Pan-American Exhibition in January–February 1931 at the Baltimore Museum of Art, it won the $500 Museum of Art Prize.

Harris's enormous ambition for a new, Modernist, spiritual art in Canada was aided and abetted by his fellow theosophist Fred Housser in his landmark book *A Canadian Art Movement: The Story of the Group of Seven* (1926). Housser's book is best deemed a polemic or tract. It may claim to be an art history treatise, but that is not its correct genre. Persuasively and elegantly written, it is a defence of the Group.

Housser may not have written his book as a riposte to *The Fine Arts in Canada* (1925) by Newton MacTavish, but it certainly functions as one. In fact, Housser's entire book counters MacTavish's opening salvo:

> Much conflicting opinion is expressed from time to time as to nationality in art, especially in literature and the fine art of painting. For that reason the term "Art in Canada" is used purposely in this book, in contradistinction to the term "Canadian Art," and also for the reason that the writer is not convinced that there is anywhere any art that is peculiarly Canadian.[9]

Convinced as he was to the contrary, Housser wrote about artists inspired by direct contact with Nature. In order to make his argument that the Group had produced a distinctly nationalistic art, Housser segregated them from European artistic influences; he also wanted to stress that they were not academic in orientation—they were "amateurs."* The book's evangelical,

---

* The Ottawa portrait painter Ernest Fosbery was particularly incensed by what he considered to be various myths promulgated by Housser: "The Amateur Myth: the fable that the members of the group were amateurs uncontaminated by European influence ... the Discovery Myth: the fable that they 'discovered' that Canadian landscape was paintable ... The National School of Painting Myth: the claim that these men are the first and only Canadian painters, in fact that a National School has arrived." "As to Certain Myths," letter to the editor, *Ottawa Journal*, February 2, 1927.

Whitmanesque tone irritated some readers, such as Clarence Gagnon; others, like Bertram Brooker, understood the need for such an argument in 1926. Another reader, Jim MacDonald (in an unmailed letter to the author), remarked that reading *A Canadian Art Movement* proved the truthfulness of Napoleon's claim that all history is an agreed-upon lie: "It seems impossible to state things exactly as they were. The historian has to deal with documents and memories. The documents are the best material if written at the time. Memories put a haze around things which falsify them, or at all events *poeticize* them." However, Housser's chief failing was that "the stage is not properly set in the beginning."[10] Of course, Housser had no wish to set the stage properly; to have done so would have invalidated the entire thesis of his narrative.

In reality, Housser was writing a theosophical history of modern Canadian art, with Lawren Harris as its protagonist. In order to accomplish this task, he had to deal with the cult of Tom Thomson. The following sentence contains measured praise, but it is also putting the dead artist in his place: "There is no trace of an intellectual philosophy, nor a theory of aesthetics; no preachment on life, no effort to impress or improve, or lift you up, or cast you down, but just pure 'being,' as though nature itself was speaking to you through a perfectly attuned and seasoned medium." Nature may have been on Thomson's side, and that is a good thing; however, Thomson had no philosophy or aesthetics, made no effort to impress or improve.[11]

In contrast to this wild child of Nature, there was Lawren Harris, who united Nature with Soul.

> Artists in all ages have painted nature from a spirit of devotion toward her but Harris paints the Lake Superior landscape out of a devotion to the life of the soul and makes it feel like the country of the soul. All of his landscapes are large and lofty in conception. Forms are moulded and felt without a suggestion of sensuality.[12]

In the context of this passage, sensuality, in opposition to spirituality, is a negative phenomenon.[13]

At the very same time that Housser was writing his dexterous, persuasively argued polemical defence of Harris and his fellow artists, Harris had established a strong, mutually supportive friendship with Housser's wife, Bess. Harris's portrait of Bess candidly reveals his admiration for her spiritual qualities. In the twenties, Harris's sense of loneliness and isolation was relieved by his friendship with her. This can be seen in four letters from about 1922. Bess, who was an artist, also aspired to write. She confessed her secret to Harris, who wrote her about what she should do.

> Why not tackle a novel?—Letting the characters come to clarity—the weavings come to so many clean-cut strands in a simple pattern . . . You have penetration, the severity of precision. You know numbers of striving characters, idle characters, sleeping, half-awake and aware characters—You see into the workings, the ferments, the seethings and simmerings of people.[14]

In the summer of 1922, Bess wrote him about the difficult place women occupied in a society dominated by the male point of view. He replied with an encouraging, sympathetic letter on August 5, 1922:

> What you say about the scattered indirection of women's lives is surely true.
> Most of them chattels for ages and ages.
> Some few, however, mistresses of their own lives as fully as it is possible in earth life for either man or woman, but complete mistress inside—no man or woman is so outside as long as they are man and woman.
> Man is no different from woman.
> Think of the games he plays. His enthusiasms, diversions, excitements, now and in the past and how he is shackled to petty ways—to endless chitter-chatterings, belittlements.[15]

The letters are chaste, supremely spiritual, written in darting, epigraphic outbursts, and filled with suppressed emotion. They reveal the quiet desperation in which Harris existed.

In the mid-twenties, there was an additional emotional burden. He had achieved the worldly success he had long sought, but was he in danger of losing his soul? Were the pictures he was painting really capturing the radiance emanating from within?

14

A LANGUAGE OF HIS OWN

(1926–1927)

He must be more dedicated, Lawren reminded himself, to find-ing new ways to capture his vision. In his mind's eye, he saw everything clearly. The precision with which he could envision a new spiritual reality staggered him, but then, when he put his hand to paper, everything fell apart. He could not leave behind his old staid language of representation.

Blocked. That was the correct word. He saw the path, but he could not walk down it.

IF HARRIS WAS PONDERING a change in direction, he was doing so very hesitantly. Rather surprisingly, he received a sharp nudge from the American artist and collector Kath-erine Sophie Dreier (1877–1952). Dreier, born in Brooklyn to emigrants from Germany who had amassed a modest fortune in the iron importing business, had from 1907 to 1914 been in Europe studying painting and exhibiting her work. There, she participated in several group exhibitions in Frankfurt, Leipzig, Dresden and Munich, visited Gertrude Stein's salon, purchased a Van Gogh, and read and been deeply influenced by Kandinsky's

Concerning the Spiritual in Art. In 1913, she exhibited her work in the Armory show and a year later founded the Cooperative Mural workshops, a combination art school and workshop modelled after the American Arts and Crafts Movement and Roger Fry's Omega Workshops. In January 1920, she, Marcel Duchamp and Man Ray founded the Société Anonyme (SA), an organization dedicated to staging regular exhibitions of advanced contemporary art. This group hosted the first American one-person shows of Kandinsky, Klee and Léger.

Katherine Dreier.
Photograph. Yale.

Harris had come to Dreier's attention when he submitted two works (*A Northern Lake* and *Ontario Hill Town*) to the Philadelphia Sesquicentennial Exposition, held from June 1 to December 1, 1926. *A Northern Lake* won the Gold Medal, but when she visited the show, the lady's eye was drawn to *Ontario Hill Town*, which she might rightly have thought looked German expressionist in style. She included a reproduction of it in the booklet *Modern Art at the Sesqui-centennial Exhibition* published by SA, and asked Harris to join SA and to exhibit in its upcoming show of "extreme Modern art" at the Brooklyn Museum, from late autumn 1926 to January 1, 1927. "Being an artist myself," she informed Harris, "my effort in arranging an exhibition is to have the pictures so balance each other in color and composition that the ensemble forms a pleasing whole."¹

In a letter to Dreier of September 1, 1926, Harris asked her to include *Miners' Houses* and, especially, the significantly larger *Mountain Forms* as his entries. Although he did not hear back from Dreier, he sent both canvases to her. On November 19, 1926, just as her exhibition was opening at the Brooklyn Museum, she finally wrote: "I wish you could come and see how very handsome your two pictures look and how much your canvas called 'Mountain Forms' has been admired . . . Several papers have asked for your 'Mountain Forms', so that we have photographed it and I hope the papers will print what the reporters have sent in."² (However, the Brooklyn catalogue reproduced *Miners' Houses*, not *Mountain Forms*.) Harris obviously wanted Dreier to see *Mountain Forms* because he knew that in her he had the ideal audience: she would see and appreciate how he was incorporating abstraction into the genre of landscape.

Deeply touched by Dreier's interest in his work, and exhilarated by his subsequent visit to the exhibition, Harris decided to do everything in his power to convince the Art Gallery of Toronto (AGT) to host a travelling version of the show. This was a difficult task, because in July 1926 the AGT's Exhibition Committee had decided this display was too revolutionary for Toronto. Harris pleaded with the members of the committee:

There is nothing in [the Brooklyn exhibition] of an offensive nature, that is, decadent in a moral sense. All the works impressed one as exemplifying sincere adventure, research and expression and whilst there are numerous attempts at unusual expression and others showing unusual uses of various media the whole exhibition leaves a clear and to me very convincing impression. The element of fake, of vociferously striving for attention, of trading on gullibility is quite absent.³

Harris canvassed members of the committee separately, and told Dreier that the Art Gallery of Toronto was one of the finest on the continent, "but the crowd that run it need a severe shaking up." He added:

> I talked with the chairman of the exhibition committee of the gallery to-day. He fears that just following a campaign for new members and trouble last spring because of our own show [of the Group] they might lose a number of members—dear me—then he talked expense—I told him I would pay half—but they are a very timid crew, his committee, so they may side step the opportunity. To-morrow I talk with another one and will press the importance of securing the exhibition with him and others.
>
> If they refuse I will secure some other place where we can hold the exhibition, advertize it in every way possible. I can get the papers here interested even if by way of ridicule. I am determined if you are agreeable and I can afford the cost to get the exhibition here for April or a part of it.[4]

Harris was successful: the exhibition was shown at the Art Gallery of Toronto from April 1 to 27, 1927. Bryne Hope Saunders of the *Evening Telegram* was thoroughly flustered by what she saw in the first exhibition of abstract art in Canada, but Fred Jacob in the *Mail and Empire*, in his sensitive response to the various approaches to Modernism he witnessed, concluded: "If these pictures awaken emotional or aesthetic responses in some men or women, or appear, for them, to have a profound significance, then they do justify themselves in a certain direction."[5]

Works by Arp, Braque, Léger, Ernst, Mondrian, Kandinsky, Miró, Klee and Man Ray were among the 175 items on display at this exhibition, the first time advanced Modernist art was shown in Toronto. Harris's two canvases shown in Brooklyn were not on display (he asked that they be excluded so that he could not be accused of conflict of interest), and even if they had been, they might have seemed a bit conservative next to many other works on display. So elated was Harris by this exhibition that he took the unusual step of volunteering to conduct explanatory tours at the gallery.

In a letter to Dreier, a fellow theosophist, of mid-December 1926, Harris spoke about moving from a "feeling of National consciousness" in his art towards a "universal consciousness."[6] In so doing, he was signalling an important change of direction in his career.

When he reviewed the SA exhibition in *Canadian Forum* in May 1927, Harris further tipped his hand as to the direction he was taking in his own career:

> Most of the pictures were abstract. These could be divided as coming from two sources. One half of them from naturalistic sources wherein the more abstract and lasting qualities of design, movement, rhythm, equilibrium, spatial relationship, light and order were extricated from the fleeting aspects of a scene or scenes to suggest its informing, persisting life. The other half, and in the main the most convincing pictures, were directly created from an inner seeing and conveyed a sense of order in a purged, pervading vitality that was positively spiritual.

Harris obviously considered his own recent work as belonging to the first group: these were works that began with naturalistic form and then moved into abstraction. The "more convincing" pictures represented the area into which he was pondering a move. In 1927, though, he was not sure he had it in him to make this move.

Harris remained convinced that Canadian art must always retain its own special integrity, no matter how experimental or "advanced" it became:

> Many people interested in the future of Canadian Art feared that the direction shown in the exhibition might lure some Canadian artists from their path. That seems very unlikely. While the exhibition did stimulate creative thought and emotion and opened new and thrilling vistas, it would be impossible now for any real Canadian artist to imitate any European artist. Our way is not that of Europe, and when we evolve abstractions, the approach, direction, and spirit

will be somewhat different. Furthermore, the exhibition has enlarged the vision of many of our people, has awakened them to a greater range of ideas and new possibilities of expression and had thus enlarged the eliciting audience for our artists. This should keep them true to their own path and help clarify their particular direction.7

The tone in this proclamation may be strong and decisive, but Harris remained tormented by the direction in which he was moving. He wanted to achieve something new, but if he veered in that direction, he might have nothing to show for it.

A strong voice of dissent to the SA show came from Franz Johnston, once Harris's colleague in the Group of Seven:

I am confident that most of the creatures that perpetrated these monstrosities have "leprous brains", if any. These people who do these things are more dangerous than many incarcerated in asylums for the insane . . . The very people in Toronto who are raving about the esoteric qualities in these works are those who raise the greatest "hullabaloo" when a side-show shows physical abortions and freaks of nature. Then why in the name of common-sense and fair-mindedness endorse these mental miscarriages.8

These vitriolic words recall some of the invectives launched against the Group. On the verge of venturing in a new direction, Johnston's harsh words—in part probably aimed at Harris—must have given him pause.

Harris's profound dilemma about abstraction was complicated in 1927 by his difficult relationship with Bertram Brooker (1888–1955). Brooker, born in England, had lived in Canada since 1905, when he and his family settled in Portage la Prairie, Manitoba. He moved to Toronto in 1921, where he continued his career in journalism at *Marketing* magazine.

Brooker's religious beliefs share some traits with Harris's. In July 1923, at Dwight on Lake of Bays in northern Ontario, Brooker had a mystical experience that transformed his life. He rejected the materialism of twentieth-century culture and placed his reliance on spiritual values. He was a great admirer of Whitman.

Like Harris, Brooker felt that musical form was spiritual form. They both were convinced that the artist uses "rhythms and moods to make a harmonious home for the imaginative and spiritual meanings [they have] evoked in him."9 However, Brooker believed in the concept of a Nietzsche-inspired artist-leader, and he rejected any kind of religious system, including theosophy.

Always looking for a way to promote a fellow artist he considered talented, Harris promoted the younger man. However, from the outset of his relationship with Harris, Brooker had serious reservations about him. On August 25, 1925, he penned a portrait of Harris as "Manchee," the protagonist in a proposed novel:

Bertram Brooker.

> Something like Harris, except in position and physical appearance. Under forty. Supremely confident of his art and rather self-centred, rather wanting to be courted, especially in his own studio. Suspicious of newcomers, cryptically sarcastic, tricking them into confessions or statements he will not like, so that he can be quickly done with them.
>
> As artist a revolutionist, yet not unimpressed by the great works of the past, which he admires as examples of tremendous technique.
>
> As a Canadian almost ferociously patriotic, with a great feeling for the country, which has been greatly bolstered by Whitman. Hesitating to go to Europe or even New York for fear of being seduced from his utterly native viewpoint . . .

As a mystic he also believes that things are going to happen in this country, indeed are happening. He feels himself in the vanguard of the movement and is looking for every sign. Unless people show some sign of it he is impatient with them . . .

His gestures are practically a language of his own. I must observe Harris closely when he comes back. The angular motions of his hands, all to bring out of him what words fail to bring out. And I must get that smile of his when his hair lifts, and something happens to his eyes.[10]

Harris turned forty in 1925, but he had visited New York several times by then.*

Acidic though this pen portrait may be, it contains some truthful threads. Harris had moments of being imperious, self-aggrandizing and difficult. He did, however, have the capacity to laugh at himself, and framed some of Lismer's satirical cartoon drawings showing him in bouts of condescension-laden mandarin behaviour. In one (not in his collection), Harris becomes Laocoön, who, attempting to warn the Trojans against the Greeks bearing gifts, was destroyed by serpents set upon him by Apollo. Here, Harris becomes the proponent of Modernism whom Hector Charlesworth and his ilk want to destroy.**

Brooker's estimate of Harris's belief system is certainly accurate. Another observer as intelligent as Brooker might have been more empathic and seen that behind Harris's facade of ease and strength resided a very uneasy person. Brooker did not perceive

---

* Gregory Betts provides convincing evidence that the protagonist in Brooker's 1936 *Think of the Earth*, which won the first Governor General's Award, "has many loose resemblances to Harris. The character is a mystic who looks to the mountains, the Canadian mountains, as the icon of northern spiritual intensity and purity, as a metaphor for the spiritual impulse in his mind." *Lawren Harris in the Ward*, 86.

** Another opponent of Harris (and the other members of the Group of Seven) was Prime Minister Mackenzie King, who found their landscapes "frightful." He especially did not like the "decayed trees" of Harris and Thomson. See Ord, *The National Gallery of Canada*, 103.

LAOCOON

Arthur Lismer.
*Lawren Harris
as Laocoön.*
Circa 1925–30.

this because he had strong feelings of competition with Harris. For his part, Harris was equally rivalrous. Brooker presented him with a vexing situation: he wanted to promote Brooker's abstractions because he himself was thinking of going in that direction; on the other hand, he envied Brooker's extraordinary talent in that form of pictorial expression.

In this instance, Harris handled his conflicted feelings by arranging the first showing of Brooker's abstractions, at the Arts and Letters Club in January 1927. However, Harris's mixed emotions were revealed in the way he did not display complete confidence in Brooker in public. Brooker was both hurt and irate, as his diary entry for January 24, 1927, makes clear.

My pictures went up at the Arts and Letters Club on Saturday and there was a curious silence around the place, relieved only by the whisperings of groups who would not come up and discuss them with me openly. I came away and walked

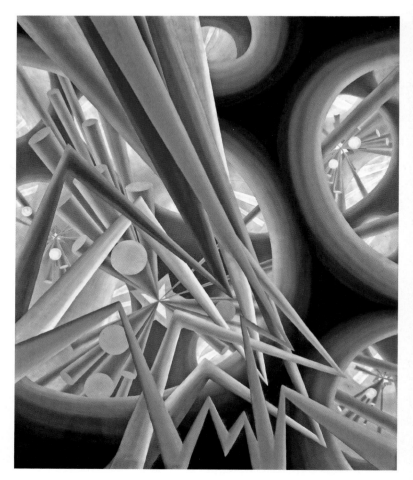

Bertram Brooker.
Sounds Ascending.
Circa 1929.

up Yonge Street with Fred [Varley] and Lawren feeling hard-
ened (in the best way) by the experience. They talked of
everything else; apparently embarrassed by the remarks they
had overheard, and not caring to tell me.

. . . Lawren and I had a fine time over [one] picture and I
felt fonder of him than ever. He and Mrs. Harris are to come
over soon to see the stuff, on her suggestion.

Today at the club it was no better. Lismer asked Lawren to
say something at 1.30, but after a while he and Lawren went
over to the fireplace, talked together for a while and then left

the club. Gradually everybody left the table and I was there alone . . . I could not help feeling let down and rather deserted by Lismer and Lawren running away without any kind of announcement, or even any notice as to whose pictures they were and what they intended to convey.[11]

In the instances cited by Brooker, Harris seems to have sinned by omission. He refused to take a direct stand in public in support of Brooker, but he had, in the first place, gone to the trouble of organizing the exhibition. He did this at some cost to his relationships with other members of the Group. In fact, on at least one occasion, an *ex cathedra* defence by Harris irked MacDonald—whose distrust of Modernism led him to dislike Cézanne—so much that he told Brooker, in what was *supposed* to be a letter of apology, on January 28, 1927, that he did not see the point of what Brooker was trying to achieve:

I do feel that art in general, nowadays, is being made too complex a matter. Intellect is squeezing the life out of it, in order to see how it is made, & I regret that I find few simple understandable things said about it. So I would like anything of the occult or secret doctrine avoided in it if at all possible . . . I cannot understand your process of working, at present, for I do not think I have any capacity of clearing my mind. I see better past memories & sensations, in that intuitional state (very rarely, of course) but I get no blanks to return from.[12]

Perhaps Harris did not defend Brooker's work ardently enough. To do so would have been to invite conflict, something Harris always tried to avoid. He would also have had to show his own hand. In 1927 he was not prepared to do this to the extent the thin-skinned Brooker wished.

A canvas such as *Sounds Ascending* must have touched Harris deeply. The irony is that Brooker, apparently because he could not find an appreciative audience in Canada, abandoned abstract painting in 1931.[13]

Caught between many rocks and hard places, Harris was tottering back and forth in 1927. His marriage remained a stale affair. That year the family vacationed in Temagami in northern Ontario. Upon their return to Toronto, as they were wont to do, the Harrises moved house, this time to one in Oriole Parkway that had been built for them.* A change of address requires a great deal of preparation, time and effort. In the case of the Harris marriage, it also provided an opportunity for them to unite in a common cause, one that allowed them to push aside their many incompatibilities.

Oriole Parkway.

That autumn in Toronto, on November 27, Harris met Emily Carr (1871–1945). The relationship would eventually bring with it many pleasures, but at that time Carr's great admiration for his accomplishments must have both elated and saddened Harris. He would have been elated because he recognized in her a kindred spirit who, like himself, was attempting to make meaningful, spiritually infused Canadian landscape paintings; he would have

---

* This house was designed by the architect Douglas Kirkland.

been saddened because he was toying with the idea of abandoning landscape art and perhaps wandering in a new direction.[14]

Fourteen years older than Harris and just as insecure, Carr, who was born in Victoria, British Columbia, had become an artist through gritty determination and exceptional fortitude of character. She attended the San Francisco Art Institute from 1890 to 1892, made her first of several sketching and painting trips to Aboriginal villages in 1898, and, realizing that she still lacked technical know-how in rendering what she saw, went to England to study at the Westminster School of Art. In 1907 she determined once again to paint the Aboriginals, and in 1910 she returned to Europe, where she studied at the Académie Colarossi and incorporated both Post-Impressionist and Fauvist techniques in her work. In 1912 she travelled to the Queen Charlotte Islands and the Skeena River, where she painted the art and architecture of the Haida, Gitksan and Tsimshian.

Emily Carr.

Her work received scant and often indifferent critical attention. For the next fifteen years, she existed in strained circumstances, running a boarding house, the House of All Sorts. Her "discovery" as a major Canadian artist came through Marius Barbeau and, later, Eric Brown, who called upon her in Victoria and was deeply moved by her work. He invited Carr to show her work in an exhibition of west coast Aboriginal art. She sent twenty-six paintings east in 1926.

Inspired in part by Fred Housser's book and in particular by the reproduction she saw of Harris's *Above Lake Superior*, she determined to meet members of the Group. On her first visit to the Studio Building, she met A.Y. Jackson and a large number of students. She liked his paintings of Native peoples.

Two days later, under a gloomy November sky, she called on Lawren Harris. As Harris, in his normal friendly manner, pulled out canvas after canvas for her to see, Carr, seated on his sofa, was "dumfounded," touched to her "very core." Harris's work was "a revelation, a getting outside of oneself and finding a new self in a place you did not know existed." The pictures moved "into the vast lovely soul of Canada." She was especially touched by Harris's drawing of a starving mother and her two malnourished children done while he was in Nova Scotia; this image had been published in the *Canadian Forum* in June 1925.

That evening, two things took hold of her "with a double clutch. Canada and Art. They were tossing me round & tearing me." She asked herself: "Oh, God, what have I seen? where have I been? Something has spoken to the very soul of me, wonderful, mighty, not of this world." Harris's work rose "into serene, uplifted planes, above the swirl into holy places." If he had found such profound spirituality in the Canadian landscape, perhaps she might be vouchsafed the same gift? In his studio had surged "through her whole being, the wonder of it all, like a great river rushing on, dark and turbulent, and rushing and irresistible, and carrying me away on its wild swirl like a helpless little bundle of wreckage."[15]

When she visited Harris's room a second time, Carr felt transported. "Lawren's studio is wonderful, all quiet and grey, nothing unnecessary. There is equipment for painting, equipment for writing, a roomy davenport and peace; that's all. It is a place to invite the soul to come and gather the riches of thought, and ponder over them and try to express them, an orderly place of an orderly mind."[16]

The studio may have looked like an austere Harris painting, but the artist himself was not in an "orderly" state of mind. When she confessed her admiration, he was grateful, but he offered blunt advice: "Don't be influenced by anything or anybody. Shun everything but your own inner promptings, your own purest reactions—like the plague. You liked my stuff, and perhaps because it was somewhat new to you, it made more of an impression than it otherwise might have. But *don't* be influenced by it, I mean—stay decidedly with your own way."[17] Varley had warned her against Harris: "He thinks Harris is going too far, brings religion in too much. For his own part, he says, he likes to stick a bit firmer to good old Earth."[18] Emily was much more on Harris's side than Varley's.

Certainly, Carr's admiration buoyed Harris's spirits. Having understood exactly what he was trying to do, she expressed her sentiments in heartfelt words of wonder. In her, Harris had found his ideal audience. He felt her greatness as a fellow artist, and her words of praise probably meant more to him than Bess Housser's. Yet he must have been more than a little troubled. Carr's admiration was unstinting. Was he right to abandon what he had only very recently and with considerable difficulty accomplished?

As well, Lawren would have noted, perhaps with a twinge of discomfort, his new friend's admiration of Trixie, whom she met on Sunday, December 11: "Mrs. Harris welcomed me [to her home] and I gave a long look to see what she was and how she influenced his work. She was beautiful, quiet, gentle, not very young, a peaceful person. I decided she would be a great help and strength to him."[19]*

"Of this I am convinced," Carr had very intuitively told herself. "He has come up to where he is now by diligent, intelligent grinding and wrestling and digging things out; that he couldn't do what he is doing now without doing what he has already done; that his religion, whatever it is, and his painting are one and the same. I wonder where he will rise to."[20] Of course, Harris was asking himself the very same question.

---

* Most people who knew the Harrises at this time would have agreed with Doris Mills Speirs: "And [Lawren] went very, very deep and Trixie just stayed where she was. She didn't grow. She was just a nice, nice woman but she didn't grow, and she couldn't possibly follow him. She couldn't follow what he was doing. She couldn't follow what he was thinking. She couldn't do it, and it meant that at home there was no one very close to him . . ." Interview with Charles Hill, October 15, 1973.

15

ABSOLUTE SILENCE

(1928–1930)

Emily gave him a voice. She asked him how she should paint, but it was he who learned from her. To her, he could confess his deepest worries about where he was going in his art. He opened up his heart to her in a way he could not do even with Bess, the great love of his life. Bess was an extremely good painter, but she was not a genius like Emily. That was the crucial difference between the two. Only Emily comprehended the ruthless dedication and complete sacrifices that must be made in order to produce great art.

Emily also understood the ups and downs in an artist's existence, grasped intuitively that we only have ourselves to blame for our failings. He told her, "But I have nowhere anything to complain about—any pickle I get into is my own silly fault, and that I know better than I know anything. I would decidedly like to alter many things in myself. I need much more good-will, buoyancy, light in the heart."[1]

"Gracious me, what we stir up when we really commence to live—when we enter the stream of creative life—then we are on our own . . . and begin to see a supreme logic behind the inner struggle."[2]

IN ADDITION to Emily Carr's rapturous adoration of him and his work, Harris could have taken considerable satisfaction in his mountain landscapes. In 1926, he was at Lake O'Hara in Yoho National Park (Lefroy Lake and Schäffer Mountain) and at Banff National Park near Lake Louise (Mount Lefroy, Mount Temple). Two years later he returned to Lake O'Hara. In 1929 he painted near Lake Louise in Banff National Park (Mont de Poilus) and at Mount Robson in Mount Robson Provincial Park. In paintings such as *Isolation Peak*, *Mount Robson* and *Mount Lefroy*, he was not only making images compelling in their own right but ones that adhered to his aesthetic and religious ideals.

Lawren Harris.
Isolation Peak.
Circa 1931.

Isolation Peak depicts Mont des Poilus. (Harris did not depict *Isolated* Peak, which is to the west of Poilus; there is no *Isolation* Peak in the Rockies.) His use of the noun "isolation" is meant to suggest the remoteness of the mountain, its separateness. In another sense, the mountain represents the plight of the artist in the modern world: his vision often sequesters him, creating an almost unbearable sense of loneliness. The pencil and oil

Lawren Harris.
Mount Robson.
Circa 1929.

sketches for this painting show how Harris would begin with a fairly realistic drawing then gradually reduce it to abstract forms. Similar working methods were used in both *Robson* (Mount Robson Provincial Park) and *Lefroy* (Banff National Park), so that the *idea* of mountain comes to predominate.

However, significant distinctions were always being made. In *Isolation Peak*, the greens and browns in the land in the foreground suggest the mountain in the background might possibly be accessible; in *Mount Robson*, the snow-covered rock formations make viewing the mountain more difficult. *Mount Lefroy* is imperiously remote. In each of these images, Harris is suggesting that such mountains are both sacred and occult, but he is also implying that man sometimes has a great deal of difficulty in knowing how to integrate his experience with these places of intense spiritual energy. In his preparatory drawings, Harris tended to stick to what he could see with his eye; his finished canvases add the abstract dimension.

Harris once revealed to a painter friend one of the principal reasons he was drawn to mountains: "[They] don't want man. They're resisting man. They're pushing man away . . . I just warn

Lawren Harris.
Mount Lefroy.
1930.

Lawren Harris.
Lynx Mountain,
Mount Robson
District. Circa
1929–30.

you about that, because you feel the antagonism of the mountains towards man, because they're afraid what man might do to the mountains."[3] Man has so much severed himself from the divinity within him that he is at war with the primal forces inhabiting mountains, which are very much aware of the ecological harm man can do to them. In some ways, painting mountains became for Harris a way of returning to the essential underlying forces governing the world.

Although Harris had received many accolades over the past decade, he had also been severely criticized. He had some severe strictures to deal with in 1928. At the sixth Group of Seven exhibition in February, he showed thirteen canvases, including two mountain landscapes and four Lake Superior ones. Fred Jacob in the *Mail and Empire* felt that Harris was having too overpowering an influence on the other members of the Group.[4] Bridle had begun to tire of what he considered

> the almost complete dehumanization of painting. Epics of solitude, chaos, and snow. Not a man, woman or child, nor any beast; scarcely a flower. Only the guest exhibitors show these human things . . . The world depicted by the Group is mainly one of force, phenomena, space, mountains, waters, skies, forlorn forests, rocks, moss and sunlight . . . It is so despairingly beautiful and inhuman.

Varley, who had earlier voiced his disdain for Harris's spiritual values to Emily Carr, was, in Bridle's opinion, the only artist to have evaded the "Harris germ."[5]*

---

* Another painting that Harris put on exhibition was *Design for a Chapel* (now known as *Figure with Rays of Light* [AGO]). In this canvas, shards of light descend upon an assemblage of ice forms; the one in the centre of the canvas (the chapel) is rendered in a quasi-abstract manner. The writer in the *Toronto Telegram* of February 18, 1928, was unimpressed: "[Harris] abandons realism for idealism . . . Imagine a peeled banana of gigantic size standing on end before a display of northern lights and you have it."

That observation was meant as a severe criticism of what Bridle considered a pernicious influence. The observations of both journalists are correct when applied, for example, to Carmichael's *Evening, North Shore, Lake Superior*. This painting may be parodic of *Above Lake Superior*, but the dark tonal ranges are Carmichael's, and the brush strokes are thicker and more luxuriously applied than in Harris's work at this time. Influence there may be, but it seems to be one that unleashed Carmichael's strengths rather than undermining them.

The all-Canadian exhibition (selected by the National Gallery) at the Vancouver Exhibition in August 1928 gave rise to the usual number of both snarling and appreciative notices. There were eighteen canvases by members of the Group on display. One notice would have given Harris a lift:

> A stranger coming to Vancouver during [the period of the exhibition] would have been convinced that the people of this city were more interested in art than the citizens of Florence, or Chelsea, or Montmartre . . . Vancouver owes this famous group a great debt, for their pictures drew crowds to the exhibit that would never have gone there otherwise, and added zest to life by inspiring heated discussions which lasted for months.[6]

The Group was showing work that could compare favourably with the best being produced in Europe; it was making Canadian subject matter interesting to Canadians; it was igniting strong responses. On those three important counts, Harris could see his efforts coming to fruition.

And yet, reluctantly, Harris may have come to see the justice in this observation by Brooker: "Until recently, of course, the effect of the Group and their painting [has been beneficial]. Young painters, and especially beginners and students, seeing their work, were encouraged to look at Canada with a fresh viewpoint—a viewpoint unencumbered by the atmospheric—realistic—photographic tendencies." For Brooker, "so long as the influence of the Group of Seven operated to release young Canadian painters from the stuffy ties of Victorian atmosphericism," that was healthy. However, the Group's influence had become so powerful that it was now fashionable to imitate them. In Brooker's opinion, this implied that the Group had become an obstacle to genuine creativity.

Harris tried to keep busy. At the end of July 1928, he joined Trixie and the children at Lake O'Hara in the Rockies. That autumn he travelled with Jackson, Carmichael and Casson to the north shore of Lake Superior (this was to be the last Group sketching trip). In 1929 he collaborated with Lismer on plans to decorate the lecture hall of the Toronto Theosophical Society. That autumn he went by car with Jackson along the south shore of the St. Lawrence as far as Father Point near Rimouski, Quebec.

Jackson very much enjoyed the "marvellous motor trip," and especially the fact that Harris's "big boat [of a car] goes like a bird." The landscape reminded him of the Lake Superior region "with a little less grandeur to it, strings of little villages all along the shore. I had no idea it was so populated. It's hard to paint, too scattered and much newer than the villages further up the river."[7]

Harris found one subject that fascinated him at Father Point, a place named after the Jesuit priest Henri Nouvel, who in 1663 celebrated the first Mass in the region. As was his usual custom, Harris first made an accurate sketch of the lighthouse. Then, with his now customary way of making his subject adapt to his inner point of view, he rendered it as a much taller and thinner structure than it was in reality, and reduced the nearby dwelling, fence, shore, water and sky to geometrical elements.

The tower reaches skyward, its lines sharp and precise. The red at the top of the tower is echoed in the roof of the nearby buildings. Red here relieves the blues, whites, blacks and dark greens that dominate the painting. In a subtle way, Harris is experimenting with expanding his colour palette, and the result here is convincing.

At the seventh Group show in April 1930, Jehanne Biétry Salinger was deeply impressed by this canvas: "Almost like a

Lawren Harris.
Father Point. 1930.

symbol of [Harris's] own work and perhaps of Canadian art, [it] is the most simplified of his paintings and is designed with the most splendid sense of space relations. It also contains an element of spiritual power which makes of it one of his strongest works."[8] In this sense, it might be possible to read the lighthouse as a source of both physical and spiritual illumination.

In the *Ottawa Citizen*, Brooker was unmoved by what he saw at the same exhibition:

> The present show at Toronto rings the deathknell of the Group of Seven as a unified and dominant influence in Canadian painting . . . They have themselves ceased to experiment. Moreover, they are much less productive . . . Jackson and Harris, the only two of the Group who have much time for painting, are represented mostly by smaller paintings than usual, all landscapes, and of a type that one has come to expect. The experimentation is over, the old aggressiveness has declined.[9]

Where Salinger saw a heightened use of simplicity to portray spiritual insight, Brooker discerned emptiness. Harris may well have agreed with Brooker that he had lost his aggressive edge. He obviously did not think *Lighthouse* was his prelude to a new type of symbolical landscape. For him, it was a magnificent dead end.

The reviewer in the *Canadian Forum* was unequivocal in his condemnation:

> The cement which once kept all the stones of this Canadian tower together has dried out and has fallen off, the stones have been disassembled and have been scattered. For the sake of sentimentalism or conservatism, bring them together if you will, but it takes more than the desire to see them, one next to the other, to make of them a unit with a symbol, having a common significance.[10]

At the very time he was struggling to create a new kind of art and to get himself out of another artistic dead end, Harris had to confront those who felt the Group had outlasted its usefulness.

In early May, Lawren and Trixie travelled to Europe for six weeks. By the early thirties, Harris had a jaded view of Europe, although he recognized that it had contributed enormously to the unfolding spirit of man. In time present, however, it consisted of imperial nations that had dedicated themselves to "conquest and exploitation, that has affected in one way or another all the peoples on this globe, and which disease contains within itself the virus of Europe's death throes." The most evident symptom of decline, he stated in 1933, was "the devilish moral cowardice of Germany today, a people who under the cloak of a fanatical belief in the superiority of the Aryan-Germanic racial strain—a myth if there ever was one—make a scapegoat of another and utterly helpless people, the Jews in their midst, and bully and butcher and crucify them."[11]

The climate in Germany must have been especially upsetting for someone who had come into being as a professional artist there. The Harrises visited at least two German cities—Stuttgart and Munich—and visited France. He implied in a letter to Emily

Carr that he had seen works by Cézanne, Picasso, Matisse and Derain. Such artists "know they belong to Europe, fit in—a logical continuation of tradition—but America, Canada, a different thing—another approach—a new dispensation."[12]

In attempting to look up Katherine Dreier, he called upon her friend Marcel Duchamp. The abstractions Harris saw did not impress him, he assured Emily: "I have seen almost no abstract things that have deep resonance that stirs and answers and satisfies the soul . . . But that does not say that some painters may not produce them to-morrow or the next day."[13]

In this observation Harris may have been leaving the door open for himself, but he was obviously conflicted because of his earlier commitment to the establishment of a school of Canadian Modernist landscape painting. If he embraced abstraction, he must have felt he would be abandoning ideals he had, until very recently, forcefully defended.

One of the reasons Lawren and Trixie went to Stuttgart was to inspect modern house designs and generate ideas for what he referred to as his "new mansion," to be built on Ava Crescent by the Russian immigrant architect Alexandra Biriukova (1893–1967). (Douglas Kirkland, who designed the Harrises' Oriole Park house, was originally supposed to tackle this assignment.) Once again, Lawren and Trixie were overlooking the obstacles in their relationship by thinking of another house move.

Standing on a lot with a curved front on Ava near Spadina in Toronto's exclusive Forest Hill area, the two-storey house extended almost two hundred feet back and was sixty-three feet across the front. Buff limestone was used for the base and sills; the major surfaces were covered in stucco. The design was intended to be severe but relieved by grille work along the windows and metalwork along the terrace.

The entrance from the flagged terrace led into an oval two-storey-high hall encircled by a spiral staircase. Off the centre hall were a living room, a dining room, a study and a kitchen. The second floor had another study, three bedrooms, three baths, a sunroom and a roof terrace over the garage. The set-back roof elevation contained two bedrooms, two baths, another study and a children's playroom. The ceilings on the ground floor were twelve feet high; concealed lighting threw rays of light down the four corners of each room; wall angles were avoided by built-in bookcases, a radio and a phonograph. Harris hired Carl Schaefer to apply silver and aluminum leaf to the ceilings of some rooms so that they would reflect light onto Harris's canvases.[14]

Ava Crescent.

Since the neighbouring houses were Georgian and English-inspired Period Revival, this Modernist structure provided a dashing, exuberant contrast. Harris may have selected Biriukova because he knew her work in completing the interior design of the Russian Orthodox church on Glen Morris Street; Thoreau Mac-Donald had carved symbols taken from the Orthodox liturgy.

This was the home of a wealthy person who wished to proclaim that he was completely comfortable with contemporary trends. While the resulting house is a splendid example of international art deco, the design on the metal grille on the two-storey central window is of pine needles, a subtle reminder that the owner was a lover of his country's flora.

Although discouraged and disillusioned with respect to any belief system he still retained about his own engagement with landscape art, Harris determined in 1930 to look at some new forms of landscape: those to be found in the Arctic. Three years earlier, Jackson and Frederick Grant Banting had travelled on the Canadian government supply ship the *Beothic* on its annual voyage to the Arctic.

Harris's account of the Arctic trip is a bit matter-of-fact:

> A few years after Jackson's and Banting's trip to the Arctic, Jackson and I joined the Government Arctic expedition. We were most fortunate on this occasion as this particular expedition made the most extensive trip ever taken in the Arctic region in one season. The ship went directly north to Godhavn on the Greenland coast, and then up the coast to Etah where Commander Peary used to winter, and then into Kane Basin. From this point we went south along the coast of Ellesmere Island into Lancaster Sound where we were held up by ice for days. For four hours on our way out the ship was in danger of being crushed by the immense weight of the huge moving ice-floes. We then went around the top of Baffin's Island, down the east coast to Hudson's straits, through the straits and across the northern waters of Hudson Bay to Chesterfield Inlet. Later we returned through the straits and proceeded southward along the Labrador coast to Nova Scotia.[15]

Well before the trip, in 1927, Jackson had reiterated many Group commonplaces: "There is a country to the north of us which is unique and distinctly Canadian." This was one further heroic landscape designed for artist heroes to paint.[16] Upon his return, the press reported that the Canadian artist, as represented by Jackson and Harris, was "more Canadian, more virile than ever."[17] For Harris, this was a difficult concept to incarnate because his ideas had changed so much since he had first conceived of the Canadian male landscape artist as the embodiment of virility. He no longer believed in such notions.

Space in which to work on the *Beothic* was difficult to come by, as were the sights to be gleaned, as Harris also recalled:

While we were on this trip Jackson and I painted a large number of sketches, although painting was difficult as we usually saw the most exciting subjects while streaming through channels or while being bumped by pack ice. On many occasions we had time only to take rapid notes. These notes we worked up into sketches, crowded into our small cabin, seated on the edge of our respective bunks with only a port-hole to let in the light.[18]

Not unexpectedly, Jackson provided a much fuller account of the voyage, including two anecdotes about Roman Meal. On that journey, "the excellent comestible got as close to the North Pole as it had ever been." Captain Falke was so exhausted that Harris "persuaded *him* to use it." At the outset of the last leg of the journey, Jackson ruefully recalled, "tragedy struck us. One morning the cook announced that the Roman Meal was all used up. We were consequently run down and listless when we got to Chesterfield." At the Hudson's Bay store, Harris, a bit despondently, asked if there was any Roman Meal. "The clerk had never heard of it. Looking about the shelves, Harris spied something familiar on a top shelf and called the clerk, who got a ladder. It was Roman Meal, four packages of it. We were saved!" Harris purchased the lot.

For Jackson, the Arctic was full of life. He had been there before, had made friends with the crew of the ship, and knew many of the Canadian inhabitants. On the Greenland coast, he and Harris stared in wonder at a "range of big reddish-violet hills covered by glaciers standing in relief against warm grey skies." There were episodes of "filthy weather," heavy fog and ice blockages.[19] For Harris, the Arctic was primordially silent.

When he arrived back, Harris was not particularly enthusiastic about what he had accomplished, probably because his frame of mind did not allow him much leeway in being generous to himself. Publicly, he exuded confidence: Canadian artists, he claimed, should place themselves "at the head of the big adventure of discovering Canada's vast northern empire."[20] He told Emily Carr his real feelings:

The arctic was an experience. I know that if it were possible for one to go up there and take one's time and go where one liked it would yield some fine things. But it is not possible. You'd have to charter a real ship.

I'm painting some of the Arctic things—not bad—but nothing to usher the soul into eternal bliss. I am striving but also not realizing and aware most moments that I'll come to the disillusionment of [not] accomplishing anything unusual. I'm trying to get to the summit of my soul and work from there—there where the universe sings.

Sometimes I feel as if my shell were creeping around me shutting me off from zest and light and pure form. I don't know a thing and yet I feel as if I'd been through enough . . . I need to get to work and disregard all the silly vagaries of personal feelings. Always somehow if one keeps working, something comes through.[21]

By most standards, what Harris accomplished was of an exceptional quality, but he simply could not grasp this truth emotionally.

Harris's photographs of the Arctic are atmospheric and almost mournful, especially those of the Inuit. Although he did not capture them on canvas, his photographs of Aboriginal existence have an elegiac edge to them. At the insistence of seventeen-year-old Peggie, Harris had even purchased a movie camera for this trip. He first showed his "Moving Pictures of the Arctic" at the Toronto Conservatory of Music on January 8, 1934.

In a canvas such as *Icebergs, Davis Strait*, the huge vertical shafts of two large icebergs are joined together by one that resembles a platform. That sculptural form, accompanied by a shallow foreground area and by the clouds and sky above, emphasizes the isolated majesty of the Arctic environment. In contrast, *Ellesmere Island* works with a variety of verticals penetrated by a mystical sunlight at the top; here, clouds obscure the top of the mountain. *Icebergs* is an open view that sublimely confronts the spectator; the other image is a closed form in which something is hidden.

Just how stripped down Harris's work had become is best seen by considering A.Y. Jackson's iceberg compositions from the same

(left)
Lawren Harris
aboard the *Beothic*.

Beothic Portfolio.
A selection of
photographs
taken by Lawren
Harris during his
trip to the Arctic
in 1930.

voyage. In one image, for instance, he places Inuit in the bottom foreground, layers boulders and an expanse of ocean water in the middle foreground, and then displays a huge iceberg juxtaposed against the sky. This landscape displays monumental form, but it is one grounded in the factual reality of what Jackson observed, whereas Harris's Arctic images deliberately transport the viewer to another world.

Under the Auspices of the
Berkeley Girls' Club

Moving Pictures of the Arctic

Shown and described by Mr. Lawren Harris who
filmed them personally

Toronto Conservatory of Music
Monday, January 8th, 1934, at 8.30 p.m.

Vocal and Instrumental Music by assisting Artists

RECITAL HALL   TICKETS 50 cents

In order to enter this level of consciousness, Harris depends heavily on yellow, blue and white. In theosophical terminology, yellow represents intellectual consciousness whereas blue is associated with religious feeling. For Kandinsky, yellow symbolized material reality, blue was "heavenly"; white for him was emblematic of a world from which all "colours as material attributes have disappeared . . . White, therefore, acts upon our psyche as a great, absolute silence." But it "is not a dead silence, but one pregnant with possibilities. White has the appeal of nothingness that is before birth, of the world in the ice age."

Put another way, Harris in his Arctic landscapes was contrasting the world of conscious thought with that of religious inspiration; the dialect between those two forces, moreover, is being set on a primeval stage. These landscapes may be about the conflicting claims of intelligence and passion, but they enact this eternal struggle in a silence filled with the *possibility* of rebirth and renewal. This is the world of awe: "great, absolute silence."[22] As one observer put it, Harris's "icebergs are strange monuments with a symbol embodied in their form and their colours. They do not freeze you when you look at them, for they are not of ice, they are what Lawren Harris feels and thinks after he has con-

Lawren Harris. *Icebergs, Davis Strait.* 1930.

Lawren Harris. *Ellesmere Island. Circa* 1930.

templated them."[23] In the Arctic, Harris confronted huge open spaces filled with monumental ice forms; he was not certain if such emptiness was for him paradisaical.

The Arctic works of Harris and of Jackson were shown together at the National Gallery in December 1930 and then at the Art Association of Montreal for two weeks in February 1931. In those two exhibitions, Harris had thirty oil sketches of the Arctic. In May 1931, when the Arctic collections went on display at the Art Gallery of Toronto, Harris added six canvases. In August 1931, this work was shown in Vancouver, and seven Arctic canvases were included in the December 1931 Group show, the last Group exhibition.

Jehanne Biétry Salinger was convinced the Arctic paintings were a dismal failure. She wrote: "Lawren Harris has not identified himself with nature or the life he found in the Arctic." These canvases "give the painter's own conception of these spectacular scenes. And these conceptions are essentially abstract and philosophical. His icebergs are strange monuments."[24] A year later, the same critic was even more vigorous in her disdain: Harris

> had retired to the sanctuary of an aristocratic spirituality, where his understandings and aesthetic appreciation of human values suddenly froze as though under the spell of a magic wand, his voice ceased to speak, his heart ceased to beat, and his mountains, and his lakes, and his rocks, and his trees in their cold blue, green, or white garment did not seem to live anymore.[25]

Privately, Emily Carr held the same opinion about Harris's Arctic work. In a diary entry of July 11, 1934, she labelled them "dead and lifeless," although they were "still beautiful in colour & light."[26]* As devastating as these words might have been if voiced to him, Harris would have agreed with his friend's assessment. He felt that he had literally painted himself into a corner. The Arctic paintings and sketches may be majestically sublime, but they are almost inhumanly beautiful.

---

* However, a bit earlier, in November 1933, Emily had visited Harris's studio. She told a friend: "am taking home one of Lawren's arctic sketches. I *chose* it. His Arctic pictures are simply glorious. I spent three long afternoons in his studio and he showed me everything he had."

Inwardly, Harris existed in a state of pure, gut-wrenching despair. He could discuss the resulting feelings only with Emily Carr, who, like him, frequently experienced black moods of self-abnegation. The advice he proffered to her can be seen as externalizations of what he must have told himself daily. Moreover, in the following passage can be heard the voice of a man who has endured harrowing losses:

> Remember, when discouraged, that there is a rhythm of elation and dejection and that we stimulate it by creative endeavor, by an acceleration of vision of work—we stir up life, essential life, and if we permit it, it will take hold of us, and at times we may wish we were humdrum, lethargic, dull and normal . . . Don't struggle against it—accept it—glory in it, if possible . . . and in the process, in the storm, a great divine calm is sometimes glimpsed . . . When we enter the stream of creative life—then we are on our own—we have to find self reliance—achieve conviction—learn to accept—and begin to see a supreme logic behind the inner struggles.

Lawren Harris at easel in the Studio Building.

Harris's language may be suffused with elements of theosophy and Eastern religious thought, but the man has stepped out from behind the mask.

The artist's conviction that his vocation requires him to pay a heavy psychic price is found in another passage, one in which he catches a glimpse of the way forward:

> Despair is periodic, a part and parcel of the life of every creative individual—some even succumb to it and are swamped for their life. It cannot be conquered—one rises out of it . . . Every creative individual despairs and always has since the beginning of time, no matter how fine the things they produce. There are still finer things to be done and still finer, ad infinitum.[27]

16

AT THE CROSSROADS

(1931–1934)

His self-portrait tells a large part of the story. His practice was to have a sitter face him, but he could not do this in painting himself. His glance is sideways, as if he was looking at himself in a mirror. Indeed, that is how he sketched the picture, but the resulting image looks as if he is attempting to run away.

The countenance bears a strong resemblance to Charlie Chaplin. Some might say it is a comic self-caricature, much in the manner of Arthur Lismer's sketches in which, as leader of the Group, Lawren was shown in not only his best patrician guise but also his pompous manner. In those days he could laugh at himself; now he wanted no part of himself. The cocked eyebrows and his now-white hair standing slightly up show a man at odds with himself.

THE FINAL Group exhibition took place in December 1931. Harris had fourteen paintings on display, including six Arctic canvases and five Lake Superiors. Thoreau MacDonald was unstinting in his disdain for the entire exhibition, although his now seriously ill father had four canvases

Lawren Harris.
Self-Portrait. 1932.

(entry numbers 108 to 111) on display. (He had planned to submit what would have been numbers 113 to 123, and those spaces were left blank in the catalogue.)

In Harris's portrait of Thoreau from about 1927, the young artist appears slightly bashful, more than a bit pinched, but also deeply ascetic and high-strung. Harris's portrait was "done for practise"; the young man was working as a designer in the Studio Building and was available as a model at the artist's convenience. He probably did not enjoy being treated as the resident office boy-cum-janitor, collector of rents and exhibition preparer. He once described Harris's space at the Studio Building as a "surgery."[1]

Lawren Harris.
Thoreau
MacDonald.
Circa 1927.

Thoreau's review raises many valid points (and Thoreau Mac-Donald certainly had a conservative Arts and Crafts outlook in that he had a penchant for old architecture and rural life), but nevertheless this notice has a malicious edge:

> The Group of Seven and their followers have always been regarded as Canadian through and through. That has been their special pride and they have never tired of praising the grandeur of the North and the great Canadian Shield. But for Canadian patriots, lovers of our Country, their present exhibit is far from cheering. For they are ever becoming more artistic, more artificial. Without any feeling for the face of our country they tiresomely express themselves in strange and unbeautiful forms, in artificially constructed scenery without life . . . In their efforts to be modern and free [they] are in danger of becoming more conventional than older societies.

Harris would have been perfectly aware that the references to "strange and unbeautiful forms" and "artificially constructed scenery without life" were aimed directly at him. MacDonald added:

> If the Group intends to be a nursery for incompetent paint-
> ers, then all right, but if they aim to raise the standard of paint-
> ing in Canada and to increase the love and understanding of
> our country, then something different must be added.[2]

In her notice, Jehanne Biétry Salinger, who had responded negatively to Harris's Arctic pictures the year before, was much kinder:

> The Group of Seven perhaps has died with this December
> exhibition. It has died, in the sense that each of the leaders,
> who were its members, has gone on by himself, that the paths
> of the Seven have parted, perhaps never to cross again, but
> their very motive for coming into existence as a group has
> grown so far and so wide that Canadian art has emerged from
> this initial Canadian art movement.[3]

At a party held at Harris's home after the opening, A.Y. Jackson declared that the

> interest in a freer form of art expression in Canada has
> become so general that we believe the time has arrived when
> the Group of Seven should expand, and the original members
> become the members of a larger group of artists, with no offi-
> cials or constitution, but held together by the common inten-
> tion of doing original and sincere work.[4]

Even from its first exhibition, the Group had moved in the direction of being a "nursery." R.B. Hewton, R. Pilot and Albert Robinson had been participants in 1920; drawings by Percy Robinson appeared in the third exhibition, work by Albert Robinson in the fourth; in 1926 were included J.M. Alfsen, A.J. Casson, Bess Housser, Thoreau MacDonald, Doris Mills, Marion Miller, George Pepper, Anne Savage and two others; in 1928, when Casson had joined the Group, the invited contributors included Charles Comfort, Bess Housser, Edwin Holgate, Thoreau Mac-Donald, Yvonne McKague and Carl Schaefer; in 1930, when Holgate joined the Group, pictures by, among others, Brooker, Carr, Thoreau MacDonald and Yvonne McKague were on display. Significantly, in the catalogue, all artists were listed in alphabetical order in a single group; a reader would get the impression that no distinction was being made between the Group and the other artists. In 1931, when LeMoine FitzGerald became a member of the Group, the same practice was followed; other artists included Brooker, Thoreau MacDonald, Bess Housser and Yvonne McKague.

The Canadian Group of Painters (CGP), founded in 1933 with Harris as its president and Fred Housser as secretary, initially had twenty-eight members. Harris stated the objective of the new federation in a letter to FitzGerald:

> We feel that it is essential to form a society of all the so-called modern painters in the country, secure a charter and make ourselves felt as a country-wide influence in terms of the creative spirit. We propose to call the society "The Canadian Group of Painters" thus retaining the word group and suggesting the enlargement of the idea.[5]

The CGP also came into being as a kind of compromise. Eric Brown's advocacy of the Group of Seven had got him into constant hot water with the members of the Royal Canadian Academy. In 1932–33, for instance, a national petition by conservative artists had called for the dismissal of Brown as director of the National Gallery because of his bias towards Modernist expression. In January 1932, Franz Johnston wrote the prime minister, R.B. Bennett, to complain about the supposed discrimination against him by the National Gallery. A counter-petition in support of Brown was organized; he survived, but he kept clear of Canadian art after this debacle. The National Gallery's annual exhibition of Canadian art was discontinued. A.Y. Jackson resigned from the Academy, Harris from the Ontario Society of Artists. By forming the CGP, a significantly larger group that was more catholic in its membership, the hope was that such anti-Modernist sentiments could be assuaged.

Harris was putting a good face on a troublesome situation. For years, he had managed to add more and more artists to the Group exhibitions (in 1931, paintings by thirty-two artists were shown) while at the same time trying to keep the Group label intact as a form of "brand recognition." Brooker told FitzGerald in 1933: "I am a little afraid that a strong nationalist bias, which always gets into the utterances of the old Group, either public or private, is going to continue very strong in the New Group."[6]

For perhaps different reasons, Brooker and Thoreau Mac-Donald wanted a new order in Canadian art to be established. They feared that the nationalist bias that had informed the Group at its founding would ultimately not allow Canadian artists to enter the world stage; they wanted the adjective "Canadian" to have a more universal meaning.

It would not be amiss, however, to see these two young artists in Oedipal terms. They were young men who wanted to overthrow the reign of the father and establish their own claims to artistic greatness. This was, in many ways, an "anxiety of influence" issue in which the sons, in order to come into being, had to rebel against father figures. In doing this, Brooker and MacDonald brought matters full circle because at its beginning the Group of Seven had created an extremely artificial construction of Canadian landscape painting as a genre that did not exist before them.

The first appearance of works by members of CGP as a group was at the Heinz Art Salon in Atlantic City in November 1933. The catalogue's anonymous foreword reiterated the standard Group of Seven claim that "modernism in Canada has almost no relation to the modernism in Europe . . . In Canada, the main concerns have been with landscapes, moods and rhythms." The first exhibition held in Canada was at the Art Gallery of Toronto. In that foreword, there was a great deal of earnest compromise at work: "Hitherto it [Canadian art as practised by the Group of Seven] has been a landscape art . . . but here and there figures and portraits have been slowly added to the subject matter, strengthening and occupying the background of landscape."7

Bridle poked fun. This was a new phase of what he labelled Group Psychology. In 1919, it had been "Whoopee"; in about 1925, "Family Compact"; now it was "New Democracy."8 In the *Canadian Forum*, Robert Ayre claimed that Canadian art was moving "toward human life, away from landscape . . . but in growing up we are beginning to show the effects of the profound disturbances in human affairs which have shaken the world."9

Doris Mills,
Fred Housser,
Gordon Mills.

Harris's former colleagues in the Group did not share his new vision. Arthur Lismer, as was his custom, dealt with this matter in a friendly, gentle manner in a drawing, in which Harris, cigarette in hand, stares in astonishment at one of his mountain landscapes. More pointedly, he composed a ditty in which he lampooned the move towards abstraction on the part of Harris and Bertram Brooker:

Ye Brookers & Ye Harris, now listen all to me.
Ye may have been to Paris but you canna draw a tree.
These stunted apparitions, with wildly waving arms
Are merely suppositions that give the public qualms
But take some consolation from the poet who wrote for thee
In the scheme of all creation only "God can make a tree."10

Lismer's reference to the well-known "Trees" by the American poet Joyce Kilmer (1886–1918) is an interesting ploy, but he seems to be equating Group of Seven landscape painting with popular verse for a large audience who would know nothing of poets such as T.S. Eliot or Ezra Pound. The implication is that Modernists such as Harris and Brooker are venturing into dangerous, experimental terrain that will leave the "public" far behind.

Arthur Lismer.
Lawren Harris
Contemplating One
of his Mountain
Images.

Harris conceived of issues in nationalistic, aesthetic and theosophical terms; he was not accustomed to thinking in terms of personal psychology, but the issues that overwhelmed him in the early thirties can be understood in employing some of that discipline's language.

His strong depressive feelings became engaged when he could no longer be the artist he wanted to be. He was deeply conflicted because his theosophical convictions pulled him in one direction, his nationalist aspirations in a seemingly opposite one. Theosophy is worldwide in its outlook, although it privileges the North as the source of a new dispensation. Harris was beginning, very much in the manner of Thoreau MacDonald and Bertram Brooker, to move in the direction of the universal as opposed to the restricted domain of the Northern.

In particular, Harris had established a distinctive signature style in his renditions of Lake Superior, the Rockies and the Arctic, but he felt he had nowhere to go with that kind of art. He had hit a wall. However, artistic issues were merely the tip of the iceberg.

By 1931, Harris had become convinced that he was living an enormous emotional lie in his marriage. At the very same time, feelings that he had long repressed had begun to take their toll; his past sorrow at the deaths of his father, brother and Tom Thomson were probably rekindled. He knew that Jim MacDonald was extremely ill. Was it enough to become a successful Canadian artist using what had become a rote way of creating Northern landscapes, or should he follow his gut feelings and move in a completely new direction?

In addition, Harris was a bit worried about Lornie. This can be glimpsed in a letter to Katherine Dreier:

> Our eldest boy wants to study painting. As far as I can tell he has real talent but I am puzzled how best to help him. The boy is twenty—decent living—but lacks as yet direction and application. I feel that the important thing is to get him in with a crowd of serious workers and have him learn to direct all his powers to one end—the development of his talent.

Harris planned to send Lornie to the Boston Museum art school, but he wondered if he had thoughts about what to do after that.[11]* Lawren's obvious pride that his son wished to follow in his footsteps is evident here, as is the careful way he approached important decisions.

During the summers of 1932 and 1933, Harris sketched at Pointe au Baril on Georgian Bay; that place was named after the "barrel on the point" that in the 1870s marked the treacherous entry to the main channel from the open water of Georgian Bay. Harris's imagination never responded strongly to that area of northern Ontario, and that may have made matters worse.

A sense of incompetence invaded Harris, even though *Above Lake Superior* took the $500 Museum of Art Prize at the Pan-American Exhibition in Baltimore. Among the other Canadian

---

* Lornie studied from 1931 to 1933 at the Boston Museum of Fine Arts, under Rodney J. Burn and Robin Guthrie, and at Central Technical School, Toronto, under Robert Ross. For three years, he taught evening classes at Northern Vocational School, Toronto, before spending a year as art master at Trinity College School, Port Hope. With the outbreak of World War II, Harris joined the war effort, first serving in a tank regiment, and then as an official war artist.

artists whose work was on show were Emily Carr and Bess Housser. On July 10–11, 1933, he attended the first North American International Intertheosophical Convention at Niagara Falls, Ontario, where he read a paper on theosophy and art. That autumn, he conducted classes for young people at the Toronto Theosophical Society. He also organized and delivered radio talks on theosophy.

For years, Lawren and Bess had maintained a strong, chaste friendship. For him, she became the representation of spiritual beauty in human form. They were kindred spirits. Fred, well aware of the relationship between his wife and his best friend, was deeply wounded because he knew he no longer came first in his wife's affections. In March 1930, he told the painter Isabel McLaughlin, who had asked him about his philosophy of life, particularly theosophy:

> But, after all, we carry our spiritual baggage with us from place to place. The creative life is an ever-changing thing . . . [With] any fruition of success, no matter what, must come a struggle to make a greater struggle necessary. Life is like that,—especially the creative life. Bess and I have almost completely changed our living and circumstances on an average of once every three years since we were married. Another change is due soon.[12]

McLaughlin had trained as a painter in Paris from 1921 to 1924 and then studied at the Ontario College of Art and the Art Students' League, where she was a pupil of Arthur Lismer. As an artist, she liked to employ bold, striking colours; as an art buyer, she was eclectic, and gathered a significant private collection of contemporary art, mostly Canadian.

In March 1930, Housser did not know what the "change" was to be. Shortly thereafter, he and Yvonne McKague fell in love. Born in 1897, McKague had studied at the Ontario College of Art from 1915 to 1920 and taught there for one year before settling in Paris to study at the Académie Grande Chaumière, the

Interior of
Housser home.
1931.

Yvonne McKague.
*Rossport,
Lake Superior.
Circa* 1929.

Académie Colarossi and the Académie Ranson. She later studied
in Mexico and then at Provincetown with Hans Hoffmann. After
she returned to Canada, she taught at the Ontario College of Art.

When, sometime in 1934, Bess was told by Fred that he and Yvonne were having an affair, she became distraught and soon thereafter went to Reno, Nevada, where she obtained a "quickie" (six-week residency) divorce.[13] Upon her return, she planned to live in Lawren's quarters in the Studio Building (Lawren took over Thoreau MacDonald's space, although he was probably still living at Ava Crescent). Bess's move into the Studio Building may have provoked Lawren's break with Trixie: he moved out of his home on June 13, 1934.[14]

The "upheaval" was not supposed to end in marriage, but Annie Raynolds, Lawren's mother, counselled her son and Bess to marry because otherwise they would be casting themselves socially adrift. Therefore, on July 6, Lawren and Bess went to Reno, where he in turn obtained a divorce. Lawren and Bess then married on August 29, 1934, probably somewhere in Nevada.*

As Bess recalled, the judge who married them was a "dear old benign soul [who] had lost his wife about two weeks before . . . His two secretaries (as witnesses), who looked as though they might be my own aunts, beamed on us afterwards."[15] The marriage particularly angered Trixie and her family, and they evidently threatened to bring charges of bigamy against Harris. This may have been the reason the couple soon fled the country.

Yvonne McKague Housser and Isabel McLaughlin.

The events as outlined above do not begin to encapsulate fully the complexities

---

* Four years later, when they were living in New Mexico, Lawren and Bess told friends that they had waited for Lawren's children to grow up before getting divorces and marrying. However, such remarks might have been invented so that they could appear to be a more conventional couple than they really were.

of what was going on. Before Harris went to Reno, he, Bess, Fred and Yvonne were apparently living together at the Housser home on Glengowan Road.[16] This is known from a letter Yvonne wrote to Isabel McLaughlin:

> Firstly—probably I did say that we might have to live together if there was no other way—I did not mean to say that Fred and I felt that way—but as you say everything was so hectic! Probably said so—and I *do feel* that way now—but dear one—that was not the remark of Aleck's that Fred was upset about—that "We were all living together up at the house"— implying rather doubtful behavior . . .[17]

In 1934 Toronto, the breakup of the Harris marriage would have caused a considerable stir on its own, but the fact that Harris had taken up with the wife of his best friend, that his best friend had taken up with a woman who was an artist, that some kind of wife swap had occurred, and that the four were living under the same roof suggested that all kinds of proprieties had been broken. In her missive, Yvonne is making the point that everything had been done with a due sense of decorum, by which she meant that the four participants had been forced briefly to live under one roof and had not conducted themselves in a louche way. The reference to A.Y. Jackson is amplified later in Yvonne's letter; the suggestion is that he was attracted to Bess and, if she were available, would have liked to have been the man with whom she took up.[18]

Another sidebar to the events of 1934 is Yvonne's revelation that Lawren, Fred and Bess had consulted the mistress of the notorious charlatan "Brother 12," Edward Arthur Wilson (1878–c. 1934), who established the theosophical-based Aquarian Foundation in British Columbia in 1927. He used that base to lure money from socialites with promises of eternal life: "But I—Lawren—Bess & I knew this man's lover—mistress—he called her Isis—what have you? She was extraordinary—an astrologist who influenced Lawren's & Bess's lives—also Fred's."[19] Isis apparently was a doctor's wife whom Wilson had seduced on a train. He claimed that he was a reincarnation of Osiris, she of Isis. The fact that Lawren, Fred and Bess consulted this woman as to what they should do with their lives demonstrates the confusion that had overcome them. There is the slight possibility that Bess and Lawren contemplated moving to British Columbia at that time.

Trixie took up the role of the wronged wife, and she had many supporters, including A.Y. Jackson, who supposedly said, referring to the CGP, that the president had run away with the secretary's wife. Harris supported Trixie financially for the remainder of her life (she died in 1962).

The Harris separation and divorce were never discussed in the newspapers, but Lawren, Bess and Trixie and her family would have been aware of a divorce that had recently created a public furor. In 1932, the Nobel laureate Frederick Banting had begun a relationship with the theosophically inclined Blodwen Davies, who published her book on Tom Thomson in 1935. At about the same time, Banting's wife, Marion, had begun to see Donat M. LeBourdais, a writer and the director of a group called the Canadian National Committee on Mental Hygiene. On February 8, 1932, Banting, accompanied by two private detectives, burst into LeBourdais's apartment, where Marion was present. The doctor grabbed LeBourdais by the throat and pushed him over a sofa. One of the detectives advised Banting: "Doctor, you can't take a dead man into Court!"[20] In the past, the Toronto newspapers had not stooped to cover such domestic upsets, but the Banting debacle changed their attitude.

In December 1932, *Hush*, the leading Canadian scandal tabloid, had included an item on the Banting divorce that, in its descriptive language, bears more than a superficial resemblance to the events leading to the Harris breakup:

> While the artistic world had been aware of the close friendship existing between Dr. Banting and Miss Blodwen Davies for many months, it assumed the association to be one actuated by kindred intellectual tastes . . . Both Dr. Banting and Miss Davies were considered to have similar mental "auras", far above the heights attainable by the rabble. If they sought the privacy of each other's company in the attic of the Ban-

ting home, the accepted belief was that it was to discuss some new abstruse theory . . . Instead, it would appear [based on Marion Banting's father's deposition] that they were drawn together for the purpose of satisfying the passions inherent in man and woman.[21]

In 1934, there was the distinct possibility that the Harris separation and divorce could become a media event, something that no one involved wished. If Lawren remained in Toronto, he might become subject to such scrutiny; that would have been a considerable worry. It was best to leave and allow the dust to settle.

The children were divided in their reactions to their father's behaviour. Twenty-four-year-old Lornie and twenty-one-year-old Peggie supported their father in his decision to leave home and follow the inclinations of his heart. Howie, fifteen at the time, may have sided with his mother. When Bess called on her friends to assure them that she and Lawren were embarking on a celibate relationship, she was rebuffed by most of them.

Bess was seen by Lawren as angelic, but that was not necessarily how others perceived her. To them, she could be overly opinionated and heavy-handed. When Bess informed Emily Carr that she and Lawren had become a couple, Emily was outraged (she may have thought that Bess had manipulated the Fred–Yvonne affair so that Lawren would run away with her). Moreover, Emily had very much approved of Trixie when she met her in 1927. She had enjoyed a wonderful evening with the Harrises at their home, relishing the symphonic music Harris had played.

Earlier, she had been candid with Lawren and Bess that theosophical belief—with which she flirted briefly—was not for her: she remained a Christian, who needed to make contact with a personal God. When she informed Bess of her feelings on that issue, she received a letter filled with condescension. Furious, Emily wrote to Lawren in complaint. His response was polite but firm. He might be a close friend of Emily, but Bess came first.

Well, well, sure I'll help you out. I saw Bess. She is writing you. She knows that nothing whatsoever can come between

you and her. But she thought the peremptory letter you wrote
her a bit uncalled for. It trampled—she is a high, gentle, sweet
soul in every way and should be so considered and treated. She
has the deepest feelings for you—you mean very much to her,
your strength fortifies her, as does the honesty and beauty of
your soul . . . But I tell you what you do when you have need
of ripping things up a bit, write me.[22]

For Harris, his soulmate could do no wrong. Emily hated Bess's
self-assuredness and lady-of-the-manor superiority. However,
such aspects of her personality did not bother Harris, who was
often lacking in confidence. Bess provided him with a deep sense
of surety, and for him this remained the anchor in their relationship.

In June 1933, in a despondent mood, Harris had told Emily:

Haven't painted for ages it seems and feel as if my painting
days are over . . . Occasionally I get a flicker of an idea then
it fades or sufficient enthusiasm is lacking and there we are.
Nothing to do about it. I am at a crossroads really and have
yet no visions to know what to do; what road to take. But my
O my, I am anxious to be on my way—and that is trying when
one doesn't know the way.[23]

Lawren's marriage to Bess and removal from Toronto quickly
revived him. Not only could he paint once again, but he could
venture into a terrain he had long been drawn to. His anxieties
vanished.

17
NEW
ADVENTURES
(1934–1936)

All artists are by definition outsiders. They see things no one else sees—or cares to witness. Lawren had always been aware of these truths, which were both comforting and unsettling. Comforting because they explained why he was different. Unsettling because they imposed a desolate loneliness.

Now he was both an outcast and an outsider. His supposed lack of morality was widely discussed in hush-hush terms. He had acted badly, the gossips claimed. He had abandoned his wife. No one cared that he and Trixie no longer had any ties holding them together. The private reality was an uninteresting topic in comparison with the public disgrace.

He could no longer exist on the surface. Pretend that everything was all right.

TORONTO SOCIETY in 1934 was rigidly hidebound. Any attempt to move beyond its narrow limits of accepted behaviour brought immediate ostracism. Trixie, the person left without a partner, was furious at Lawren: she destroyed all papers and documents relating to their past. After the house on Ava Crescent was sold, she moved to 79 Farnham Avenue and, later, 561 Avenue Road, an apartment building. Bess soon discovered that many previously open doors were closed to her. There were possible legal repercussions. In a perhaps misguided effort to purge himself, Harris attempted to destroy many sketches and drawings.*

Up to 1934, Lawren had been a man who did not embody the idea of the artist as bohemian, a notion that separates the artist from other members of society and implies that he may live a picaresque existence that flirts with illegalities. Such ideas were not well received in Canada in the thirties. Tom Thomson had embodied some aspects of this fantasy. In addition to being the self-taught genius who died young, there were suspicions that he might have been murdered because he had trifled with someone else's wife or girlfriend.

But what about the gentleman-artist, the wealthy man who, out of a sense of noblesse oblige, becomes a propagandist for Canadian art? In the early thirties, Harris was certainly seen as a revolutionary, someone who was trying to infuse a new spirit into Canadian painting. Up to 1934, however, he was a safe rebel because he launched his Modernist campaign from the vantage point of privilege. He was not the incarnation of the poverty-stricken, starving artist, someone who can easily become a threat to society's norms. For example, Harris almost always worked at his easel dressed in a suit. He may have been an artist, but he was also a gentleman.

In 1931, he had constructed a grand new house in Forest Hill, a structure that embodied accepted ideas of wealth, taste and sophistication. From an outsider's perspective, he then abandoned his wife, his family and this mansion. (In reality, his marriage had been in disarray for many years and his two older children backed

---

* Thoreau MacDonald recalled that before an obviously distraught and upset "Lawren left, he threw all his outdoor sketches and drawings in a heap on the basement floor [of the Studio Building] and gave orders to get rid of them." Peter Larisey interview with Thoreau MacDonald, September 27, 1976. In fact, many of these canvases and sketches were stored in an opening under the stairs and retrieved years later by Bess Harris.

his decision to leave.) If, from Toronto society's point of view, he acted in this aberrant way, what would stop other people, perhaps not as wealthy, from doing the same? Such behaviour could be seen to undermine long-held notions of propriety. The resulting brouhaha produced gossip, some of it malicious.

Harris's behaviour was especially shocking because of his position within the Toronto hierarchy. When his friend and tennis partner, the artist Peter Haworth, visited him, Lawren assured him that "sex" had no part in his relationship with Bess. "There's to be none of that."[1] If Lawren had been strongly sexually attracted to Bess, his sense of guilt would likely have repressed those feelings; the relationship would have foundered. Since it was—and remained—a spiritual one, he could give himself the licence to leave his wife.

When Doris and Gordon Mills were divorcing, Lawren wrote her about his recent experiences in somewhat convoluted language that nevertheless reveals that he had found, despite society's strictures, a large measure of inner peace in his relationship with Bess:

> Once in a lifetime every man Jack of us and every lady Jill of us is brought face to face with his or her incarnational problem. The problem arises from the chrysalis of thought, belief and ideas formed by ourselves in the past and the solution consists in permitting the expanding pressure of a greater life. To breakup and disperse that chrysalis, so that we may be born into a new life—an increase of creative freedom—and so on and on until eventually we achieve real spiritual oneness with all life.[2]

In 1934, Harris knew he had dispersed the chrysalis and had achieved the sense of oneness that had long been evading him.

Emily Carr in faraway British Columbia was extremely disapproving of Bess and Lawren. Bess had broken the news to her face to face. In her journal, Emily wrote that "they'd been living falsely" and she could "never quite trust them again."[3] Harris was not immune to barbs from Emily, whose anger at him found different points of egress. In a letter to Harris, she had spoken disparagingly of Edward VIII, his renunciation of the throne and his decision to marry Wallis Simpson. Harris replied: "Can't agree with you about the Duke of Windsor. I don't believe he preferred a 'designing hussy' to the Empire. He could have had one hundred thousand mistresses and the Empire would not have batted an eye at any of them. But he wanted a wife . . . He was too damn decent to play hypocrite."[4] If she had intended to draw blood by criticizing the Duke, Emily succeeded admirably. In defending the former king, Harris was also justifying his own behaviour in taking up with Bess.

Bess's distress can be seen in a letter she wrote to a close friend in November 1934. "It is still so near.—The upheaval.—The venomous hate it aroused in the world when one endeavours to move [in a new direction guided by] the spirit's dictates." At first, she remained convinced that she had been treated badly by Fred and the new Mrs. Housser:

> Yvonne and Fred have been my greatest difficulty—My personal self tells me that they have used me with a ruthless cunning and cruelty—to their own ends—but I'm beginning now to see with their eyes and how they see—and I'm losing my resentment there—that they were not quite able to live up to the grade that my idealism made for them.[5]

Bess was angry because she felt that Fred and Yvonne were claiming they had become involved in an adulterous relationship because she had emotionally excused herself from her husband in order to pursue Lawren. Bess may be a bit self-serving in these reflections, but she and Lawren were able, within a relatively short period of time, to set aside any bitterness they felt towards the Houssers, to whom they remained joined in the fraternity of theosophy.

That November, the recently married Harrises arrived in Hanover, New Hampshire, to visit William and Ethel Stewart, with whom he had lived in Berlin twenty years earlier. Stewart, now head of the German department at Dartmouth College, welcomed his nephew and Bess warmly. Ethel was a warm and gracious friend.

Hanover is located on the western side of New Hampshire in the upper Connecticut River valley. The river forms the border between Vermont and New Hampshire. The town, chartered in July 1761, was named in honour of Hanover Parish, the home base of settlers from Lisbon, Connecticut. Hanover's first inhabitants arrived in 1765–66, and in 1769 the Reverend Eleazar Wheelock received a charter to establish a college; he named it after a supporter, William Legge, the second Earl of Dartmouth. From 1777 to 1791, Hanover joined with other disgruntled New Hampshire towns along the Connecticut River to form the independent Republic of Vermont. This government issued coins called Vermont Coppers and even operated a postal system. Eventually, when Vermont became the fourteenth state in 1791, Hanover became part of the state of New Hampshire.

Lawren and Bess fitted in extremely well with the faculty, who regularly dressed for dinner together on Saturday nights. One art historian remembered that the "entire art department found [Harris] most congenial and we had many social evenings at his house and he had such at ours."[6] Bess wore white or pale grey dresses, and the couple exuded elegance. They practised yoga and meditation in the morning. They were slim, poised and always at ease with each other.

Between 1932 and 1934, José Clemente Orozco had painted his fresco *The Epic of American Civilization* in the lower level of the college's Baker Library. Although Harris's art did not encompass this type of Modernism, he would have appreciated its brilliant colours. Members of the art department at Dartmouth were fascinated with contemporary art and glad to have a practitioner of it in their midst. Moreover, the art department had studio space but no funds to pay an artist in residence; Harris needed studio space and did not need a stipend. This situation led to an excellent marriage of convenience.

While Harris was at Dartmouth, the architect Walter Gropius, founder of the Bauhaus, spoke there; so did Alvar Aalto, Mies van der Rohe and R. Buckminster Fuller. The abstract painter and colour theorist Josef Albers also visited. Harris read everything on modern art he could lay his hands on in the college library.

New York City was not far away, and Harris made considerable effort to see everything he could. He probably attended the one-man shows by Miró, Léger, Kandinsky and Klee held there; he was present at the exhibitions at the Museum of Modern Art, including the landmark Cubism and Abstract Art exhibition in March and April 1936. Earlier, the Whitney showed Abstract Painting in America in February and March 1935. In the spring of 1938, the Harrises travelled to Charleston, South Carolina, to see the Solomon R. Guggenheim Collection of Non-Objective Paintings at the Gibbes Memorial Art Gallery. In Manhattan, they may well have visited Alfred Stieglitz's famous gallery, An American Place.

New York City itself, however, was repulsive as far as Harris was concerned. "Most things in the place are terrifically overrated by advertising. It's an ugly place, a very ugly place in the main. Rockefeller Center is the only coherent unified expression . . . It's grand and points the way. So does Frank Lloyd Wright's big and carefully worked out model of Broadacre City, which we saw at an exhibition." Wright's utopian socio-political project that would have given every American family a one-acre plot of land obviously appealed to Harris. However, his practical side recognized that this "swell job . . . presupposes a different social order as does anything that suggests worthwhileness."

Within two weeks of their arrival in New Hampshire, Lawren and Bess were travelling into the nearby White Mountains, where Lawren began to work productively once again. The White Mountains cover about a quarter of New Hampshire and extend into Maine. They are part of the Appalachian range and are the most rugged mountains in the state, a feature that would have attracted Harris, who was extremely familiar with the Rockies. The origin of the name is much debated: the snow-capped high peaks may have been observed from shipboard by early settlers; the alternate theory is that the mica-laden granite of the summits looked "white" to early observers.

In his sketches, Harris abstracted various elements of the mountains. A century earlier, the English-born Thomas Cole (1801–48), the founder of the Hudson River School, had found these mountains "magnificent":

> There the bare peaks of granite, broken and desolate, cradle the clouds; while the valleys and broad bases of the mountains rest under the shade of noble and varied forests . . . Although in some regions of the globe nature has wrought on a more stupendous scale, yet she has nowhere so completely married together grandeur and loveliness—there he sees the sublime melting into the beautiful, the savage tempered by the magnificent.[7]

The Boston artist E. Ambrose Webster (1869–1935) painted winter landscapes there in the 1910s that bear a passing resemblance to Harris's 1913 winter images. In the middle and late 1920s, Marsden Hartley (1877–1943) found scenery that assisted him, in a Harris-like manner, to "uncover the principle of conscious unity in all things" and the "living essence present everywhere." In his own White Mountains images, Harris emphasized their primal, geological origins. His *Mount Washington*, for example, depicts the highest point in the range in terms reminiscent of Fuji or Everest. For him, this mountain became symbolic of the spiritual regeneration that now animated his personal life.

The couple would work in their studio in the morning, walk into Hanover for a sandwich-and-milkshake lunch, and then rest, walk or motor in the afternoon. For some years before this, Harris may have painted with music playing on a phonograph; in New Hampshire, one friend recalled that he always painted to the accompaniment of extremely loud music.[8] Annie Raynolds rented a house in Hanover; in that way, she could be in close proximity to her son and her brother. Another visitor from Toronto was Doris Mills, who rented a room near Lawren and Bess. She and the Harrises would often go out for drives, during which Lawren would tease his friend, an expert ornithologist, about the names given to various species and sometimes make up new ones.

New Hampshire
house.

Even old comrades remained at odds with Harris. Arthur Lismer, a fellow theosophist, directed a barb against Harris's "unhumanistic" inclinations in 1936. An artist like Harris, he said, "turns from the world of other men's making and goes to the vast unexplored world of abstract thought . . . into a world of order and mathematical divination but which takes from him all contact with his fellow men into a stratosphere of rarified purity of design and colour."[9] Harris crisply rejoined: "Many folks have the idea that so-called abstract art is not in terms of Humanity. This, because most folks don't know its language and therefore mistake their limitations for infallible criteria."[10]

One stalwart supporter of the "new" Lawren Harris was his close friend John Robins (1884–1952), whom Harris met when they were teaching musketry at Camp Borden. In about 1925, Harris painted Robins's portrait. Although known to be gregarious and high-spirited, in Harris's portrait he looks placidly at the viewer, his hands resting before him. This is not the John Robins most people knew, but it is the person with whom Harris had formed a close understanding.

Robins, who was born in Windsor, had been educated at Victoria College at the University of Toronto, Freiburg and Marburg in Germany, and finally the University of Chicago, from which he received his doctorate. Like Harris's uncle, William Kilborne Stewart, he had taught German; he later switched to English. A man of an extremely eclectic background (at various times a cub reporter, lumberjack, cattle puncher, conductor and actor), his *Incomplete Anglers* won the Governor General's Award for non-fiction in 1943.

For Robins, his friend was a master of paradox, one who "contradicts flatly and with finality" an opinion he has espoused a moment before. An acquaintance asked Robins one day, "If Lawren Harris is so much interested in art for the people, why doesn't he paint pictures that people can understand?" The same person complained: "He's so doggone inconsistent. There was a time when he painted houses in the Ward that looked like houses and then apparently he didn't give a hoot about the people. Now he wants every ditch-digger to be an art connoisseur, and he paints nightmare geometry."

Given that Harris and Robins had discussed the turning points in Harris's art many times, the professor felt himself competent to talk about the remarkable new directions in his friend's art. According to him, Harris still retained his love of the houses and landscapes he had shown in earlier works, but "its [new] expression, while just as natural, is certainly less direct." The theory to which Harris had turned suggested that there was "a graphic or tonal symbol of universal intelligibility for every activity of the human consciousness." Coupled with this, Harris had performed "an act of faith in the perfectibility of man, and more narrowly in the receptivity of the average man." This interest in "significant form" might have *seemed* to be leading the artist away from humanity. According to Robins, this was a superficial view.

So when Harris began painting his gaunt Algoma rampikes and rocks, his interest in form led him to eliminate to an even greater extent . . . the endearing little cozy accidentals that the majority of us demand in landscape. A certain austere simplicity in his temperament probably had its influence as well. The result in his painting was an aloofness that was often stigmatized as inhuman.

There was no inhumanity. Absence of humanity, yes, and even of the artist's consciousness of humanity at times. In what may have been an almost mystical sense, Harris recognized character in that Superior country, and he painted the pattern of that character, its moods, its contemplation, rarely its activity. He may have over-simplified it. But in any case he was selecting the symbols that seemed to him to signify the character of that land.

Without resorting to any kind of theosophical language and with due recognition that Harris had an "austere simplicity in his temperament," Robins provides a deft reading of the changes that had taken place in his friend's art.

With a dry sense of humour, Robins observes that when Harris painted the Rockies,

> their own mothers would not have known them and would have disowned them if they had recognized them . . . I am not familiar enough with the Rockies to have an opinion as to whether they [Harris's paintings] brought out the character, revealed the Informing Spirit of mountains or not. At any rate they were no abiding place, and the transition to abstract painting soon followed.

Harris may have pursued a new form of representation, but he was not painting for a select or elite audience. "He believes art to be essential, not to the pretty life, but to the good life, the good citizen, the Canadian community. No man I know has a keener sense of civic responsibility."[11] Harris's target audience, Robins maintained, had never changed despite the fact that his modes of representation underwent several major transformations. If Harris no longer chose to depict houses, say, that did not mean he had abandoned his concern for the people who lived in those houses; he had simply advanced to a new way of expressing his distress.

Emily Carr and Lawren were able to agree to disagree about religion and abstract art. When she prodded him with questions about the latter, he was exceptionally forthcoming in telling her how he was now infused with new creative juices, although he was abandoning the kind of work that had made him celebrated.

Abstraction seems the best way for me. I have done quite a number of things and with each one learn a little more or increase that articular way of perceiving. Feeling can be as deep, as human, as spiritual or resonant in an abstraction as in representational work. But because one has less to rely on by way of association it requires a greater precision. One must be sure and the conviction sure. It is a struggle all right. There is no doubt in my mind that it enlarges the range, the scope of painting enormously. It replaces nothing, it adds to the realm of painting. It makes possible an incalculable range of ideas that the representational painting is closed to. It increases the field of experience, enhances it and that is entirely to the good . . .

As for me, there is for the present no other way. I had as you know come to a complete full stop in painting and in life. The new opportunity means new life and a new way of life and a new outlook and new adventure. So too, for Bess. She paints less than I do and goes her own particular way in painting and has done a few beautiful things. We have a large studio, work together and mutually assist each other in every way.

Some day I may return to representational painting. I don't know. Can't tell. At present I am engrossed in the abstract way and ideas flow and it looks as though it would take the rest of my days to catch up with them.[12]

In another letter, he rephrased his convictions. He was well aware that Emily had serious misgivings about what he was doing, but in writing to an artist whom he admired unstintingly, he was in a way talking out loud:

You ask about our abstract endeavours. Well, they are all different and yet alike—some more abstract than others—some verging on the representational—one never knows where the specific work in hand will lead. I try always to keep away from the representational however—for it seems the further I can keep away and into abstract idiom the more expressive the things become—yet one has in mind and heart the informing spirit of great Nature . . . [Abstract art] contains the possibility of expressing everything. It takes the expression away from the specific, the incidental and can lift it into another place, where the experience is enhanced, clarified—and it's great fun—there is so much adventure in it and an intensity of concentration that I like.[13]

The fog in which Harris had dwelt for so long had been lifted. The language of this letter is vivid and forceful; it is written by a man whose life has been irrevocably transformed by love.

Bess and Lawren.

Harris was now able to engender the metamorphosis he had long sought, from landscape artist to one whose work was centred on abstraction. Earlier, he had written about two different branches of abstraction, one that departs from but is nevertheless dependent on realistic elements and one that moves only in the realm of the abstract. Harris hankered after the latter, but he soon found that he worked best when combining realistic elements with each other. The resulting canvases thus have a surrealistic touch because objects that ordinarily have no direct relationship are placed next to each other. The laws of causality are suspended.

As a landscape painter, Harris had moved in the direction of abstracting realistic elements, reducing them to essentials, decreasing his colour palette, and allowing his surfaces to have clear, uncluttered brush work. Not surprisingly, many of those techniques soon found their way into the abstract work that he began in the White Mountains of New Hampshire. In a letter to Fred and Yvonne Housser, he mentioned that Hanover "is in the Boreal Zone. I don't know how it got there, but it's colder and more northern in feeling than all of Southern Ontario."[14]

There are surviving drawings of New Hampshire landscapes, and the first painting he completed after two years was of Mount Washington, the tallest peak in the American Northeast. Rendered in white, blue and brown with black outlining, it resembles his Lake Superior and Arctic pieces. He also completed another painting, *Winter Comes from the Arctic to the Temperate Zone*, in which a deep blue Arctic island and a soaring mountain are foregrounded by boughs of snow, an important motif for the artist in his decorative landscapes in 1913. This work looks backwards, but Harris uses it as the basis for *Mountain Experience*, a canvas that shows a bold leap into unknown territory as the mountain form lengthens to become a geometric triangle surrounded by other forms. The verticals here are extremely powerful, giving the image a thrilling upward surge. Here is a work in which the artist's belief in the sacredness of mountains is rendered in a completely new way.

Becoming much bolder in his zest for experimentation, he employed a quasi-realist setting in *Poise*. Here the background is composed of architectural elements that resemble skyscrapers; in the foreground, two vertical forms are in opposition to each other; the bottom one (feminine) is made from rounded shapes whereas the top one (male) is drawn at sharp angles. This relationship can be seen as gender related, or it can be seen as an opposition between two contrary forces. In any event, these two forms

Lawren Harris.
*Mountain
Experience.
Circa* 1936.

have reached stability and thus the large circular form can rest at the top of one of them.

Similar experimentations can be witnessed in *Equations in Space*, but the range of colours is greatly expanded to make use of a wide variety of yellows and oranges in a brightly coloured canvas in which the flat, semi-transparent vertical form on the left is contrasted with the sculptural horizontal one on the right. The colour range in the top background intertwines pale blues and yellow whereas the bottom is in much darker colours. Once again, opposites have separate identities but are attracted to each other.

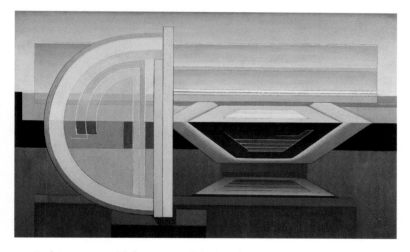

Lawren Harris.
Equations in Space.
Circa 1936.

In his personal life, Harris felt that he had finally obtained balance and poise, and this new state of being was being described pictorially. In terms of sources, there are many possibilities, but perhaps the most direct influence on him was his fellow propagandist and theosophist Katherine Dreier. She frequently uses clearly representational elements but places them in relationships to each other that ultimately produce an abstract design.

There can be no doubt that Harris was also employing "dynamic symmetry," wherein proportions in a work of art are carefully regulated according to principles found in classical Greek art and in nature. The Canadian-born Jay Hambidge (1867–1924) was the principal theorist of this approach, but Harris may well have heard C.W. Jefferys's lectures on this theory in Toronto in the mid-twenties. Of course, dynamic symmetry fits very well into theosophical ideas about order and balance. (Arthur Lismer called it "Dynamic Cemetery.")

In August 1934, reflecting on the whirlwind of gossip to which he and Yvonne had been subjected, Fred Housser told Isabel McLaughlin: "I suppose we must have found the peace that is supposed to pass understanding, for while all our friends were stewing about us and our plans, and the gossip of those who knew nothing, and those who knew better, we have not felt that it touched us. How people take it is *their* problem."[15]

When Fred died of a heart attack at the end of December 1936, Lawren told Yvonne:

> We have you in our mind and heart constantly these last several days—and Fred also. You both seem close to us, closer than you ever were and I hope that feeling has been a sustaining one. We did feel so poignantly that it was a great pity that Fred could not have had another nice stretch of years with you.
>
> You know, I have often wondered what I would do should Bess slip out of her body before I do. In one way it seems a devastating thing to contemplate but one or the other of us has to go first. So should I be the one left in my present outward body I have determined to try and convert my feelings—those deep reactions that [surge] from within the heart—into a more shining love than I have known, free from any [subtlety] of self seeking and direct them to her heart.[16]

18

AT EASE IN ZION

(1937–1940)

Lilias Newton's portrait was almost too perfect as far as Lawren was concerned. Was this an image of the artist as a successful middle-aged dandy? Or did it show a whitened sepulchre? He still asked himself this kind of question on a daily basis, but he had become a happy man. He shared all his deepest feelings with Bess. She never judged him harshly. In fact, she often provided him with insights he was incapable of reaching on his own.

Contentment. That was the name of the stage of life he had reached. But that was an especially dangerous feeling for an artist to experience, since it might allow complacency to rear its ugly head.

HARRIS WAS EXULTANT after he arrived by serendipity in Santa Fe, New Mexico. If there was a heaven on earth, he was certain he had discovered it. The place was "swell-elegant," a term Harris often used to express a moment of happiness.

And what do you think has happened to us? We feel we have found our place here in Santa Fe. Life opens up for us here as it did nowhere in the East—both creatively and in terms of

Lilias Torrance
Newton. *Lawren
Harris*. 1938.

usefulness. We both felt the place the day we motored in. It has
an unseen atmosphere that is at ease in Zion—creatively free
and stimulating—the district is spiritually magnetized—unan-
alyzable but potent. Right from the start things commenced
to happen as if prearranged, we became useful and our being
spread naturally into the creative life of the place . . . and there
are a goodly number of rather swell folks. We have made
some good [friends] and they are the real creative folk just
now moving into the new creative shape or vortex I spoke
of—spiritual abstraction. Yes, there is something on the make
here that I doubt can occur in the same way anywhere else on
the continent.[1]

Bess and Lawren had left Hanover in a blizzard on the last day of February 1938 and arrived three weeks later in a sunny, warm place seven thousand feet above sea level surrounded by the Sangre de Cristo Mountains, part of the Rockies. At that point, they knew they had reached their new home. Immediately, "we felt that this was the peak in *every* way and we promptly rented a charming little adobe house of four rooms with its own surrounding wall and 'patio,' got out our paints and panels and are hard at it." She could not contain their enthusiasm: "Lawren is on the bit—teeming with ideas and humming with energy. It is a land of great beauty and a wonderful quality of air which seems to invite creative activity."[2]

When Lawren and Bess left Toronto in 1934, they were escaping. They journeyed to Hanover because Lawren's uncle lived there. They made friends; they shared a studio; they enjoyed themselves. However, Hanover presented them with problems about housing; there, they had been forced to move five or six times, on each occasion to relatively small quarters. When they left Hanover in 1938, they were not sure what they were doing. Certain they wanted to escape cold winter weather, they may have allowed serendipity to guide them.

Nevertheless, Harris, who probably visited Stieglitz's An American Place in Manhattan, would have been well aware that the proprietor's celebrated wife, Georgia O'Keeffe, had painted in Taos, New Mexico, from 1929 and then, from 1934, at Abiquiu, between Taos and Santa Fe. He would have been aware of her spiritually charged canvases, and this may have drawn him to New Mexico. He might well have heard of a group of painters in New Mexico who were experimenting with abstraction in a similar manner to himself.

More generally, he would have been aware of the reputation of Santa Fe and Taos as home to many colonies of artists. The crooked streets, hollyhock-flanked walls and cobalt-blue skies were perfect accompaniments to the sun-drenched, primeval-looking landscape that seemed to be earth's nearest equivalent to living on the moon. The residents of Santa Fe, as the American painter Marsden Hartley rhapsodized, were especially welcoming of artists: "It is so seldom that the artist is considered in the scheme of things, that it sounds like a miracle."[3] In this regard, he considered Santa Fe to be European.

So many artists lived in Santa Fe that one visitor in 1926 observed, "I learned to distinguish an artist's house from a Mexican's by only one fact; both were yellow-red mud; both indulged in bright blue door and window frames; but the Mexican usually had a goat tethered by the front door and the artist didn't."[4]

Quite soon after the Harrises arrived in Santa Fe, they were spotted by the painter Raymond Jonson and his wife, Vera, who saw a "stunning looking couple walking past our home and studio in Santa Fe. I went out and introduced myself to them and they to us."[5]

Raymond Jonson.
1944.

The Iowa-born Jonson had moved to Santa Fe in 1924. Although he was not a theosophist, his work was permeated by religious interests (Rudolf Steiner's anthroposophy) similar to Harris's. In fact, he was already an admirer of Lawren's work, which he had seen at the Roerich Museum's Exhibition of Paintings by Contemporary Canadian Artists in New York in March 1932.*

The American and Canadian held each other in mutual esteem: Bess and Lawren purchased Jonson's *Cosmic Rhythm No. 4* that May, a canvas that husband and wife admired "immensely, unboundedly." Harris informed Jonson, "We like your work very very much, but a number of your later things exceeded our expectations—They are noble works, worthy to hang in any of the world's great collections."[6]

---

* Harris had from about 1924 a strong interest in the paintings of the Russian-born mystical artist and writer Nicholas Roerich (1874–1947) and had visited the museum at West 107th Street.

As it turned out, the Harrises' timing could not have been better. Almost immediately, Jonson introduced them to a circle of painters who were interested in abstraction, the esoteric and the occult. The couple had no choice but to stay.[7]

They rented a house on Manhattan Avenue, arranged to have a studio addition built, and soon settled in. They remained there until the summer, at which time they vacationed at Prouts Neck, Maine. On the way to Maine, they stopped in Colorado at Pikes Peak and Colorado Springs and then at Yellowstone Park in Wyoming. At Colorado Springs, they were disconcerted to witness an unseemly alliance: sewer pipe was being laid in the "Garden of the Gods." When they motored up Pikes Peak, they were greeted with thunder and lightning. There was snow at the top, but "the glimpses we got in between storms . . . were very exciting."[8]

Lawren Harris at Pikes Peak.

Before they reached Maine, Lawren and Bess had to deal with an emergency. The couple had agreed to meet up with nineteen-year-old Howie in Boston, a convenient meeting place. During the visit, the young man unexpectedly developed symptoms of diabetes:

> he looked very well but within a few days was down with diabetic coma from lack of proper training and instruction—For twenty-four hours it was a nip and tuck fight with two doctors and three nurses on the job—but he is meant to live— and pulled through nicely and is now back to his normal and rather happy attitude and condition.

As a result of this crisis, Lawren and Bess were "designing to keep [Howie] with us" if there was a specialist in diabetes in Santa Fe.[9] There may have been no such person, because this plan did not materialize. The weather in Maine was rainy and "soupy," and "sweltering."[10] The Harrises continued on to Montreal so that Lawren could sit for his portrait by Lilias Torrance Newton (commissioned by Harry Southam).

Even during his absence from Canada, Harris worried about the state of contemporary art there. In a letter to Eric Brown of October 7, 1937, Harris proposed to sell two paintings to the National Gallery (one by A.Y. Jackson, the other by Tom Thomson) for about $1,200. The resulting funds would be used to establish the Tom Thomson Memorial Fund. This project demonstrates the exiled Harris's continuing commitment to the "encouragement of original, indigenous painting in Canada."[11]

In October, the Harrises moved into their new home, one of three adobes in a large walled compound, Plaza Chamisal, on Acequia Madre, one of the oldest streets in the city. It was exactly what they were looking for after the cramped conditions in which they had existed since fleeing Toronto. These buildings had stuccoed walls, flat roofs with parapets, and porches supported by carved wooden posts and corbels. The walls had rounded corners; some of the windows were wood crowned, typical of the Territorial style common in New Mexico. The resulting atmosphere was tranquil and hushed.[12] From the dusty main street, the Harrises would drive into the bright green of their enclave.

In the Harris home, there was a large studio at the end of the living room with a ten-foot hall between the two spaces.* The

---

* The house was designed by Katherine Stinson Otero (1891–1977), an aviatrix turned architect. In June 1938, she entered into an agreement with Harris whereby he lent her $2,100 to construct a studio building, to be designated No. 1 Plaza Chamisal. In return for the loan, Harris was to rent the house and studio for $110 per month. (University of New Mexico, CSWR, OSFP, Box 10, Folder 11)

The Plaza Chamisal was the home of, among others, the architect Mary Colter, Miner Tillotson, the regional director of the National Park Service, and Louise Carr, a radio personality.

"music box"—the gramophone—was placed in one corner of the studio and the music it produced travelled about forty feet before reaching the living room. Music and painting were thus gloriously at hand. The living room was painted white, the upholstered furniture was white, and the Harris paintings on the wall (mainly of Arctic subjects) obviously had a great deal of white in them. White upon white upon white gave visitors the impression they were being received in an austere, overly refined atmosphere, although the general impression was of understated elegance. Guests would be treated to their hosts' excellent sound system; much of the time the music was Scandinavian—Grieg and Sibelius.

Santa Fe house,
Plaza Chamisal.

Lawren and Bess were exceptionally polished, accomplished hosts, but they gave visitors the impression that they would not tolerate an abundance of intimacy. Such a perception may have come into being because the Americans quickly perceived a difference in attitude in the Canadian Harrises. Lawren and Bess, still reeling from how they had been shunned in Toronto, may have become overly reticent, even wary about protecting their privacy.

Lawren Harris
at Taos Pueblo,
New Mexico.

When the Harrises first arrived in New Mexico, the circle of artists to whom Jonson introduced them was on the verge of forming the Transcendental Painting Group (TPG); their manifesto declared that they were dedicated to the goal of carrying "painting beyond the appearance of the physical world, through new concepts of space, color, light and design, to imaginative realms that are idealistic and spiritual."

In addition to Jonson, this group included Bill Lumpkins, Emil Bisttram (1895–1976), Agnes Pelton and four others. At initial discussions at Jonson's artists' supply store, the group wanted to band together to protect themselves "from realist swarms."[13] At the time he met Harris, Jonson recalled, "we were just in the phase of organization and he immediately joined with us and was a vital personality in the meetings and discussions we could arrange."[14]

In Jonson, Harris had met a kindred spirit. For one thing, Jonson had initially been drawn to New Mexico because of the possibilities it offered a landscape painter. However, in 1938 he was trying to move into abstraction. Their manifesto also included a declaration by the theosophist, writer and astrologer Dane Rudhyar (1895–1985) that the TPG consisted of a minority of "creative personalities" whose task was to confront the materialism of their age. "Great art always emerges out of . . . historical necessity—and in no other way." Those ringing words would have reminded Harris of his own rhetorical flourishes in the founding of the Group of Seven.

When they had lived in New York City, Emil and Maryan Bisttram had been active theosophists. At their apartment in Taos, Rudhyar conducted weekly meetings about religious subjects. The Bisttrams had drifted in the direction of "Tibetan yoga." In contrast to the extremely polished Harris, Maryan recalled, her husband was a bit of a diamond in the rough. Nevertheless, the two got on extremely well.

Harris's physical appearance at the age of fifty-two was imposing. He was tall and slim, had rosy, fair skin and a shock of white hair. He held his shoulders back, walked with dignity and "carried his head as if he wore a crown."[15] Harris, always immaculately turned out, was usually dressed in white.

With the Bisttrams, the Harrises discussed marriage in general terms. The four agreed: "Marriage isn't always a necessity, nor are the activities of marriage necessary." In the eso- teric philosophies of the East, Maryan reflected, "the final step is celibacy."[16] She was sure that the Harrises shared that conviction.

Lawren Harris at the age of fifty-two.

Their new circle were, Bess told Doris Mills, "mostly painters—and the modern group—they are grand—stim- ulating—and very friendly— the people here are generally less rigid and more open to ideas than in the east."[17] In a later let- ter to Isabel McLaughlin, in January 1940, Bess described her and Lawren's social life in more jaded terms:

We have been as busy as ever, life never seems to slow up much,—now we have two groups coming to the house regu- larly.—one on Wednesday evenings for study—and the other on Saturday for music . . . We had dinner at Rudhyar's house and met his wife. A strange little person who looks like a child, dark curly hair—but I should guess a willful disposition. Rudhyar seemed less strange and exotic in his own house—perhaps because he was in ordinary clothes—not colored corduroys—or perhaps because he was quiet and in happy spirits—we saw Emil the other day—the Jonsons we see very often.[18]

Perhaps as a result of the fallout from his earlier involvement as "leader" of the Group of Seven, Harris tried to take a back seat within the TPG. He agreed to be a member, but he advocated the formation of the Transcendental Painting Foundation (eventually agreeing to be its president) as an ancillary arm to support TPG's business side; he put up the money for the incorporation fees. When Jonson became confused by exactly what his new friend wanted to accomplish, Harris set the record straight:

The Group as a band of active Transcendental painters interests me first and foremost—before anything else and a good long way before anything else . . . The Foundation is not basic, fundamental, primary. It can only become a success when the painters themselves produce works to justify it. And how many such works are there?—a good many of yours and damn little else as yet . . . As for me, I would rather be the humblest painter in the Transcendental Group than ten thousand times president of any Foundation however excellent . . . So, I only accept the office of the president of the foundation pro tem.[19]

Once bitten, twice stung. Harris did not really wish to be directly involved with the administration of this new group, but he felt compelled to offer what assistance he could.

If he had hoped not to be scratched once again by art politics, that hope was not realized. In 1931 Harris had assisted Roland McKinney in the selection of Canadian work for the Pan-American Exposition in Baltimore. When McKinney was selecting artists for the Golden Gate Exposition in 1939, Harris suggested that he consider the TPG. That mention later led to the allegation that he was trying to rig the entries from the Santa Fe area in favour of members of the TPG.[20]

The TPG's first exhibition was held in April 1939. Harris's work was not mentioned in any reviews, but in the *Santa Fe New Mexican*, Alfred Morang, a violinist, writer and landscape artist, reviewed the exhibition at the Arsuna School of Fine Arts in Santa Fe (likely the same as the one in April). Harris's work, he observed, "has a three dimensional quality that makes his Transcendental painting akin to certain constructions. His color has subdued force and subtlety but it is his masterly creative design that places him in the front ranks of leading non-representational artists."[21] In September, the same writer critiqued the work Harris had submitted to a regional exhibition: *Composition 10* is "filled with intense nonrepresentational significance. The painter has succeeded in the difficult task of making abstractions into what may be termed objective mental forms."

Even in paradise, Harris's work did not always go well. In February 1938, Bess told Isabel: "Neither of us have been successful we feel in our painting—worked too conscientiously perhaps—rather than feelingly—Maybe like winter wardrobes they look worn in the spring light after too close an application and will look better to use when we come back in September . . . Lawren thinks he may experiment with abstract equivalents done 'on the spot'."

In the same letter, Bess told her friend what she considered to be the basic differences between men and women: "Men are dynamic and travel—direct lives—Women are but a background for them—and soil if you like for their roots.—Neither need to lose their individuality so.—but find a creative momentum when the adjustment is right—Women have a natural genius for the creative in relationships."[22] Even for 1938, these observations may represent extremely conservative thinking on the status of women, but they reflect Bess's personal credo.

She explains exactly what she has decided to do to assist her husband in a letter of December 28:

I am studying Dynamic Symmetry you will be surprised to hear. Taking a course with two other (younger) married women with an artist [Emil Bisttram] who lives 75 miles away! But it takes all my spare time . . . I must move into the abstract if I am to continue painting both for inner and outer reason. I need to be in the house and available,—even to be in the studio.—It is needful. It is also a joy that I can be really useful to Lawren in his own creative work.—and that the usefulness increases.—I am blessed with more painting perception than I am blessed with to do.—so it is good to use it.—Whenever Lawren finds himself in a questioning place he comes for me and we go and talk it over . . . The more one looks, the more meaningful the non-objective forms and spaces become.[23]

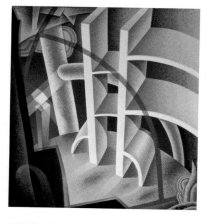

Raymond Jonson.
Variations on a Rhythm. 1931.

Here, Bess is explicit: her role as the wife of Lawren Harris is to act as a helpmate, someone actively involved in his work. Such a wife is obviously the opposite of Trixie. Bess places her husband's career first, especially as she recognizes that she is much better at thinking about art than making it.

There can be no doubt that Bisttram exerted a tremendous influence over both Harrises. In New Hampshire (and perhaps before), Harris had been intrigued by dynamic symmetry, about which Bisttram was not as didactic as Hambidge: "I do not consider it a formula that ties me down to specific limitations . . . I find it releases

Emil Bisttram.
Upward.
Circa 1940.

the imaginative powers, liberating the creative forces towards a final unquestionable order."[24]

Harris's work in 1938–39 certainly shows the influence of the Hungarian-born artist in its use of large circle/bubble shapes as well as transparent, overlapping planes. This approach to painting Harris also considered musical in that its principles embodied mathematical formulae similar to those used by composers.

Lawren Harris.
Painting No. 4
(Abstraction 94).
Circa 1939.

Lawren Harris.
*Composition
(Abstraction
No. 99).
Circa* 1938.

Painting No. 4 (Abstraction 94), Composition (Abstraction No. 99) and *Abstraction (Involvement 2)* were probably completed in New Mexico. The vertical movements in these three paintings are carried out with an extremely accomplished hand; the principles of dynamic symmetry are in evidence. However, each uses a different organizing principle. In *Painting No. 4*, various triangular shapes play against each other and are complemented by the circular forms; the downward thrust in *Composition* may be dramatic, but the yellow, greens and cream bestow a countervailing sense of quietude; in *Abstraction*, the verticals are interrupted by the transparent triangular forms that whirl in space, and the entire composition is deliberately weighed down by the two orange/yellow circles.

Lawren Harris.
*Abstraction
(Involvement 2).*
Circa 1939.

Despite some trepidation on his part, Harris's second generation of abstract forms display his increasing mastery of the kind
of Modernist expression he wished to pursue. The "mountain"

feel of the first generation has been reduced significantly; these new paintings have the kind of refinement he had long wished to achieve.

In June 1940, when lights were going out all over Europe, even people in faraway New Mexico, as Bess observed, "were worked up." Women were collecting clothing for a possible war. Bess had stripped her and Lawren's clothes closets and turned in fifteen men's pullover sweaters. She was restless and had discovered there were "few people" there who made her long "for their *steady* companionship." She was disgusted by Jonson's pacifism and wondered what he would do if his "new moth-proof, fire-proof, earthquake-proof painting store room" was attacked. In any event, she had now come to the conclusion that there was "nothing new or fresh in his work." However, Bisttram's was "alive and darn interesting."[25]

Despite occasional bouts of boredom, Bess and Lawren would have remained in New Mexico but for the outbreak of World War II. Although the United States did not enter the conflict until Pearl Harbor in December 1941, the transfer of Canadian funds abroad became prohibited in 1940. In addition to their own finances, Bess and Lawren had to be concerned with those of Annie Raynolds, who was now living in Pasadena, California. She was there because her frail health responded well to the climate and so that she could be within a reasonable distance for her son to visit regularly.

Annie decided to move to Victoria, British Columbia, because it had the most temperate climate in Canada. There, she was a guest at the Empress Hotel. The Harrises felt they were too far from Annie in New Mexico and thus determined to move to Vancouver. On September 18, 1940, Bess told Doris:

> Just a hurried few lines to tell you we are beginning to pack our goods and chattels for a return to Canada. The Finance Board cut off Mrs. Raynolds' funds unless a certificate from a Doctor said she could not live in Canada.—We could not see our way to procure that as she is strong physically though

alas her faculties are steadily getting fussier—Her interests are those of a fifteen year old girl.—which makes for certain problems, as you may guess, so Lawren must be fairly close to her.

Bess then raised the issue of why the return was not to Toronto: "First we thought Toronto.—but at present Victoria is pleasing. Mrs. Raynolds and her tempo have slowed down considerably, which is good for her,—many contacts and people seem to be confusing—and Toronto of course would suggest old habits of life which she could not possibly meet or move into."[26] Bess does not mention that she and Lawren might have objected to Toronto on other grounds. In fact, on December 24, 1940, Lawren told Jonson: "We have sent for our goods but that doesn't say we're settling [in Vancouver] for good. We've rented a house for six months—and then we'll see wots wot."[27]

19

EQUIVALENTS

(1940–1948)

Lawren did not wish to leave Santa Fe: perfect weather, won-derful friends, astounding mountain ranges. But he realized that he had to push such misgivings aside.

Both Lawren and Bess were relieved that they did not have to seriously consider returning to Toronto. That would have been a form of hell. His mother, he knew, was as content as she could be in Victoria. Vancouver would be an entirely new experience and a genuine adventure. Hadn't he always welcomed new exploits?

D URING HIS TIME in Hanover and Santa Fe, Harris had kept in touch with the art world in Canada. He sent four abstractions to the Canadian Group of Painters exhibition in November 1937, organized the display of Canadian art at the Golden Gate Exhibition in 1939, and showed some of his Group of Seven canvases at the Art Association of Montreal Spring Exhibition in March 1939 and again at the Canadian National Exhibition that August. His first Santa Fe abstractions were shown with the Canadian Group of Painters in late October 1939. In March 1940 he was chosen as one of the participants in a four-person show at the Art Gallery of Toronto.

Lawren had visited Lornie and Howie in Toronto in 1938. Peggie had stayed with him and Bess in both Hanover and Santa Fe; and then in September 1940 the Harrises visited Peggie, who was living in St. Catharines, Ontario. In October 1940, the couple called upon Lawren's mother in Victoria and also on Emily Carr.

As far as Emily was concerned, she experienced a rapprochement with Lawren but not with Bess:

> I think it staggered her to see me crawling round so slow, not even dressed yet, but in gown & bedroom slippers. I don't think Bess ever gets much further than herself & her ailments of which she always keeps herself well stocked. She is a bit of a "poser". Lawren is genuinely fond of me I know. A faithful correspondent and although we have not the same outlook now that he has gone abstract, we are thoroughly interested in each other's work, and lives, and our friendship is a deep one.[1]

From Vancouver, Lawren and Bess took the train to Toronto, where they stayed at the Windsor Arms Hotel. From there, he wrote to Raymond Jonson.

> The month here has been packed, jammed with visits, dinners, lunches, conferences, meetings and an endless program of renewing friendships.
>
> We leave here Sunday for Vancouver and will stop over a few days in Banff to rest and to view the mountains in what is now their winter.
>
> Then we go to Vancouver to settle for the winter and spring. We have a house there—haven't seen it—but know its plan and location and fancy it will suit us and that we can paint therein.[2]

Their new home had been rented for them by one of Bess's sisters and was in the exclusive Point Grey neighbourhood of Vancouver, high above English Bay. Bess told some New Hampshire friends: "Our little house is set high on a slope which stretches down to an ocean inlet, across the inlet the land rises sharply to dark fir-covered slopes and white snow hooded mountains."[3] Up and down the inlet ocean-going vessels could be seen.

In addition to settling into a house in a splendid setting, the domestic arrangements of the Harrises were congenial, as Bess assured a friend: "As for me, I'm a *very* proficient house keeper—provide excellent meals.—paint some—play with the new spaniel puppy [called Judith, Judy for short]—try to be agreeable—read the *Bhagavad Gita*.—knit in odd moments—and play hostess—we seem to have quite a number come in, usually for dinner."[4] Lawren told Raymond Jonson: "We have built a wooden shack of a studio a few jumps from the house. It has a grand light, is a good workshop and we are both busy therein." He added: "Mother loves Victoria . . . so that solves our problem. So long as she remains contented in Victoria we will remain here."[5]

All in all, Lawren and Bess were happily settled by the late winter of 1941, as Bess told Doris: "The blossoming trees are exquisite and almost astound the eye—It's a heavenly place to live." All reservations had been set aside: "I was not really enthusiastic about coming—neither was Lawren.—now we are grateful that Life took us in hand and landed us in these beauteous parts."[6] Harris did have regrets about leaving New Mexico: he liked the Plaza Chamisal and his many friends. In September 1942, he wrote to his former landlord: "I presume that all the houses in Plaza Chamisal are filled. I hear a number of Californians moved inland when the threat of Japanese bombing first emerged and a number of these settled in Santa Fe. The wise ones would."[7] The Canadian government forced Harris to withdraw all his money from the States, but he did not mind: "This country has shut down on everything—conserving and directing everything to one end—to defeat the Nazis."[8]

As part of his contribution to the war effort, Harris volunteered as a civil warden (auxiliary policeman). At the time, there was considerable fear that the Japanese might invade, and there were, for example, gun emplacements along Spanish Banks. In his new role, Harris would have ensured that all regulations concerned with protecting the municipality were followed by its residents.

At home, the Harrises established set routines. At various times, there were gardeners and drivers. There was a succession of cooks; the key criterion was whether the candidate could prepare a coconut cake with a "seven-minute" icing. The wine served at meals was almost always Mateus, the medium-sweet frizzante rosé wine from Portugal.

Lawren Harris
at easel at
Belmont Avenue.

In his wonderfully dry, best sarcastic manner, A.Y. Jackson observed: Harris "should liven up the boys round there, or he may merely get them interested in reincarnation." To a certain degree, both prophecies came to fruition.

Long before Harris settled in Vancouver, a controversy had erupted when eighteen Group paintings were shown there at the 1928 Exposition. According to a letter sent to the *Daily Province* by the Reverend J. Williams Ogden, an amateur artist and long-time member of the B.C. Art League, those canvases should have been burnt: "We know that these 'freakists' by political influence and press manipulation have, for the time, captured the seats of power in connection with the National Gallery of this Dominion and that good public money is being paid for the

Lawren Harris as civil warden.

purchase of the works of these men." The condemnatory remarks were aimed squarely at Harris and MacDonald, and the resulting controversy was aired coast to coast. This *succès de scandale* led to an attendance of 65,000. Not one canvas sold. Having contributed in his absence to a tempest in a teapot that had taken over the city twelve years earlier, Harris now welcomed the opportunity to pitch his tent there and perhaps continue the battle in person.

In the winter of 1941, Lawren, at the age of fifty-six, was especially content: "I am having a show here at the end of April," he told Jonson, "and am busy putting my stuff in shape."9 Harris's reputation had preceded him. He was known as the founder of the Group of Seven, a passionate advocate of Canadian art, the first president of the CGP, and an exile who had chosen to return to Canada by way of Vancouver. The local arts community was deeply gratified to have this famous person among them.

The exhibition of twenty-seven canvases was shown for two weeks at the Vancouver Art Gallery and was then moved to the campus of the University of British Columbia. Since the work—

all abstracts—departed completely from the kind of art for which he was known in Canada, Harris was asked to prepare a statement of intent. In his statement, he affirmed his conviction that "abstract or non-objective painting" embraces concepts that "can only be expressed or embodied in visual language"; nevertheless, he assured the skeptical, such work is "a natural outgrowth from representational painting," enlarges the field of painting, and "does not and cannot replace any of the painting of the past."

Harris's reasonable and mild-mannered positioning of his work had a mainly calming effect, although Browni Wingate in the *Vancouver News Herald* was not convinced: "Is it worth it? This is art in its most limited form, dealing with only raw materials . . . It lacks . . . emotional power on the part of the artist. Mr. Harris is an exquisite colorist, a fine painter, but he expresses nothing more than a certain artistic good taste."

In the *Vancouver Sun*, Mildred Valley Thornton (1890–1967), a well-known local artist who worked in a representational mode, was quite welcoming of what she beheld:

Many people today are aware that the so-called natural world of which we are so cognizant is but a more dense and gross manifestation of that which moves at a much higher rate of vibration on higher planes, so it is right and natural that artists should be the bridge of interpretation between these two realms. The effort to do this is not really comprehended by the materialistic mind and an understanding of these things must be earned by patient study and the complete abolition of prejudice and preconceived ideas.

As such, the canvases for her conveyed "various ideas of motion, peace, space, quiet, calm, fury, sanctity, haven, growth, etc."

For her part, Bess did not need convincing of the significance of abstract art, but she was ecstatic about how her husband's work had been presented by the Vancouver Art Gallery:

Lawren's show . . . looked wonderfully well in the Gallery here—it was good to see a whole room full of his work—all abstracts too.—it was very converting.—if one was inclined to be doubtful—they—the doubts—just disappeared.—A lively interest was awakened in the public—and according to the Gallery Director a very unusual one for Vancouver.

In sharp contrast to Toronto, she felt,

> Vancouver is rather a large small town in many ways and it's great fun—The people are most pleasant and friendly—not sophisticated.—and certainly the women are not "smartly" dressed according to Eastern standards.—but no wonder considering the shops—Life has a very pleasant tempo.—very different and *much* slower than Toronto, Montreal etc.—No one is excited or hurried.[10]

Still stung by what had happened to her in Toronto, slower, less sophisticated Vancouver offered many comforts.

Shortly after his one-man show, Harris was elected to the council of the Vancouver Art Gallery. To the businessmen who populated this group, he was an ideal choice because of his birth and business connections. They did not know enough about art politics to realize that they might have landed a firebrand.

Little known to the captains of industry, there was a Modernist artist already resident in Vancouver. J.W.G. (Jock) Macdonald was born in Thurso, Scotland, in 1897 and began his art education at the Edinburgh College of Art in 1922. Four years later, the Vancouver School of Decorative and Applied Arts hired both Macdonald and Fred Varley. After a dispute with the head of that institution, the two men in 1933 opened the British Columbia School of Arts in a garage on a vacant car dealership in downtown Vancouver; Harry Taüber, a theatre designer, joined them. This institution survived for only two years. After Macdonald peremptorily closed it without consulting him, Varley never spoke to him again.

The Macdonalds moved to Nootka on the west coast of Vancouver Island, where they stayed for eighteen months. In that new environment, Jock began to see his art in a fresh, transforming way. Not unlike Harris, he started to paint in a manner inspired by the elemental forces he witnessed; he decided to emphasize spiritual expression rather than external representation. He created what he called "modalities," which he defined as "expressions of thought in relation to nature"; these were "creative expressions which could not be said to relate to nature (objectively) nor relate to abstract thoughts (subjectively) about nature, but rather included both expressions."[11]

In extremely poor health and plagued by financial difficulties, he attempted to find work in Hollywood, California, but soon returned to Vancouver. He wistfully reflected: "B.C. has that vapour quality which seems to me to be much more clairvoyant in its inspiration than that blazing and relentless sunshine down south."[12] Deeply discouraged in 1939, he nevertheless clung to his new vision: "Expressions of beauty and truth are the most

Jock Macdonald.

essential qualities of life, and this endeavour of study must not be smothered under any conditions."[13]

When Harris arrived in Vancouver, Varley had been gone from the city for four years and Macdonald was supporting himself (barely) by teaching at Vancouver Technical High School. Like Harris, Macdonald was fascinated by Eastern religious systems and theosophical thought; more importantly, he had been experimenting with abstract art for five years. His "modalities" look very much like the work Harris was doing in 1939–40.

Temperamentally, Macdonald was completely different from the mercurial Varley. He was of a philosophical turn of mind that allowed an easy friendship between him and Harris. When Har-

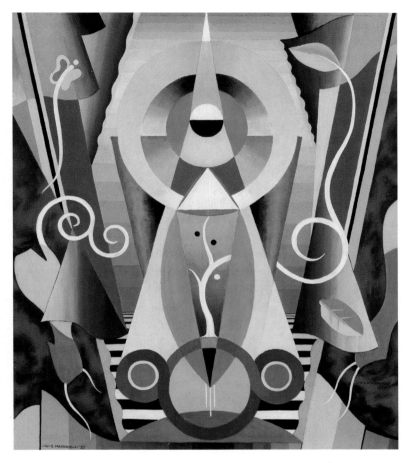

Jock Macdonald.
Fall (Modality 16).
1937.

ris met him, Macdonald had been a member of the gallery council for nine years.*

Like Harris, Macdonald was spellbound by mountains, by
their physical majesty and sublime aloofness. By 1941, both men
tended (but not exclusively) to use such landscapes as sources of

---

* The work of Beatrice Lennie (1904–87) would also have been of great interest to
Harris because she was, together with Macdonald, the Vancouver artist in the early
forties most interested in abstraction. In the late twenties she had been a pupil of
both Varley and Macdonald at the Vancouver School of Decorative and Applied
Arts; she later taught with both men at the British Columbia School of Arts. In a
canvas such as *The Atom* (1938) she mixes representational and abstract elements
in a manner reminiscent of Harris's New Mexico paintings.

inspiration rather than as natural phenomena to be given realistic form in sketches or paintings. To be in the mountains was to be touched by supernatural wonders. In August 1941, Harris, Bess, Jock and his wife Barbara spent six weeks at Lake O'Hara Lodge in Yoho National Park. Harris's experience that summer was probably enhanced by Macdonald's presence:

> We did very little work but a great deal of climbing and even more clambering around, imbibing the elevation of the spirit the mountains afford in the hope that it will convert itself into plastic ideas for painting . . . There is an austere starkness about them that braces me no end. But there is an almost complete divorce between the naturalistic—representation—and non-objective painting. The one won't go into t'other, yet on seeing marvelous mountains and having exciting experiences among and on them I am convinced that there are equivalents in non-objective painting which are more expressive, moving and elevating than any possible representation of them in paint.[14]

Lawren Harris in the Rockies.

Despite his inclination to the contrary, Harris would sometimes still simply draw the mountains. However, he and Macdonald were really allowing the spiritual values they discerned in such sublime landscapes to quicken their creative juices.

Another contact was revived because of a shared fascination with mountains. The Winnipeg-based LeMoine FitzGerald had shown two paintings with the Group of Seven and became a member of it in 1932 after Jim MacDonald's death. However, Harris and FitzGerald actually met only in August 1942, when FitzGerald and his wife summered on Bowen Island near Vancouver. Much earlier, in February 1928, Harris, very much taken with FitzGerald's drawings at an exhibition at the Arts and Letters Club, had written the younger man: "I particularly like the way you extricate a suggestion of celestial structure and spirit from objective nature in your drawings." He also admired the "restrained radiant colour," "fine form" and "harmonious sounds" with which he created a "heavenly garden of Eden" in his work.[15] The following year, when he saw some more work by FitzGerald at Dent's in Toronto, he told him: "Sometime later I will try and write down what little I know about abstract painting. You seem to suggest a feeling in that direction."[16] Of course, Harris was seeing his own struggles mirrored in the other artist's work, and it was typical of him to reach out to someone experiencing the same artistic turmoil.

Lawren and Bess were at ease in Vancouver, but Lawren had the constant worry of keeping tabs on Annie at the Empress Hotel in Victoria. By December 1941, her condition had so deteriorated that she had to

Belmont Avenue.

be settled in Vancouver. The Harrises moved across the street to 4760 Belmont Avenue—a large clapboard house high on a hill— and Annie moved into their old house at 4749. The shift was done in this way because 4749 had bedrooms and a bathroom on the ground floor, conditions that would make Annie's life tolerable. Soon the Harrises were running what Bess termed "a very exclusive little hospital."[17] Annie died quite soon afterwards, on March 26, 1942. Throughout his moth-

Interior, Belmont Avenue.

er's last illness, Lawren was "faithful, devoted and patient—and yet detached."[18] A son who had always had tender feelings for his mother, he remained careful and considerate in his care for her.

Their second house on Belmont was much more spacious, as Bess informed Doris: "the old hall-through-the-centre plan with dining room and kitchen on one side so that we get no kitchen noises in the living room.—The living room used to be two rooms—each with a fireplace—one fireplace was moved out to the hall and a partition taken down. The walls are ivory—the curtains natural and cream."[19]

Music remained an essential component in Harris's everyday life. An audiophile, he always had the best sound systems available. "We have continued our 'Musical Evenings' here," Bess told a friend. "There are still a number of young people coming with an increase of older people, so that we sometimes have almost thirty sitting around our living room.—They sit for three hours listening to records."[20] One guest, Geoffrey Andrews, had warm memories of evenings at the Harrises': "The food was absolutely superb . . . The table was a work of art: the mahogany, the silver, the flower arrangements, the food." Dinner talk was wide-ranging and stimulating, but what impressed him most was the "joint creative energy"[21] of Bess and Lawren.* The Harrises also hosted what Lawren facetiously called "tycoon parties" to raise money for worthy causes such as the Vancouver Art Gallery—and to thank those who had been generous to their philanthropic activities. Harris and H.R. MacMillan (1885–1976), the forestry magnate, called upon various businessmen to solicit money for an expansion to the VAG.

In January 1941, one guest, the portrait painter Nan Cheney (1897–1985), provided an extensive description of her experience at one of these events:

---

* The young architect Arthur Erickson (1924–2009) attended some of these evenings: "The Harrises were the centre of Vancouver's modest artistic life at that time, opening their home to anyone who wished to come to hear music in the dark through a then unheard of 'high fidelity' sound system. With the accumulation of refugees from Europe, conductors like Sir John Barbirolli might be there, or composers like Arthur Benjamin, besides dancers, poets and painters." *The Architecture of Arthur Erickson* (New York: HarperCollins, 1988), 12. Another frequent guest at these events was the violinist Harry Adaskin (1901–94), the founder of the Hart House Orchestra in 1923. He was the head of music at the University of British Columbia from 1946 to 1958.

Last Sat. we went to the Harris's [*sic*] for the evening & were simply stunned by his abstracts—They are really beautiful in a cold impersonal way & yet they fascinated you & the colour is gorgeous—. . . Mrs. H. was dressed in a long white crepe—form fitting—dress with flowing sleeves & she sat on the floor in graceful poses on white angora goat hair mats which they brought from New Mexico . . . —We spent most of the evening in the dark listening to the gramophone—the music box, they call it, & the last word in recording. They have *all* the symphonies & thousands of records. It was very nice but too loud for my tender ears.

Drinks and sandwiches were served afterwards. In contrast to Harris, Nan found Jock Macdonald a person with "immature" opinions.[22]

These musical evenings, held every second Saturday, continued until someone—presumably someone who had been invited to the soirees and knew the ground plan of the Harris house—broke in and stole the records. Many of the recordings were replaced; the musical evenings, however, ceased. Harris continued listening to music while painting, a custom that was especially stimulating when working on abstracts.

The painter B.C. Binning, who became a close friend of Lawren's, argued that Harris brought "enormous prestige" to Vancouver. However, he felt Harris was too generous and uncritical of other painters. "Harris just couldn't say no to anybody. All men were his friends . . . It wasn't really sentimental. It was a kind of almost spiritual thing: We must all be brothers."[23]

However, just as Harris had been seen as autocratic some years earlier by Bertram Brooker and Thoreau MacDonald, he acquired the same reputation in Vancouver. G.H. Tyler, who later became director of the Vancouver Art Gallery, recalled the time the gallery "had a show from Calgary and there was a flower painting by somebody. Harris hated flower paintings. I hung the show and went out for lunch. When I came back the painting was gone. Harris had ordered it down and had put it in the basement."[24] Tyler returned the painting to the spot it had occupied and attached its frame to be wall by a six-inch spike in the event Harris tried to remove it again.

Not surprisingly, Harris's prudishness extended to nudes. One evening Lawren arrived at the gallery for the opening of a small exhibition of the work of the English artist Matthew Smith. Harris objected to two nudes and had them removed before the other guests arrived.[25]

Jack Shadbolt, who had been a frequent guest at the musical evenings, which he dubbed "music séances" conducted in an "exclusive minor temple," fell out of favour when he dared to take exception to some of Harris's pronouncements.[26] Another painter, Joe Plaskett, felt that Harris sometimes acted as a dictator, insulated in a Shangri-La atmosphere because of his wealth.[27]

The charges against Harris are fair, but they have to be counterbalanced by his extraordinary generosity to many artists, including Plaskett, who were struggling to survive. For example, rather than hang his walls with his own work, they were usually filled with the work of others. Those paintings were for sale, and if need be, Harris could be an engaged, passionate salesperson.

After his return to Vancouver, Harris saw his role as an advocate for Canadian art in a completely different way than he had during the Group of Seven years. Earlier, he had promoted the Group as *the* Canadian Modernist group. As an older man, he felt passionately that Canadian art as an entity was an endangered species to be protected and nourished. His embrace of what was Canadian became more catholic, in large part because he himself had moved from representational to abstract art: he was more aware of and sensitive to the wide gamut of artistic expression. In "Democracy and the Arts," he gave voice to those sentiments: "The totality of production of the arts should form an unbroken creative chain from the poorest and most fleeting efforts to the most inspiring and enduring expressions. So that no link is missing and thus no one is left out."

Those words came partially in response to the grim realities of World War II and the realization that after the war Canada would have to find of way of ensuring that artists joined together in a single, powerful unit. Given his earlier role in Canadian art, it was natural that Harris would agree to become the British Columbia representative of the Federation of Canadian Artists when it was formed in 1941: he was of the opinion that "all of the art societies in Canada and the staffs of all the art colleges in Canada could unite in one federation and work together toward their own creative and social enlightenment."[28] In 1944, Harris became the group's second president, a position he held until 1947. He expressed his credo in these words:

> The chief aim [of the Federation], as I see it, is to make the creative and replenishing life in art an inseparable part of the life of Canadians from coast to coast. All other aims stem from this one and are secondary. In other words, as a Federation, we will serve the arts and the needs of the artist best, if our aim is first to serve our own people.[29]

During Harris's presidency, the chief issue was the "National Art Centre Plan," according to which twenty-five major cultural community centres were to be built from coast to coast. Like two parallel institutions, the National Film Board and the Canadian Broadcasting Centre, these centres would ensure the establishment and dissemination of Canadian art throughout the entire country rather than have it concentrated in a few urban areas. "Moreover," Harris argued,

> the needs of the artist generally and the problems of art and the artists and culture generally in the country are now bound to undergo great changes and these problems and changes can only be met by a country wide Federation of artists which can and should become a power in every part of Canada.[30]

The federal government did not readily accept these ideas, which would have resulted in a substantial diminishment of funds for the National Gallery. But Harris's major disappointment was that his lobbying brought him into conflict with Arthur Lismer, whose career was now centred on art education for children. Lismer was dependent on the Carnegie Foundation for funding and was afraid that the FCA would approach the same organization for funding and thus diminish the resources available for Canadian projects. Once again, Harris was caught within the competing, sometimes bitter and frequently disruptive world of art politics.

On a significantly smaller scale was Lawren's conflicted relationship with Emily Carr. As her letter to a mutual friend, the CBC's Ira Dilworth, makes clear, she had never forgiven Lawren for his marriage to Bess. Responding to bits and pieces of gossip about the Harrises in Vancouver, she told Dilworth:

> Perhaps the Harrises are just paying back eat entertainments. I know Lawren used to loathe that sort of stuff. His work always came first. But since he married Bess—Bess likes posing a bit—charming hostess etc.—I do not think she has strengthened him. Is it good for folks to be tooooo happy Ira? Isn't it a *little* dangerous?[31]

Emily is implying that Harris might be a better artist if he were unhappy. She is also suggesting that Bess, a woman and an artist far below her in worth, had displaced her. However, Lawren knew Bess well before he met Emily. The issue for Carr was emotional jealousy.

There was another problem in their relationship. From the time he arrived in Vancouver, Harris acted as a quasi-dealer for Emily. He had a number of her canvases on hand and would promote them to would-be buyers. A sticking point for her was that Harris had purchased and enthusiastically talked up *Indian Church* from 1929, arguably one of her masterpieces.* However, by the early forties Emily did not like that painting and was angered by her friend's espousal of it: she felt that she had advanced far beyond that work. Harris later sold the painting to the Toronto

---

* When Harris returned from Europe in June 1930, he informed Emily: "We saw considerable art in Europe—but I would rather have 'The Indian Church' than anything I *saw*. When we got back it looked better than ever—it's one swell thing."

collector Charles Band on condition that he eventually give it to the Art Gallery of Toronto (now the AGO).

With Emily, Harris often could not win for losing. After she died in 1945, Harris, who was one of the trustees of the Emily Carr Foundation, worked steadfastly to locate promising artists to whom the available funds could be dispensed.

Composition No. 1 was the highlight of Harris's exhibition at the Vancouver Art Gallery in 1941. It is a summation of the abstract work done in New Hampshire and New Mexico. Even more geometrically precise than his previous work, it has a stolidity lacking in the earlier abstractions. It is both powerful and imposing, although it lacks the lyrical whimsy that had been achieved in Santa Fe. It is also a canvas in which ideas about mountains are obviously present, especially in the dark blue vertical thrusting upwards towards the centre of the picture plane.

Lawren Harris.
Composition No. 1.
1940.

Following his trip to Lake O'Hara with Harris in the summer of 1941, Macdonald held his second one-man show at the Vancouver Art Gallery (his first had overlapped with Harris's); it consisted of mountain landscapes. Two months later, Harris organized an exhibition of abstract paintings at the same place and included work by himself, Macdonald, Bisttram, Jonson and others.

The simple fact was that Harris could try to escape landscape, but he remained in its thrall. He may no longer have wanted to be a representational artist, but that calling was an intrinsic part of his makeup. Pictures inspired by flames became one way of escaping the net of representation. So was a canvas such as *Abstract Painting No. 20*, which began as an experiment looking at the complexities of wood grain. From what were supposed to be blow-ups of such observations, he produced *20*.

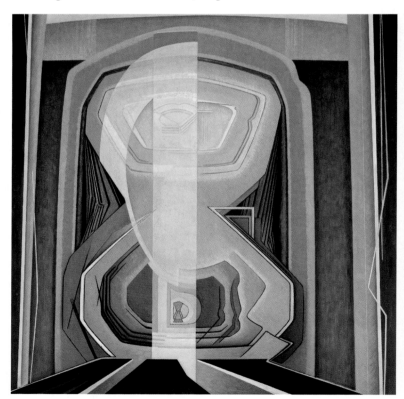

Lawren Harris.
Abstract Painting
No. 20. Circa 1943.

However, the painting becomes a meditation on the notion of doors and keys. A series of vertical frames enclose the space; on top of each other are two abstract shapes, each with a key shape in the centre; the transparent yellows of the top are echoed in the deep orange opaque at the bottom. *20* has a surrealistic element and suggests a world where the abstract and the representational find common ground. The two planes, one on top of the other, also suggest Mark Rothko, a painter whom Harris would come to admire greatly in the fifties.

Harris became puzzled as to exactly where his own late paintings fit into the larger panorama of Canadian art. Didn't Canadian painting have to represent something intrinsically Canadian? If it did not, how should it be classified? When Isabel McLaughlin asked him in 1945 if his earlier work could be placed next to his new work, he hedged:

> No, I would not feel that my present stuff could be included in a collection of Canadian paintings "just as well as work of my earlier period." The present work is not Canadian in subject matter which makes a difference in the actual hanging of pictures. In the present CGP show you have hung a gallery with abstractions because no doubt they hang better together than mixed in with representational works. Whether the present pictures are Canadian in spirit I wouldn't know but I fancy they must be so in some sense or degree.[32]

Harris might have argued about applying the adjective *Canadian*, but he was thrilled when the Art Gallery of Toronto approached him in 1947 about mounting a retrospective: he would be the first Canadian artist ever accorded this tribute. Harris co-operated fully with the gallery, although he was careful to impress upon everyone involved that he wanted his abstracts to be given their due. He freshened up or retouched several early canvases and sent a list of the changes, at which point Martin Baldwin, the director of the gallery, asked him to stop this practice: "Do you seriously think it would be a good thing to repaint canvases done years before?"[33] Harris responded:

Re retouching and repainting.—this would be minor in every case—changes I have had in mind for years. I have made changes on several of the older canvases which I have here and unless people were told they had been repainted in parts, no one would know it. In every case the painting has been improved but this has been done in terms of the day the painting was painted.[34]*

In the months leading up to the exhibition, while Harris may have posed many questions, he was characteristically generous in answering queries directed at him by the curator, Sydney Key. He was especially pleased that, at his suggestion, *Abstract (War Painting)* (*circa* 1944) was shown on the cover of the catalogue. This painting in its stark contrast between black and yellow suggests that the darkness of war in the background can be offset by the golden, spiritual forms that inhabit the foreground. Put another way, evil can inhabit human existence and seem to be the underpinning of all existence; however, this is an illusion to be banished. Evil is a void; goodness will prevail. The ovoid form implies spiritual rebirth.

The resulting exhibition contained seventy-five canvases; entries 58 to 75 were abstracts. Two reviews would have especially gratified Harris. In the *Toronto Daily Star*, Augustus Bridle obviously felt that it was correct that Harris had been given the honour of the first "over-all" showing the "evolution of one Canadian in art." He spoke of the "spectacular-ectoplasmic boreal scenes . . . idiomatic expressionisms of an inner mentality, with a positive genius for interpreted color-graphs; magnificent dreams of semi-abstraction in color, textures, form, and always that exquisite color-

---

* In the 1950s, Harris painted landscapes from earlier sketches, such as the Algoma painting on Masonite at the Winnipeg Art Gallery. Some Arctic canvases were undertaken after Harris had begun to concentrate on abstracts.

Harris also routinely repainted earlier canvases by himself that remained in his possession. As well, while in Vancouver, for example, if he had lent or given a painting to Peggie or Howie, he would sometimes borrow it back if he did not like something in it. He would then rework a passage or two before returning the canvas.

sensitivity. The more abstractionized design-scenes in the east room are the apex."

Another visitor, Northrop Frye, a colleague of John Robins at Victoria College and a masterful expositor of archetypal criticism, was mesmerized by what he saw in the east room:

> When we enter the "abstract" room we are conscious first of all of a great release of power. The painter has come home;

Lawren Harris.
*Abstract
(War Painting). Circa
1943.*

his forms have been emancipated, and the exuberance of their swirling and plunging lines takes one's breath away . . .

But they are pictures and not cryptograms, and have no single explanation or key, just as music can suggest any number of emotions or ideas without being programme music. With interpretation or without it, Lawren Harris's best abstractions are a unique and major contribution to Canadian painting.[35]

20
BEYOND
ABSTRACTION
(1949–1970)

He was often very frail in body; he could not concentrate the way he used to. He told himself, you're getting old. Happens to everybody. Nothing much to be done. He decided to muddle through.

Trying to make a virtue of necessity, he cagily wondered if there was any way old age would allow him to move in yet another new direction.

I am not myself anymore, he muttered. Some days he no longer envisioned bright, blinding colours. Rather, he saw them. In fact, they had become part of him.

I N VANCOUVER, Harris's time was more sharply divided than before. He spent a large amount of time in administrative tasks. For example, he was appointed in 1950 to the board of trustees of the National Gallery and would attend meetings in Ottawa twice a year until 1961.

During Harris's years as a trustee, the directors were Harry McCurry, Alan Jarvis and Charles Comfort. Jarvis shared Harris's vision of a National Gallery without walls, that is, an institution with many locations throughout Canada. (This goal had been the central mandate during Harris's presidency of the Canadian Group of Painters.) In 1956, when the trustees reaffirmed the gallery's policy of not purchasing American abstract art, Harris may have experienced some trepidation; however, his nationalist sentiments allowed him to vote in favour of this decision.

In 1959, Harris publicly aired his discontent with the governing Progressive Conservatives' indifference to the arts when he condemned them and openly supported the policies of the Liberal Party. He told the *Toronto Daily Star* that the Tories "have never shown any interest whatsoever in art." However, he had decided not to follow the lead of others and resign: "I am staying on until they kick me off. Every person who resigns leaves a place open for a government appointee, and I don't intend to resign." Harris was enraged by the government's "welching" on the purchase of two European masterworks for $440,000. After allowing Jarvis and the trustees to enter into serious negotiations with a New York dealer, the government reversed its decision. "This was a mistake," declared Harris. "It gives this country a bad reputation with art dealers all over the world. They will be more careful in future in dealing with us."[1]

Harris was the first artist to serve on this board. Among other responsibilities, he administered the Emily Carr Trust, which provided scholarships for young artists; he wrote letters of reference for many other artists. The remainder of his time was devoted to sketching and painting. This procedure is different from his Group of Seven years, in that he had once been a propagandist for his own art and that of the members of the Group; in Vancouver, he was a famous artist who was quite willing to come to the assistance of other artists of all persuasions to boost their careers.

Katherine Dreier got back in touch. Years before, Harris had given two sketches to Société Anonyme. In June 1949, she was completing the catalogue of the SA collection, which had been given to Yale in 1941. Perhaps he wanted to be represented by a "more important" work. She pointed out: "It seems a pity not to be better represented than just by those sketches, though they are interesting."[2] She had a fond memory of *Miners' Houses*. Might it be available? Harris offered to donate either a Canadian land-scape or an abstraction, with the proviso that the sketches be returned. She chose *Abstract No. 3*.

The artist John Koerner (b. 1913), who became a good friend of Harris's, noticed something else:

> It was widely reported at the time [forties, fifties and sixties] and has since been repeated as gospel that Lawren was deeply involved in Theosophy. This simply was not the case. His interest had been satisfied while he was in New Mexico in the 1940s, and by the time he moved to Vancouver he had long since relinquished any ties with Theosophy . . . However, after he left Theosophy behind, his abstract style showed he maintained a strong belief in the spiritual sphere of life.[3]

Koerner is correct. A strong sense of spirituality informed the latter part of Harris's life, but after the crisis of 1934 the influence of theosophy gradually evaporated. If Harris had been doctrinaire in the 1930s, he abandoned that stance. He did retain a strong admiration for Eastern religious traditions, as can be seen in a late canvas of 1962, which he named *Atma Buddhi Manas*.[4] However, in a 1948 interview he observed,

> Theosophy provided a temporary balm for my troubles at a time. It never impacted directly upon my work. I was affected only by the material that lay before me, although my relationship to the same theme could change from sketch to sketch. I painted snow caps white because they were white and skies blue because they were blue. My palette differs between the Algoma period and my Arctic sketches because what lay before me was totally different. Madame Blavatsky did not paint my pictures.[5]

Harris remained an excellent salesperson for the work of other artists, some of whose canvases were always on display in his home. If a young collector came to see him to buy a picture, he offered advice: "You're not ready for me." When the collector asked how

to get ready, Harris would recommend the purchase of a painting by one of the young Vancouver artists (Alistair Bell, Gordon
Smith, Takao Tanabe). The collector would do this and eventually come back. "Am I ready now?" Yes, Harris would answer, and
then sell one of his canvases for $200 that would usually have gone
for $800 (although the collector would not be aware of this at the
time). Harris was helping to develop the taste of the collector at
the same time as he was assisting young artists.[6] Gordon Smith
had fond memories of time spent with Harris. He found the older
man completely open to all the new movements in art, but he
noticed that Harris never liked to engage in small talk; if Harris encountered someone he considered foolish, he would simply
clam up.

He still liked to engage in scrapes, as he told a friend:

The critics—Gawd bless 'em and teach 'em a little humility. In practically every instance they are much less intelligent than the artists—so what to do. I do *not* favour ignoring
them, which leaves them free, much too free to vent their
notions and frequently, too frequently, mislead the public.
Whenever any one of them makes a glaring mistake in judgment I favour [him with] a reply, spoof 'em, explain where
they [went] wrong & why. The Group of 7 did this in its early
days as you know and the results were very much worthwhile.
We'll only get better and more intelligent critics if we show
up the poor ones.[7]

When R.H. Hubbard from the National Gallery visited Harris in Vancouver in 1955, he saw a seventy-year-old man still resolutely dedicated to his craft:

In the large living-room which is also his studio he paints
beside a great window looking towards the mountains. I saw
several of his free compositions in the making, that is to say at
a stage when he could still turn them on their sides or upside-
down with impunity and discuss with his friends which way
he would continue to develop them. This he did with a com-

position of rarified yellows in flowing rhythms, which was his latest work. Among those which were "finished" I was struck by the great number of variations possible in the gamut between natural forms and complete abstraction.[8]

The home life of the Harrises retained its quiet refinement and comforts. Zealously, Bess worked on this, as she told Doris: "The house is run for Lawren and his work primarily—. I could not be comfortable—with my philosophy doing anything less—also the female in me likes to please."[9] Their home's outlook was, Bess told Raymond Jonson, "incredibly beautiful." The garden "[is] a labour of love and has a great variety of texture and form—So many things will grow in this part of the world—hot weather things such as camellias and rhododendrons—magnolias—and the range of form and color in the evergreens is quite fantastic."[10]

Lawren Harris and Peggie Knox.

Lawren Harris circa 1948–50.

Harris certainly liked his home, as Bess recalled: "From the moment we leave Vancouver, Lawren's great urge is to be back again!—Which of course is a very happy condition for work and living."[11] Harris had a set routine: He was at his easel for three hours, from 10:30 to 1:30. After lunch, he did garden chores or took a walk, and then worked for another hour in the afternoon. After dinner, Lawren and Bess discussed his work of that day, "what has taken place—the pros and cons of colour and composition."[12] In 1949, the Harrises added a studio window to their living room, incorporating a veranda ten feet wide and twenty-five feet long. "What used to be a long narrowish room now flows out into a fine curve towards the sea," Bess told Doris. "As we are quite above the water—there is the delightful illusion of being in a ship's lounge and one is just about to move out to sea."[13]

The Harrises were devoted to each other, but there was a ruthlessness to Bess in the maintenance of calm and order. Since she handled all financial transactions, Bess could exert a great deal of control over her husband's business affairs. She did so in personal matters as well. When a Toronto friend of long standing, a woman who had stood by Trixie in 1934, attempted to see Lawren, Bess blocked access by telling her that he was unavailable. Harris was furious when he discovered his wife's behind-his-back machinations.[14]

Bess's own sister once claimed that she liked to play the role of Lady Bountiful. If a family friend gave Bess a gift she did not like, she would simply hand it back as unacceptable. There was the afternoon someone asked if she would like a cup of tea and she huffily replied: "Tea in the afternoon is *never* a good idea!" When Lawren was about to give one of his granddaughters a wedding gift of $1,000 in hundred-dollar bills, he was surprised to find that one of the bills was not in the envelope. Bess, who had obviously felt the gift was too substantial and had removed the money, was nonchalant.[15]

Lawren kept in close touch with Lornie. He and his wife, Elizabeth (née Hammond), saw Trixie on a regular basis until she died in 1962. When the couple were living in Sackville, New Brunswick, where he taught at Mount Allison, Trixie would often take the train from Toronto to Nova Scotia to stay with the Harrises and their two daughters (Gillian, later Godfrey, and Susan, later Richie) and son (Scott). Lawren and Lornie, who became a distinguished painter in his own right, always remained on excellent terms and often saw each other when Harris travelled east. Peggie married Barton Sheppard; with him, she had two children,

Toni Ann (later Chowne) and Stewart. After she and Barton were divorced, Peggie married James Knox, settled in Vancouver, and saw her father and Bess frequently. All five grandchildren have vivid memories of the card and sleight-of-hand tricks that Lawren would gleefully perform for them.

Howie, a graphic designer, who also settled in Vancouver, married three times and often quarrelled with his father. Towards the end of his life Lawren even denied Howie entrance to Belmont Avenue.

One visitor to Belmont Avenue in the sixties was the young curator Dennis Reid. The door was opened for him by a Chinese houseboy.[16] Bess greeted Reid warmly and took him into the sitting room, where Lawren walked towards him to take his hand. The young man was impressed with the halo of white hair surrounding Harris's face and by the older man's serene, otherworldly manner; he felt that he was meeting someone who lived in a realm of consciousness far beyond ordinary human reality.[17]

The houseboys were live-in help who served meals and cleaned. One of them, Leon Tuey, who became a distinguished stock market analyst, remembered the disciplined regime followed by Harris. After breakfast, he would answer letters, go for a walk, and then paint; after lunch, he would take a nap and then paint again.

In those days, Harris had discarded working in suit and tie; he would be immaculately dressed in a white shirt, the top button undone, and dress pants. He refused to place a plastic sheet on the white rug on the floor of that portion of the living room in which he worked, but no drop of paint ever reached the carpet. A visitor to Belmont Avenue could often smell the oil paints; Gordon Smith recalled the pieces of corrugated cardboard that were placed on a side table to hold securely paints and brushes so that they did not tumble to the floor.

Harris's charm and elegance were genuine, but so was his rigidity at times in the realm of art politics. One of the most welcoming of the local critics in 1941 had been the painter Mildred Valley Thornton, the representational artist who had responded warmly to the Harris one-man show. In 1951, she was outraged

Lawren Harris on Belmont Avenue with two of his abstract canvases.

by the actions of the selection committee: "A clique in the Vancouver Art Gallery is ministering to the vanity of a small minority of abstract artists. This is dictatorship of the most insidious kind. The sooner these disruptive influences are eliminated from the gallery the better for art in British Columbia."[18]

Thornton did not hurl an accusation directly at Harris, but he was her target. Harris was dismissive: "Nothing could be more ridiculous. The most vital among our young people are falling into the new idiom of painting because it excites them. We choose our paintings to cover the widest possible range of art activity." Not satisfied, Thornton shot back: "There is no balance between extreme distortion and musty decadence. Acquiescent juries with no moral fortitude of their own are simply clay in the hands of the potter." One of her supporters joined in: "One man is directing art in British Columbia. If you're not on the bandwagon, you don't stand much of a chance." The gallery defended Harris by stating that 1,500 members had elected him. The "potter" replied: "It's inescapable that direction eventually settles on one or two individuals. But the inference that I run the exhibition committee is ridiculous. In at least half the cases, the other members do not agree with me."[19]

Bess was a bit nostalgic about this spat, which she saw as "quite like the old Group of Seven controversy—and has its useful as well as its foolish side."

In the 1950s, Harris's conception of what was good abstract art moved in the direction of the Abstract Expressionists in the United States, particularly the work of Mark Rothko:

Lawren Harris in old age.

> But the recent expansion of abstract painting into the realm of Abstract Expressionism has inevitably led the artists to employ many different styles and invent new ones to accommodate the great increase in expressive and vital visual ideas. In other words, Abstract Expressionism is not a style like impressionism, cubism, magic realism or geometrical abstract painting. It is a new realm in which the imagination is released into an illimitable range of new subjects and has already created a number of new styles and will create many more.[20]

Harris certainly had the opportunity to see a great deal of Abstract Expressionist works when he was in Manhattan in the springs of both 1947 and 1948, the fall of 1948, and in 1950 and 1952.

Rothko, Pollock, Kline, de Kooning and the other members of this movement emphasized the release, in various ways, of the character of the painter onto the canvas. They rejected objectivity in favour of subjectivity; they insisted on leaving behind traces of the personality of the creator. Such artists also favoured what is often referred to as gestural painting: sweeping brush strokes and intense passages that proclaim the creator's individuality. Such artists are, in their own distinct way, Whitmanesque in singing the truths of their souls.

In 1954, Harris was also a bit more open about the effectiveness of surrealism:

> Surrealism is automatic painting, wherein the whole process comes from and is controlled by the unconscious. Whereas the process of abstract painting is a creative interplay between the conscious and the unconscious with the conscious mind making all the final decisions and in control throughout. This leads to quite different results in that it draws upon the full powers of the practitioner and therefore contains a much fuller range of communication and significance.[21]

Harris still disdained the complete relinquishment of control to the unconscious, but he had become slightly more welcoming of the unconscious as a factor in creativity.

Ten years earlier, in 1943, the American artist and psychoanalyst Grace Pailthorpe (1883–1971) had visited Vancouver, where she espoused automatism (what Harris called automatic painting). She influenced Macdonald, Harris less so. However, in the fifties Harris began to experiment with "automatic drawing," whereby he sometimes allowed his pencil to be moved by a superior power.*

Harris's new thinking about abstract art led to canvases that express his versions of Abstract Expressionism. For example, in *Northern Image* (c. 1952), Harris has begun to impose himself into the texture of his painting in ways that previously evaded him. He does not need any kind of representational borders; he works with transparency in a new, heightened fashion; his colours employ a full palette. The spirit of exuberance is palpable.

---

* In about 1944, in a talk entitled "The ABC of Abstract Painting," Harris discussed the emotional values in certain shapes, and then demonstrated how these various shapes and lines could be put together in an abstract painting.

Lawren Harris.
Untitled. Circa 1952.

Lawren Harris.
Abstraction No. 74.
Circa 1950.

In Hanover, in Santa Fe, and during his early years in Vancouver, Harris had worked largely in styles of painting that blend representation with abstraction. Now he moved in the direction

Lawren Harris.
Painting. 1958.

Lawren Harris.
Painting. 1958–62.

of release, of pure abstract form. Perhaps he could only do this after the 1948 retrospective, after his career up to that point had been enshrined. That done, he could move on to another new adventure.

In addition to tiring cross-country train trips to Ottawa and Toronto, Harris returned to Europe twice in the fifties (his first visits there since the one with Trixie in 1930). In March and April 1956, Lawren and Bess went by way of the Italian Line from New York. They arrived in Lisbon and then sailed on to Italy, where they visited Florence, Assisi, Siena, Genoa, Naples, Rome and Arezzo. Two weeks were spent at Revello in the hills above Amalfi so that Lawren could climb. Bess, who had never been to Europe and was restored to full health after the removal of her gall bladder the previous year, told Yvonne Housser: "Florence was like living Poetry to me, though when I say Florence I am thinking of the Umbrian countryside."[22] Upon their return to Vancouver, Bess remarked to the same friend: "Lawren has been working steadily ever since we returned from Italy, not that he did not before—but it seems to me there is a fresh creative wave up his beach.—Things just 'come off'.—without too much prodding."[23]

Three years later, the couple sailed on a Holland-American passenger freighter to England by way of the Panama Canal. They then went to the Continent and returned to New York on the *Andrea Doria*, the last completed westbound voyage of that vessel.

By 1953, concern for Bess's health had led the couple to abandon their annual treks in the Rockies. They substituted those trips with motoring holidays to Tucson, Arizona, in 1953 and 1954 and Yuma, Arizona, in 1955.

In between his two trips to Europe, on April 10, 1958, Harris was operated on for an aneurism of the aorta. He recovered well but slowly, as the seventy-three-year-old told A.Y. Jackson on the eighth of May: "Yep, had a very serious operation and came through it remarkable well . . . I bust[ed] all records, walked out of the hospital on the 12th day after the operation. I have been home two weeks and though up all day and taking short walks I find it slow going toward a complete recovery." He found it difficult to work but felt that he was entering yet another new, creative period. Physically, though, he never completely recovered.

He kept himself busy organizing exhibitions of his own work and that of others. He selected the British Columbia entries for the CNE that August, including five of his own abstractions. The following month he attended the CGP show held at the Vancouver Art Gallery; he exhibited two paintings. He arranged a show of some of his abstract paintings (and Group of Seven sketches) at the Laing Galleries in Toronto.*

When the National Gallery mounted its Harris retrospective in 1963, he was too ill to attend the opening on June 6, but

---

* In January 1960, there was another exhibition at the Laing Galleries in Toronto; the Dominion Gallery in Montreal purchased a number of his 1957–58 abstractions; he consigned some other canvases to the Roberts Gallery in Toronto. He showed a canvas with the BCFSA and at the CGP exhibition in Montreal in 1960. He had another exhibition of abstracts at the Art Gallery of Greater Victoria in October 1961, and he showed a large painting at the VAG that November.

Lawren Harris.
Untitled Abstraction P.
Circa 1968.

he was able to travel to Ottawa later in the month to view it.

In 1964, he had another major heart problem, a coronary. As Bess told a friend: "Early in August Lawren was very ill—it was a coronary.—He was in the Hospital for a month. The first half of that month was not easy—Then home and nurses for another month.—He has made an excellent recovery—and we are blessed—and we know it."

He was hospitalized again for a month in the autumn of 1966 but was able to travel to Ottawa for the Three Hundred Years of Canadian Art exhibition in June 1967. He claimed that he really made the trip in order to see Canada once again. Back home, he was content to walk a mile every day no matter what the weather.

When he was well enough, Harris continued to paint. He worked with Bess on a book about him that she was co-editing with R.G.P. Colgrove. The resulting volume contains a series of colour reproductions of Harris's work interspersed with selections from his writings. Painstakingly done, the book deftly emphasizes Harris's enormous dexterity in talking about art at the same time as the reader is invited to glance at splendid examples of his skills as a painter. Words and images are organized almost musically (and chronologically), like a series of meditations. The emphasis may be on the abstracts, but images from Harris's entire career are on view. As a piece of influence making, it is a wonderfully crafted form of spiritual autobiography in which the artist summarizes the truths revealed to him.

Lawren Harris.
Untitled.
Circa 1970.

Although Bess had seen herself as Lawren's caretaker, her life ended first. In September 1969, she was hospitalized and died of an aneurism of the aorta. She saw a copy of *Lawren Harris* two days before she was taken ill. In his last months, the dementia from which Harris was now suffering became more pronounced. He frequently stayed in his bedroom, often watching hockey games with the sound blaring. He listened every day to his recording of Rossini's *Stabat Mater*. His daughter, Peggie, sometimes held him up so that he could paint, as she recalled.

> He would sit looking north to the mountains and then at the half finished painting on the easel—and call for help. I would help him over to the painting and stand behind him with my arms around his waist, feet braced, while he leaned over the palette table trying to mix and paint, forgetting he was being held upright, until I was ready to drop with fatigue. Finally he'd put the brush down and let me take him back to his chair, often to find that what he had just done, he did not like at all.[24]

He died four months after Bess on January 29, 1970.

In his final paintings, Harris moved completely into the realms of abstraction. For years, although he was never able to articulate it fully, what Harris had pined for was a way of painting in which he could stamp his own mark irrevocably into a canvas. He wanted to *impose* his vision *and* his personality. He had been successful in this regard, but not according to his own exacting standards.

As a child, Lawren had endured the death of his father. That loss made him suspicious of the tangible world. He placed his reliance on art because in that pursuit he could find a sense of emotional surety. Then he suffered the losses of his brother and of Tom Thomson. He retreated more and more into his exploration of spiritual realities. Having achieved a breakthrough in his work as an artist, he realized that he had in his marriage allowed himself to be entrapped in material security. Slowly but surely he righted himself by changing his entire way of life. He divorced and remarried. At the very same time, he rejected the landscape style that had made him famous. He had no other choice but to explore the spiritual realities that he found in abstraction. For a time he became a wanderer before settling in Vancouver, where he continued his relentless journey into the innermost regions of his soul.

This journey can be described in a slightly different way. As a young man, Harris had marvelled at how successfully an artist such as Caspar David Friedrich had imposed his vision of a spiritual world into landscape. Throughout much of his own career in that genre, Harris emulated that predecessor. In the middle thirties, when he could no longer do this, he tried to infuse transcendental values into his abstracts. Those efforts brought him great pleasure, but he remained convinced that he could enter even further and deeper into the divine. In this regard, the spare, haunting abstracts of Mark Rothko inspired him.

Harris would have fully agreed with Rothko's passionate defence of the spirituality inhabiting his canvases:

I am not interested in relationships of color or form or anything else . . . I am interested only in expressing the basic human emotions—tragedy, ecstasy, doom, and so on—and the fact that lots of people break down and cry when confronted with my pictures shows that I *communicate* with those basic human emotions. The people who weep before my pictures are having the same religious experience I had when I painted them. And if you . . . are moved only by their color relationships, then you miss the point![25]

Harris's final canvases are filled with dense patches of pure, sensuous colour. Their feeling resides completely on the surface. They embrace life simply, vigorously and wholeheartedly. Harris found a way to insert himself fully—his complete subjectivity—into these last triumphant works. In so doing, he won his final race against time. In these canvases, he created the perfect talismans to prepare himself to enter a new terrain, the landscape of death. His journey had been a long and at times precarious one, but he had finally reached his destination.

MANUSCRIPT SOURCES
AND SHORT TITLES

ARCHIVES

Archives, National Gallery of Canada, Ottawa. Short title: ANG
Various correspondence, including Bess Harris to J. Russell Harper;
Lawren Harris to Eric Brown; Lawren Harris to the National Gallery
while he was a member of the Board of Trustees.

Art Gallery of Ontario Archives. Short title: AGO
This holding includes a 32-page questionnaire completed by Harris;
the Bess Harris–Doris Speirs correspondence; and a letter from Lawren Harris to the AGT exhibition committee (1927).

Beinecke Library, Yale. Short title: Yale
Correspondence between Katherine Dreier and Lawren Harris.

Special Collections, Dartmouth College Library, Hanover. Short
title: Dartmouth
Correspondence between Lawren and Bess Harris and Clyde and
Betty Danker; Bess Harris interview with Churchill P. Lathrop.

Library and Archives Canada, Ottawa. Short title: LAC
The Lawren Harris *fonds* includes letters to Lawren Harris, his notebooks from *c.* 1910 to 1954 and the manuscripts of various essays. There
are letters from Harris to people such as Carl Schaefer and, especially,

Emily Carr. (LAC has copies of the letters from Harris; the holographs are in the British Columbia archives.) By agreement with Carr, Lawren Harris destroyed all her letters to him.

McMichael Collection of Canadian Art. Short title: McMichael
A series of letters from Lawren Harris to J.E.H. MacDonald.

Queen's University. Short title: Queen's
Isabel McLaughlin correspondence.

Raymond Jonson Collection, University of New Mexico. Short title: NM
Correspondence between Lawren Harris and Raymond Jonson; plus letters to Jonson from various researchers asking about his friendship with Lawren Harris.

Special Collections, E.J. Pratt Library, Victoria University, University of Toronto. Short title: Victoria
Yvonne McKague Housser correspondence.

Thomas Fisher Library, University of Toronto. Short title: Fisher
Doris Mills Speirs correspondence.

BOOKS

The limited-edition version of Robert Fulford and Joan Murray's *The Beginning of Vision* contains Margaret Knox's "Personal Reminiscences" of her father (see Bibliography). This account is nine pages long. Short title: Knox

For ease of reference, the following books have been given short titles; full bibliographical references are in the Selected Bibliography, beginning on page 335.

Emily Carr, *Hundreds and Thousands*: Hundreds
Lawren Harris, "The Story of the Group of Seven": Story
Charles C. Hill, *The Group of Seven: Art for a Nation*: Hill
F.B. Housser, *A Canadian Art Movement*: Housser
A.Y. Jackson, *A Painter's Country*: Jackson
Peter Larisey, *Light for a Cold Land*: Larisey

NOTES

In the notes and index, Lawren Harris is referred to as LH.

CHAPTER ONE: EARLY JOYS AND SORROWS (1885–1894)

1. Knox, 222.
2. Ibid.
3. Ibid.
4. Ibid.
5. *The Canadian Album: Men of Canada; Success by Example . . .* (Brantford: Bradley, Garreton & Co., 1891), 254.
6. Ibid.
7. As cited in Shannon Stewart, *Berea College: An Illustrated History* (Lexington: University Press of Kentucky, 2006), 59.
8. *The Canadian Album: Men of Canada; Success by Example . . .* (Brantford: Bradley, Garreton & Co., 1891), 254.
9. Much earlier, in the seventeenth century, the Attawandaron (or Neutral Nation) occupied the valley area on the Grand River. The main village of their chief, Kandoucho, was located in what is now the city of Brantford. In 1784, Captain Joseph Brant and the Six Nations Indians left New York State for Canada. As a reward for their loyalty to the British Crown, they were given a large land grant called the Haldimand Tract on the Grand. This settlement was on the south edge of the city because it was an ideal location for landing canoes.

By 1847, Europeans were settling farther up the river, and named their village Brantford (Brant's Ford).

10. Housser, 34.

11. Knox, 222–23. In 1884, Pauline Johnson moved to 7 Napoleon Street (now Dufferin Avenue). Johnson's house on Dufferin backed onto Brant and thus provided the brothers with the opportunity to attack her laundry.

12. Ibid., 222.

13. Ibid.

14. Ibid., 223.

15. "Memorial of T.M. Harris," *Brantford Expositor*, August 31, 1894. 3–4.

16. Ibid., 16.

17. Notebook [1954], file 4-2, MG30, D208, vol. 4. LAC.

CHAPTER TWO: YOUTHFUL AMBITION (1894–1903)

1. Knox, 223.

2. Bess Harris to J. Russell Harper, July 14, 1962. ANG.

3. Knox, 224.

4. Ibid.

5. Ibid.

6. Housser, 34–35.

7. In addition to serving as Dean of Arts at the University of Toronto and president of the Arts and Letters Club in Toronto, the Canadian-born DeLury was an avid collector of works of the Irish literary revival, and was a correspondent of many of its members, including W.B. Yeats, George Russell and Lennox Robertson.

CHAPTER THREE: THE ARTIST AS A YOUNG OBSERVER (1904–1908)

1. Bess Harris to J. Russell Harper, July 14, 1962. ANG.

2. Charles W. Haxthausen, "'A New Beauty': Ernst Ludwig Kirchner's Images of Berlin," in Charles W. Haxthausen and Suhr Heidrum, *Berlin: Culture and Metropolis* (Minneapolis: University of Minnesota Press, 1991), 59.

3. As cited in Paret, 25.

4. Ibid., 27.

5. Ibid., 83.

6. Lawren Harris to Sydney Key, May 8, 1948. AGO.
7. Larisey, 8.
8. In his landmark study *Modern Painting and the Northern Romantic Tradition, Friedrich to Rothko*, Robert Rosenblum demonstrates convincingly that there is an alternate history within Modernism wherein strong spiritual values were infused into various genres, particularly landscape.
9. Duncan, 651, 661.
10. Ibid., 790.
11. Ibid., 524–25.
12. Information from Stewart Sheppard and Toni Chowne.

CHAPTER FOUR: SPIRITUAL REALITIES (1909–1910)

1. Housser, 37.
2. Lawren Harris to Sydney Key, May 8, 1948. AGO.
3. Quoted by Reid, *A Concise History*, 135.
4. *Memory's Wall: The Autobiography of Flora McCrea Eaton* (Toronto: Clarke, Irwin, 1956).
5. Housser, 35.
6. "Notes On Pictures at the Ontario Society of Artists Exhibition." All artists who had works on display were invited to comment on their work.
7. Bess Harris to Russell Harper, July 14, 1962. ANG.
8. Bridle, 21–22.
9. Roy Mitchell, "Motion and the Actor," in *Yearbook of the Arts in Canada, 1928–9* (Toronto: Macmillan, 1929), 191.
10. Ibid., 193.
11. In the autumn of 1918, while visiting Vancouver, Mitchell came upon a chest containing six viols for sale for $1,500 by an antiques dealer. Mitchell approached seven friends at the Arts and Letters Club, including Harris, MacCallum and Vincent Massey, to co-purchase this treasure trove. These musical instruments were eventually given to Hart House at the University of Toronto.
12. Cited in Davis, *Logic of Ecstasy*, 114. On March 19, 1924, Harris became "affiliated to" the Toronto Theosophical Society, but he had been a "member at large" of the International Theosophical Society well before that. In February 1922 and in January 1923, Harris was a member of the Toronto branch's Decorating Committee.

CHAPTER FIVE: NEW ADVENTURES (1911–1914)

1. "Points about Pictures: What is Canadian Art Doing for Canada?" *Canadian Courier* IX, no. 21 (April 22, 1911).
2. Duval lists these possible sources in *Lawren Harris*, 32, 34.
3. "Heming's Black and White," *Lamps* I (October 1911).
4. "Canadian Art," *Canadian Theosophist* 5, no. 12 (February 15, 1925): 179.
5. "Creative Art and Canada," in *Yearbook of the Arts in Canada, 1928–1929*, ed. Bertram Brooker (Toronto: MacMillan, 1929), 182.
6. "MacDonald's Sketches," *Lamps* (December 1911): 12.
7. "The Group of Seven," talk delivered at the Vancouver Art Gallery, April 1954. LAC.
8. As cited by Harris in *Canadian Bookman* 6, no. 2 (February 1924): 38.
9. *Leaves of Grass* (New York: Dunlap, 1971), 111.
10. *Notes on Pictures at the O.S.A. Exhibition* [1911].
11. Cottaging in the Go Home Bay area began in 1898 when the Madawaska Club was formed by a group associated with the University of Toronto who were interested in combining scientific research with recreation. The name was chosen because they originally hoped to acquire land along the Madawaska River south of Algonquin Park. Early activities focused around a clubhouse and research station, but over the next few decades members spread out and established private cottages, many of which still exist. For almost a hundred years, cottaging in the Go Home Bay area was restricted to people associated with the University of Toronto under the terms of the original charter, but that restriction has been lifted.
12. The land on which the Studio Building was constructed was purchased from Edward Dodington (the original Crown patent for this parcel of land dates to 1796; it was granted to George Playter, a United Empire Loyalist). The land was purchased for $4,793.75, but the mortgage taken out by Harris was for $10,000 (presumably to include the actual construction of the Studio Building).
13. *Lawren Harris, Paintings 1910–1948*, 8.
14. "The Federal Art Commission," *Globe* (Toronto), June 4, 1914.
15. The house had been built by D'Arcy Boulton in his park lot. The reign of the Boultons ended in 1875 when William Boulton's widow married Professor Goldwin Smith, formerly of Oxford and Cornell. Smith then became known as "The Sage of the Grange."
16. "The National Art Gallery of Canada," *Globe* (Toronto), May 4, 1912.
17. Ibid.

18. ANG.
19. Harris, "The Group of Seven in Canadian History," 31.
20. "Scandinavian Art," Public Lecture, Art Gallery of Toronto, April 17, 1931. Typescript, AGO.
21. *Exhibition of Contemporary Scandinavian Art* (Buffalo: Albright, 1913), 58.
22. "Landscape Art in Canada," in *Art of the British Empire Overseas* (London, Paris and New York: Studio Limited, 1917), 7.
23. "Tendencies in Art," *Lamps* I, no. 2 (December 1911): 16.
24. C.W. Jefferys, ["The Toronto Art Students' League"], untitled, undated holograph MS of *c.* 1944 lecture, AGO.
25. Unsent letter to Housser of December 10, 1926. McMichael.
26. Jackson, 11.
27. Harris, "The Story of the Group of Seven," 27.

CHAPTER SIX: CAMARADERIE (1913–1916)

1. As cited by Duval, *The Tangled Garden*, 24.
2. Ibid., 23.
3. Quoted by McKay, 191.
4. Housser, 32.
5. Ibid., 85–6.
6. Wayne Larsen, *A.Y. Jackson, the Life of a Landscape Painter* (Toronto: Dundurn, 2009) 56.
7. *Toronto Star*, December 12, 1913.
8. *Toronto Star*, December 18, 1913.
9. "Arting Among the Artists," *Saturday Night* XXIX, no. 26 (April 8, 1916): 5.
10. A.Y. Jackson, "Lawren Harris, A Biographical Sketch," in *Lawren Harris, Paintings, 1910–1948,* 9.
11. LH to Emily Carr, March 20, 1932. ANG.
12. Story, 28.
13. MacCallum to A.L. Beatty, May 14, 1937. AGO.
14. Story, 28.
15. Story, 27.
16. Allandale is now part of Barrie.
17. To Ethel Varley, May 16, 1914. Quoted in Reid, *The Group of Seven*, 66.
18. At the University of Toronto, he was a member of Delta Kappa Epsilon; after university, he joined the Banker's Bond Company and was a lieutenant in the Forty-eighth Highlanders of Canada.
19. Wilson, ed., lxxiii.

20. Ibid., lxxii.
21. Ibid., xlix.
22. "The Arts and the War," *Maclean's*, February 1916.
23. March 16, 1916.
24. "Pictures That Can Be Heard: A Survey of the Ontario Society of Artists' Exhibition," *Saturday Night* XXIV, no. 26 (March 18, 1916).

CHAPTER SEVEN: PARADISE LOST, PARADISE REGAINED (1917–1919)

1. "Good Pictures at O.S.A. Exhibition," *Saturday Night* XXX, no. 24 (March 24, 1917): 2.
2. "In the Garden and at the Station," *Weekly Sun* (Toronto), March 26, 1919.
3. "O.S.A. Exhibition a Brilliant Show," *Toronto Sunday World* [1919].
4. Blodwen Davies, *Paddle and Palette: The Story of Tom Thomson* (Toronto: Ryerson, 1930), 123.
5. Story, 28.
6. Ibid.
7. Lawren Harris to MacDonald. Undated. McMichael.
8. Ibid.
9. Housser (136–37) avoids any discussion of the loss of Howard Harris and Tom Thomson by stating that Harris's sense of idealism was punctured by the war: "In him the national spirit of the day provoked a desire to express what he felt about the country in a more creative and magnificent communion than a communion of war. It must be on a grander scale than anything hitherto attempted, heroic enough to stir the national pulse when the stimulus of struggle had been withdrawn. He became nervous and unstrung under the discipline of the machine. His health gave out. In 1917 he received his discharge from the army."
10. Housser, 138.
11. Undated letter from LH to MacDonald. McMichael.
12. As quoted by Duval in *Tangled Garden*, 86–87.
13. Story, 29.

CHAPTER EIGHT: ASCENDING (1918–1921)

1. LH to MacDonald. Undated. McMichael.
2. Ibid.
3. Ibid.

4. Knox, 228.
5. Information from Stewart Sheppard and Toni Chowne.
6. ANG.
7. LH to Katherine Dreier. Undated but 1926. MS Yale.
8. "The Drama of the Ward," *Canadian Magazine* XXXIV, no. 1 (November 1909): 6.
9. "Noisy Chaos of Colour in O.S.A. Exhibition," *Telegram* (Toronto), March 8, 1919.

CHAPTER NINE: CONFEDERATES (1919–1922)

1. "[Works Rejected] Action Criticized," *Toronto Star*, March 26, 1919.
2. "Noisy Chaos of Colour in O.S.A. Exhibition," *Telegram* (Toronto), March 8, 1919.
3. *Toronto Daily Star*, May 3, 1919.
4. "The New Canadian Art," *Mail and Empire* (Toronto), May 10, 1919.
5. J.E.H. MacDonald, "A.C.R. 10577," *Lamps* (December 1919): 35.
6. A.Y. Jackson, 46.
7. "The Group of Seven in Canadian History," 34.
8. MacDonald, "A.C.R. 10577," *Lamps* (December 1919): 37.
9. "New and Interesting Pictures on View," *Toronto Daily Star*, May 10, 1920.
10. "Are These New Canadian-Canadian Painters Crazy?" *Canadian Courier* XXV, no. 17 (May 22, 1920).
11. Hundreds, 28.
12. For example, she reviewed the fourth Group of Seven show in the *Canadian Bookman* in February 1925: "Canada is an entity with a spiritual form drawn from the significant character of her environment." In that piece she was somewhat hesitant about MacDonald's accomplishment: he "has found in the mountains a playground for his great feeling for design. There his real interest seems to have stopped and the colour has the effect of being filled in."
13. Larisey, 118.
14. *Toronto Daily Star*, August 30, 1920.
15. Ibid.
16. F.W. Coburn, *Boston Herald*, December 19, 1920.
17. *Buffalo Evening News*, September 28, 1921.
18. *Edmonton Journal*, April 2, 1921.
19. King, 351.
20. *Canadian Forum*, December 1920.
21. "Some Canadian Painters: Lawren Harris," 278.

22. Charles C. Hill, interview with Doris Huestis Speirs. Canadian-art1930.gallery.ca.
23. Ibid.
24. *"Contrasts* by Lawren Harris," 120, 122.
25. *Essays: First and Second Series* (New York: Crowell, 1926), 93.
26. *Contrasts,* 11.
27. Ibid., 31.
28. Ibid., 45.
29. "Some Canadian Painters: Lawren Harris."
30. "Unusual Art Cult Breaks Loose Again," *Toronto Daily Star,* May 7, 1921.
31. "Pictures of the Group of Seven Show 'Art Must Take the Road,'" *Toronto Daily Star,* May 20, 1922.

CHAPTER TEN: BREAKTHROUGH (1921–1924)

1. A.Y. Jackson, 58.
2. Ibid.
3. Ibid.
4. Ibid., 57.
5. Undated letter to his wife, quoted in Hunter, *J.E.H. MacDonald,* 21.
6. "The Group of Seven in Canadian History," op. cit. 34.
7. Harris's landscapes deliberately eschew Christian symbolism, but it is possible that remnants of his Baptist childhood find their way into landscapes such as *Above Lake Superior.*
8. Information provided by Margaret Knox in August 1981 to Douglas Worts in an interview. Mrs. Knox said 1924, but the date was probably later.
9. "Ontario Painters Doing Vital Work," March 17, 1924.
10. "Past and Present Among the Painters," *Saturday Night* XXXVII (April 1, 1922).
11. Housser, 189.
12. Ibid.
13. "Revelation of Art in Canada," 37.
14. Housser, 191.
15. Quoted in Harris and Colgrove, 103.

CHAPTER ELEVEN: LIVING WHITENESS (1922–1923)

1. Harris, "The Greatest Book by a Canadian and Another," 38.
2. Ibid.

3. Undated letter. McMichael.
4. Jessie E. Rittenhouse, "A.E.; A Study of George Russell, the Celtic Mystic, Who Has Been the Predominant Influence in the 'Celtic Revival,'" *New York Times*, December 15, 1912.
5. "Lawren Harris: An Interpretation," *Canadian Bookman* X, no. 2 (February 1928): 43.
6. "The Group of Seven Display Their Annual Symbolisms," *Toronto Star*, February 8, 1928.

CHAPTER TWELVE: MOUNT HARRISES (1923–1925)

1. Quoted in Harris and Colgrove, 62.
2. Story, 30.
3. A.Y. Jackson, 107.
4. Story, 29–30.
5. Housser, 194–95.
6. *Toronto Star*, January 13, 1925.
7. "'School of Seven' Exhibition is Riot of Impressions," *Star Weekly*, January 10, 1925.
8. *Canadian Forum* V, no. 53 (February 1925), 144–47.
9. A.Y. Jackson, *Banting as an Artist* (Toronto: Ryerson, 1943), 11.
10. Bliss, 167. In April 1925, Harris nominated Banting for membership in the Arts and Letters Club.
11. Ibid., 167.
12. "Triple Group at Brooklyn Museum," *Brooklyn Daily Eagle*, sec. B, May 25, 1924, 2.
13. "Canada's Art at Empire Fair," *Saturday Night* XXXVIII, no. 44 (September 15, 1923): 5.
14. Eric Brown, Wembley catalogue, 3.
15. *The Times*, May 28, 1924.
16. "Freak Pictures at Wembley," *Saturday Night* XXXIX, no. 43 (September 13, 1924): 1.
17. "Sir Edmund Walker," 109.
18. *Toronto Daily Star*, April 25, 1925.
19. "Disdainful of Prettiness New Art Aims at Sublimity," *Toronto Star*, May 6, 1926.
20. Thoreau MacDonald to Larry Pfaff, March 14, 1977. AGO.
21. "Art at the Canadian National Exhibition," *Canadian Bookman* VII, no. 9 (September 1925): 180.

CHAPTER THIRTEEN: JOYFUL VISION, INNER SORROW
(1926–1927)

1. "New Member is Added to Group of Seven," May 8, 1926.
2. May 6, 1926.
3. "Group of Seven Betrays No Signs of Repentance," May 8, 1926.
4. "Toronto and Montreal Painters," *Saturday Night* XLI, no. 27 (May 22, 1926): 3.
5. Harris, "Revelation of Art in Canada."
6. Knox, 226.
7. Quoted in Sixten Ringbom, "The Sounding Cosmos: A Study in the Spiritualism of Kandinsky and the Genesis of Abstract Painting," *Acta Academiae Aboensis*, ser. A, vol. XXXVIII, no. 2 (1970): 47.
8. A.Y. Jackson, 59.
9. *The Fine Arts in Canada* (Toronto: Macmillan, 1925), v.
10. A photocopy of this unsent letter of December 20, 1926, is in the MacDonald papers at LAC.
11. The book contains twelve illustrations, with Thomson's *The West Wind* as the frontispiece. Harris's *Elevator Court* and *Above Lake Superior* are reproduced. The others are *Northern Village* (Carmichael), *The Edge of the Maple Wood* (Jackson), *The Tangled Garden* (MacDonald), *Solemn Land* (MacDonald), *Winter Road, Quebec* (Jackson), *September Gale* (Lismer), *Islands of Spruce* (Lismer), *Jackfish Village* (Carmichael) and *Stormy Weather, Georgian Bay* (Varley).
12. Housser, 187.
13. Macmillan of Canada printed a thousand copies of the book in 1926. More than a hundred copies were sent out for review and 570 were sold for the retail price of $2.50. In the autumn of 1927 the book was reprinted, and 731 copies were sold at a slightly reduced price. By 1929, when the book was remaindered, 1,500 copies had been sold. For its time, this was a good market performance for such a title.
14. LAC.
15. LAC.

CHAPTER FOURTEEN: A LANGUAGE OF HIS OWN (1926–1927)

1. Katherine Dreier to LH, September 2, 1926. MS: Yale.
2. Katherine Dreier to LH, November 19, 1926. MS copy: Yale.
3. LH to Exhibition Committee, undated but November 1926. MS: Yale.
4. LH to Katherine Dreier, [late November or early December 1926]. Yale.

5. "An Attempt to Understand This 'Amazing' Modern Art," *Evening Telegram*, April 16, 1927; and "Amazing Paintings by Ultra-modernists," *Mail and Empire*, April 2, 1927.

6. Holograph is undated. MS: Yale.

7. *Canadian Forum* VII (May 1927): 239–42.

8. Johnston's riposte appeared in the same issue of the *Forum*.

9. Harris, "Revelation of Art in Canada," 86.

10. MS: University of Manitoba.

11. Ibid.

12. J.E.H. MacDonald to Bertram Brooker, January 28, 1927. Cited in Joyce Zemans, "The Art and Weltanschung of Bertram Brooker," *artscanada* XXX (February/March 1973): 1965.

13. Harris owned a Brooker abstraction from *c.* 1927 (now at the Vancouver Art Gallery).

14. Harris maintained an unusual practice in his painting, as he told Emily Carr on December 20, 1931: "I go back and paint again an old subject once or twice a year—not from habit but because it gives me a perspective on my present attempts. I find it somewhat reassuring in that I go to present work with added conviction and a little greater freedom."

15. Hundreds, 25–26.

16. Ibid., 38.

17. LH to Emily Carr, January 8, 1928.

18. Hundreds, 42.

19. Ibid., 35–36.

20. Ibid., 38.

CHAPTER FIFTEEN: ABSOLUTE SILENCE (1928–1930)

1. LH to Emily Carr, November 30, 1930. MS: LA.

2. LH to Emily Carr. Undated. MS: LA.

3. Doris Mills Speirs, interview with Charles C. Hill.

4. "In the Art Galleries," *Mail and Empire* (Toronto), March 19, 1927.

5. "Group of Seven Display Their Annual Symbolism," *Toronto Daily Star*, February 8, 1928.

6. *New Western Tribune*, June 29, 1929.

7. A.Y. Jackson to Norah Thomson, October 14, 1929. MS: LAC.

8. "Canada Splendidly Launched in Career of National Art," *London Morning Advertiser*, January 25, 1930.

9. See Hill, 264.

10. June 1930.

11. "An Epitome of Europe," *Canadian Theosophist* XIV, no. 7 (September 1933).

12. LH to Emily Carr, June [1930]. LAC.

13. Ibid.

14. Peter Larisey, "The Landscape Painting of Lawren Stewart Harris," 70–71.

15. "The Group of Seven in Canadian History," 36.

16. "Artist-Explorer," *Canadian Bookman* IX, no. 6 (July 1927): 216.

17. Quoted in Mellen, *The Group of Seven*, 176.

18. Story, 30.

19. A.Y. Jackson, 129–35.

20. Quoted in Mellen, *The Group of Seven*, 176.

21. LH to Emily Carr, December 26, 1930. MS: LAC.

22. Wassily Kandinsky, *Concerning the Spiritual in Art*, 58–60.

23. Jehanne Biétry Salinger, "Far North Is Pictured by Two Artists," *Regina Leader-Post*, May 1, 1931.

24. "Paintings Depict Canadian Arctic," *Gazette* (Montreal), May 1, 1931.

25. "Comment on Art: The Group of Seven," *Canadian Forum* (January 1932): 143.

26. Tippett, *Emily Carr*, 211.

27. LH to Emily Carr, undated but *circa* 1932. LAC.

CHAPTER SIXTEEN: AT THE CROSSROADS (1931–1934)

1. Duval, *Lawren Harris*, 224.

2. "Decline of the Group of Seven," *Canadian Forum* XII, no. 136 (January 1932): 144.

3. "Group of Seven Begins Expansion," *Mail and Empire* (Toronto), December 7, 1931.

4. Duval, *Four Decades*, 12.

5. January 1, 1939. University of Manitoba, FitzGerald, box 7.

6. March 15, 1933. MS: University of Manitoba.

7. Duval, *Four Decades*, 17–18.

8. *Toronto Daily Star*, November 3, 1933.

9. *Canadian Forum* XIV, no. 159 (December 1933): 98–99.

10. Thom, *The Cartoons of Arthur Lismer*, 122.

11. LH to Katherine Dreier, April 19, 1931. MS: Yale.

12. March 8, 1930.

13. Yvonne and Fred did not marry until June 28, 1935.

14. Frances Loring to Eric Brown, July [15], 1934. MS: ANG.

15. Bess Harris to Isabel McLaughlin. Undated. MS: Queen's.

16. Housser subsequently lived at 158 Madison Avenue.

17. Undated. MS: Queen's.

18. In an undated letter *circa* 1934–35 to Isabel, Yvonne revisits this point: Jackson's behaviour may be put "down to his fondness for Bess—and that he was hurt and worked it off" inappropriately. MS: Queen's.

19. Yvonne Housser to Isabel McLaughlin, January 26, 1975. MS: Queen's.

20. Bliss, 197.

21. Quoted by Bliss, 202.

22. Undated. LAC.

23. MS: LAC.

CHAPTER SEVENTEEN: NEW ADVENTURES (1934–1936)

1. See Larisey, 119. This information is based on an interview Larisey conducted with Peter Haworth and his wife.

2. Draft of a letter from LH to Doris Mills, October 1939. The letter was not posted. MS: LAC.

3. Journal entry for July 11, 1934. LAC.

4. December 30, 1936.

5. Bess Harris to Doris Mills Speirs. MS: Fisher.

6. Larisey, 124. This information is based on an interview Larisey conducted with Mr. and Mrs. Churchill P. Lathrop on October 9, 1973.

7. "Essay on American Scenery," 1835.

8. Churchill P. Lathrop provided this information to Peter Larisey.

9. "Art in a Changing World," *Canadian Comment* IV, no. 2 (February 1935): 23. See Hill, 76.

10. Quoted in Fred Housser to Lismer, July 20, 1936. McMichael Collection. See Hill, 76.

11. "Lawren Harris," 13–14, 18.

12. May 3, 1936.

13. April 15, 1937.

14. May 14, 1935.

15. Isabel McLaughlin Archives. MS: Queen's.

16. LH to Yvonne Housser, December 31, 1936. MS: Victoria.

CHAPTER EIGHTEEN: AT EASE IN ZION (1937–1940)

1. LH to Harry Adaskin, May 15, 1938. MS: LA.

2. Bess Harris to Betty and Clyde Dankert, April 24, 1938. MS: Dartmouth.

3. Letter of January 26, 1917. Hewett Collection, NM.

4. *Santa Fe New Mexican*, September 17, 1926.

5. Raymond Jonson to Peter Larisey, November 14, 1973. See Larisey, 137.

6. LH to Jonson, June 1938. MS: NM.

7. According to Margaret Knox, Harris, during his time in New Mexico, called upon Frank Lloyd Wright at Taliesin West, his winter home and studio complex in Scottsdale, Arizona, but was rudely received by the architect. As mentioned in chapter 17, Harris was an admirer of Wright's social policies; he would also have been fascinated by the architect's Modernist designs.

8. LH to Raymond Jonson, [June 1938]. MS: Jonson Collection, NM.

9. LH to Jonson, August 3 [1938]. MS: NM.

10. Ibid.

11. MS: LA. Ten years earlier, Harris gave three Thomson paintings to the Art Gallery of Toronto (now the AGO): *Black Spruce and Maple, Autumn Birches* and *A Rapid*.

12. Arnold Berke, *Mary Colter: Architect of the Southwest* (Princeton: Princeton University Press, 2002), 264.

13. Peter Larisey interview with Bill Lumpkins, June 1, 1982. See Larisey, 137.

14. Raymond Jonson to Peter Larisey, November 14, 1973. MS: NM.

15. Information from Maryan Bisttram. See Larisey, 138.

16. Ibid.

17. Bess Harris to Doris Mills Speirs, December 28, 1938. MS: Fisher.

18. June 13, 1940. MS: Queen's.

19. LH to Raymond Jonson, August 19 [1938]. MS: NM.

20. On March 16, 1939, Harris sent a letter to the editor of the *Santa Fe New Mexican*: "Some years ago Mr. McKinney requested me to assemble a collection of Canadian pictures for the Sesqui-Centennial exhibition in the Baltimore Art Gallery. A few months ago he again requested me to select twenty-five canvases from Canada for the present San Francisco exhibition. During the time of our correspondence about Canadian pictures I had visited the opening of the Famous Guggenheim Foundation collection of non-objective or abstract pictures at Charleston, N.C., the largest collection of its kind in the world. A few weeks later I saw some of the works of the local non-objective or abstract painters. I knew Mr. McKinney was having a fairly large representation from the Guggenheim collection in San Francisco and was so deeply impressed by the local works in the same idiom that I suggested to him that he see these pictures on his way west . . . Mr. McKinney accepted my suggestion and visited Santa Fe and Taos and

was as deeply impressed by the abstract pictures he saw as I had been. Here was something new and to his mind vital and he was immensely pleased. He expressed himself by saying that in these paintings he saw a spirit he had not seen in similar works anywhere in the East. Thereupon he arranged for a small group of those pictures for the San Francisco exhibition. At the time of my correspondence with Mr. McKinney and during his visit in Santa Fe I was not a member of the local group of abstract painters called the transcendental painting group."

21. May 19, 1939.
22. February 21, 1938. MS: Queen's.
23. December 28, 1938. MS: Fisher.
24. Ralph Pearson, *The Modern Renaissance in American Art* (New York: Harper, [1954?]), 83.
25. Bess Harris to Isabel McLaughlin, June 23, 1940. MS: Queen's.
26. MS: Fisher.
27. LH to Jonson, December 29, 1940. MS: NM.

CHAPTER NINETEEN: EQUIVALENTS (1940–1948)

1. Emily Carr to Nan Cheney, November 7 [1940]. Quoted in Walker, ed.
2. November 28, 1940.
3. Bess Harris to Betty and Clyde Dankert, May 29, 1941. MS: Dartmouth.
4. Bess Harris to Doris Mills Speirs, June 3, 1941. MS: Fisher.
5. March 6, 1941. MS: NM.
6. Bess Harris to Doris Mills Speirs, March 6, 1941. MS: Fisher.
7. LH to Katherine Stinson Otero, September 18, 1942. MS: NM.
8. LH to Raymond Jonson, March 6, 1941. MS: NM.
9. Ibid.
10. Bess Harris to Isabel McLaughlin, May 16, 1941. MS: Queen's.
11. Macdonald to H.O. McCurry, July 22, 1938. MS: ANG.
12. Macdonald to H.O. McCurry, October 21, 1937. MS: ANG.
13. Macdonald to H.O. McCurry, December 2, 1939. ANG.
14. LH to Raymond Jonson, August 3, 1941.
15. LH to LeMoine FitzGerald, undated but *c.* February 1928. MS: FitzGerald Study Centre, University of Manitoba.
16. LH to LeMoine FitzGerald, December 29, 1929. MS: FitzGerald Study Centre, University of Manitoba.
17. Bess Harris to Isabel McLaughlin, December 27, 1941. MS: Queen's. Both of Bess's parents died in 1941.

18. Bess Harris to Isabel McLaughlin, December 25, 1941. MS: Queen's.
19. Bess Harris to Doris Mills Speirs, December 27, 1941. MS: Fisher.
20. Bess Harris to Isabel McLaughlin. MS: Queen's.
21. Larisey, 152.
22. Nan Cheney to Humphrey Toms, January 14, 1941. Quoted in Walker, ed. 287.
23. Peter Larisey interview with Binning, December 1973.
24. Tyler is quoted in Tony Robertson, "The First Fifty Years: The Vancouver Art Gallery, 1931–1983," *Vanguard* 12, no. 8 (October 1983): 16.
25. See Larisey, 152.
26. Peter Larisey interview with Shadbolt, December 1973.
27. Peter Larisey interview with Joe Plaskett, October 24, 1983.
28. LH to André Bieler, June 14, 1941. See Larisey, 154–55.
29. LH, Letter Number 1 (1944). FCA papers. MS: Queen's.
30. Ibid.
31. November 19, 1941. Quoted in Morra, ed., 57.
32. MS: Queen's.
33. Martin Baldwin to LH, March 25, 1948. MS: NAC.
34. LH to Martin Baldwin, March 28, [1948]. MS: AGO.
35. "The Pursuit of Form," 54–57.

CHAPTER TWENTY: BEYOND ABSTRACTION (1949–1970)

1. William McGuffin, "'Tories Never Show Interest in Art,'" *Toronto Daily Star*, October 28, 1959.
2. Katherine Dreier to LH, June 20, 1949. MS: Yale.
3. Koerner, 31.
4. The Manas represents the highest intellectual state of mind; the middle of the painting represents the Buddhi figure; Atma, the highest, represents the Godhead. See Reid, *Atma Buddhi Manas*, 59.
5. Duval, *Lawren Harris: Where the Universe Sings*, 23, 334.
6. This information was supplied by Stewart Sheppard.
7. LH to Isabel McLaughlin, December 8 [c. 1950–52]. MS: Queen's.
8. R.H. Hubbard, "A Climate for the Arts," in *A Modern Life: Art and Design in British Columbia 1945–60*, 42–3.
9. January 8, 1950.
10. Bess Harris to Raymond Jonson, April 26, 1955. MS: NM.
11. December 3, 1950.
12. Bess Harris to Doris Mills Speirs, January 12, 1952. MS: Fisher.
13. Bess Harris to Doris Mills Speirs, January 8, 1950. MS: Fisher.

14. Information supplied by Toni Ann Chowne.
15. Ibid.
16. There were various young men employed in this capacity.
17. JK interview with Dennis Reid.
18. *Vancouver Sun*, December 13, 1951.
19. Ibid.
20. *A Disquisition on Abstract Painting*, 10, 11.
21. Ibid., 8.
22. Bess Harris to Yvonne Housser, August 1, 1956. MS: Victoria.
23. Bess Harris to Doris Mills Speirs, undated. MS: Fisher.
24. Knox 230.
25. In Selden Rodman, *Conversations with Artists* (New York: 1957), 93–94.

SELECTED
BIBLIOGRAPHY

Adamson, Jeremy. *Lawren S. Harris: Urban Scenes and Wilderness Landscapes 1906–1930*. Toronto: Art Gallery of Ontario, 1978.

———. "Lawren Stewart Harris: Towards an Art of the Spiritual." In *The Thomson Collection at the Art Gallery of Ontario*, 69–87. Toronto: Skylet, 2008.

Betts, Gregory, ed. *Lawren Harris in the Ward: His Urban Poetry and Paintings*. Toronto: Exile Editions, 2007.

Blanchard, Paula. *The Life of Emily Carr*. Vancouver: Douglas & McIntyre, 1987.

Blankenship, Tiska. *Vision and Spirit: The Transcendental Painting Group*. Albuquerque: Jonson Gallery of the University of New Mexico Art Museum, 1997.

Bliss, Michael. *Banting: A Biography*. Toronto: University of Toronto Press, 1993.

Bridle, Augustus. *The Story of the Club*. Toronto: Arts and Letters Club, 1945.

Brooker, Bertram. *Think of the Earth*. Toronto: Brown Bear Press, 2000.

———. *The Wrong World: Selected Stories & Essays*. Edited by Gregory Betts. Ottawa: University of Ottawa Press, 2009.

Burley, David G. *A Particular Condition in Life: Self-Employment and Social Mobility in Mid-Victorian Brantford, Ontario*. Kingston and Montreal: McGill–Queen's University Press, 1994.

Careless, J.M.S. *Toronto to 1918: An Illustrated History.* Toronto: James Lorimer and National Museum of Man, 1984.

Carr, Angela. "Portrait of Dr. Salem Bland: Another Spiritual Journey for Lawren S. Harris." *Journal of Canadian Art History* 19, no. 2 (1998): 6–27.

Carr, Emily. *Hundreds and Thousands.* Vancouver: Douglas & McIntyre, 2006.

Christensen, Lisa. *A Hiker's Guide to Art of the Canadian Rockies.* Calgary: Fifth House, 1999.

———. *A Hiker's Guide to the Rocky Mountain Art of Lawren Harris.* Calgary: Fifth House, 2000.

Coke, Van Deren. *Taos and Santa Fe: The Artists' Environment, 1882–1942.* Albuquerque: University of New Mexico Press, 1963.

Cole, Douglas. "Artists, Patrons and Public: An Inquiry into the Success of the Group of Seven." *Revue d'études canadiennes/Journal of Canadian Studies* 13 (1978): 69–78.

Cook, Ramsay. *The Regenerators: Social Criticism in Late Victorian English Canada.* Toronto: University of Toronto Press, 1985.

Davis, Ann. *The Logic of Ecstasy: Canadian Mystical Painting, 1920–1940.* Toronto: University of Toronto Press, 1992.

———. "A Study in Modernism: The Group of Seven as an Unexpectedly Typical Case." *Journal of Canadian Studies* 33 (Spring 1998): 108–20.

Dawn, Leslie. *National Visions, National Blindness: Canadian Art and Identities in the 1920s.* Vancouver: UBC Press, 2006.

Dejardin, Ian, ed. *Painting Canada: Tom Thomson and the Group of Seven.* London: Dulwich Picture Gallery, 2011.

Duncan, Norman. "Going Down to Jerusalem." In *The Narrative of a Sentimental Traveller.* London and New York: Harper, 1909.

Duval, Paul. *Four Decades: The Canadian Group of Painters and Their Contemporaries, 1930–1970.* Toronto: Clarke Irwin, 1972.

———. *Lawren Harris: Where the Universe Sings.* Toronto: Cerebrus Publishing, 2011.

———. *The Tangled Garden.* Toronto: Cerebrus/Prentice-Hall, 1978.

Elder, Alan C., Ian M. Thom, and others. *A Modern Life: Art and Design in British Columbia 1945–1960.* Vancouver: Vancouver Art Gallery and Arsenal Pulp Press, 2004.

Fairley, Barker. "*Contrasts* by Lawren Harris." *Canadian Forum* III, no. 28 (January 1923).

————. "Some Canadian Painters: Lawren Harris." *Canadian Forum* I, no. 9 (June 1921).

Fritzsche, Peter. *Reading Berlin 1900.* Cambridge, MA: Harvard University Press, 1996.

Frye, Northrop. "The Pursuit of Form." *Canadian Art* VI, no. 2 (Christmas 1948).

Fulford, Robert, and Joan Murray. *The Beginning of Vision: The Drawings of Lawren S. Harris.* Toronto and Vancouver: Douglas & McIntyre in association with Mira Godard Editions, 1982.

Garman, Ed. *The Art of Raymond Jonson, Painter.* Albuquerque: University of New Mexico Press, 1976.

Gibson, Arrell Morgan. *The Santa Fe and Taos Colonies: Age of the Muses, 1900–1942.* Norman: University of Oklahoma Press, 1983.

Grace, Sherrill E. *Canada and the Idea of North.* Montreal and Kingston: McGill–Queen's University Press, 2004.

Gray, Charlotte. *Flint & Feathers: The Life and Times of E. Pauline Johnson, Tekahionwake.* Toronto: HarperCollins, 2002.

Gross, Jennifer R., ed. *The Société Anonyme: Modernism for America.* New Haven, CT: Yale University Press, 2006.

Harris, Bess, and R.G.P. Colgrove. *Lawren Harris.* Toronto: Macmillan, 1969.

Harris, Lawren. "Artist and Audience." *Canadian Bookman* VII, no. 12 (December 1925).

————. "The Canadian Art Club." *Yearbook of Canadian Art 1913.* London and Toronto: Dent, 1913.

————. *Contrasts, A Book of Verse.* Toronto: McClelland and Stewart, 1922.

————. "Creative Art and Canada." In *Yearbook of the Arts in Canada, 1928–29.* Toronto: Macmillan, 1929.

————. *A Disquisition on Abstract Painting.* Toronto: Rouse and Mann, 1954.

————. "Emily Carr and her Work." *Canadian Forum* XXI, no. 251 (December 1941).

————. "An Essay on Abstract Painting." *Journal of the Royal Architectural Institute of Canada* XXVI, no. 1 (January 1949).

————. "The Function of Art." *Art Gallery Bulletin* [of the Vancouver Art Gallery] II, no. 2 (October 1943).

———. "The Greatest Book by a Canadian and Another." *Canadian Bookman* VI, no. 2 (February 1924).

———. "The Group of Seven." *Group of Seven Exhibition Catalogue*. Vancouver: Vancouver Art Gallery, 1954.

———. "The Group of Seven in Canadian History." *Canadian Historical Association Report of the Annual Meeting Held at Victoria and Vancouver June 16–19, 1948*. Toronto: Canadian Historical Association, 1948.

———. "Heming's Black and Whites." *Lamps* (October 1911).

———. "The Philosopher's Stone." *Canadian Bookman* VI, no. 7 (July 1924).

———. "The R.C.A. Reviewed." *Lamps* (December 1911).

———. "The Revelation of Art in Canada." *Canadian Theosophist* VII, no. 5 (15 July 1926).

———. "Sir Edmund Walker." *Canadian Bookman* VI, no. 5 (May 1924).

———. "The Story of the Group of Seven." In *The Best of the Group of Seven*, by Joan Murray. Toronto: McClelland and Stewart, 1984.

———. "Theosophy and Art." *Canadian Theosophist* XIV, nos. 5 and 6 (15 July 1933; 15 August 1933)

———. "Theosophy and the Modern World: War and Europe." *Canadian Theosophist* XIV, no. 9 (15 November 1933).

———. "Winning a Canadian Background." *Canadian Bookman* V, no. 2 (February 1923).

Hill, Charles C. *Canadian Painting in the Thirties*. Ottawa: National Gallery of Canada, 1975.

———. *The Group of Seven: Art for a Nation*. Ottawa: National Gallery of Canada, 1995.

———. Interview with Doris Huestis Mills. October 15, 1973. canadianart1930.gallery.ca.

Hordes, Stanley M. "The Architectural Career of Katherine Stinson Otero." Unpublished paper.

Horrall, Andrew. *Bringing Art to Life: A Biography of Alan Jarvis*. Montreal and Kingston: McGill–Queen's University Press, 2009.

Housser, F.B. *A Canadian Art Movement: The Story of the Group of Seven*. Toronto: Macmillan, 1926.

Hunter, Andrew. *Lawren Harris: A Painter's Progress*. New York: The Americas Society, 2002.

Hunter, Edmund Robert. *J.E.H. MacDonald: A Biography and Catalogue of his Work.* Toronto: Ryerson Press, 1940.

Jackson, A.Y. *A Painter's Country: The Autobiography of A.Y. Jackson.* Toronto: Clarke, Irwin, 1967.

Jackson, Christopher. *Lawren Harris: North by West: The Arctic and Rocky Mountain Paintings of Lawren Harris, 1924–1931.* Calgary: Glenbow Museum, 1991.

Kandinsky, Wassily. *Concerning the Spiritual in Art.* Translated with an introduction by M.T.H. Sadler. New York: Dover, 1977.

King, Ross. *Defiant Spirits: The Modernist Revolution of the Group of Seven.* Kleinburg, ON, and Vancouver: McMichael Canadian Art Collection and Douglas & McIntyre, 2010.

Knox, Margaret. "Personal Reminizscences." In the limited edition of *The Beginning of Vision: The Drawings of Lawren S. Harris*, by Robert Fulford and Joan Murray, 222–30. Toronto and Vancouver: Douglas & McIntyre in association with Mira Godard Editions, 1982.

Koerner, John. *A Brush with Life.* Vancouver: Ronsdale Press, 2005.

Larisey, Peter. "The Landscape Painting of Lawren Stewart Harris." Ph.D. diss., Columbia University, 1982.

———. *Light for a Cold Land: Lawren Harris's Work and Life—An Interpretation.* Toronto: Dundurn Press, 1993.

Larsen, Wayne. *A.Y. Jackson: The Life of a Landscape Painter.* Toronto: Dundurn Press, 2009.

Lawren Harris, Paintings, 1910–1948. Toronto: Art Gallery of Toronto, 1948.

Lawren Harris Retrospective Exhibition 1963. Ottawa: National Gallery of Canada, 1963.

Linsley, Robert. "Landscapes in Motion: Lawren Harris and the Heterogeneous Modern Nation." *Oxford Art Journal* 19 (1996): 80–95.

Martin, Constance. *The Odyssey of Rockwell Kent.* Chesterfield: Chameleon, 2000.

Mason, Roger Burford. *A Grand Eye for Glory: A Life of Franz Johnston.* Toronto: Dundurn Press, 1998.

Mastin, Catharine M., ed. *The Group of Seven in Western Canada.* Toronto: Key Porter Books, 2002.

McBurney, Margaret. *The Great Adventure: 100 Years at the Arts & Letters Club.* Toronto: Arts and Letters Club, 2007.

McGrath, Robert L. *Gods in Granite: The Art of the White Mountains of New Hampshire*. Syracuse, NY: Syracuse University Press, 2001.

McKay, Marilyn J. *Picturing the Land: Narrating Territories in Canadian Landscape Art, 1500–1900*. Montreal and Kingston: McGill–Queen's University Press, 2011.

McKenzie, Karen, and Larry Pfaff. "The Art Gallery of Ontario: Sixty Years of Exhibitions, 1906–1966." *Revue d'art canadienne/Canadian Art Review* VII, nos. 1–2 (1976): 62–91.

Mellen, Peter. *The Group of Seven*. Toronto: McClelland and Stewart, 1970.

Modern Life: Art and Design in British Columbia 1945–1960. Vancouver: Vancouver Art Gallery and Arsenal Press, 2004.

Morra, Linda, ed. *Corresponding Influences: Selected Letters of Emily Carr and Ira Dilworth*. Toronto: University of Toronto Press, 2006.

Murray, Joan. *The Art of Yvonne McKague Housser*. Oshawa, ON: McLaughlin Gallery, 1995.

———. *The Isabel McLaughlin Gift. Part One*. Oshawa, ON: McLaughlin Gallery, 1987.

Murray, Joan, and Robert Fulford. *The Beginning of Vision: The Drawings of Lawren S. Harris*. Toronto and Vancouver: Douglas & McIntyre, 1982.

Nasgaard, Roald. *Abstract Painting in Canada*. Vancouver: Douglas & McIntyre, 2007.

———. *The Mystic North: Symbolist Landscape Painting in Northern Europe and North America, 1890–1940*. Toronto: Art Gallery of Ontario/ University of Toronto Press, 1984.

O'Brian, John, and Peter White. *Beyond Wilderness: The Group of Seven, Canadian Identity and Contemporary Art*. Montreal and Kingston: McGill–Queen's University Press, 2007.

Ord, Douglas. *The National Gallery of Canada: Ideas, Art, Architecture*. Montreal and Kingston: McGill–Queen's University Press, 2003.

Paret, Peter. *The Berlin Secession: Modernism and Its Enemies in Imperial Germany*. Cambridge, MA: Harvard University Press, 1980.

Pfaff, L.R. "Lawren Harris and the International Exhibition of Modern Art: Rectification to the Toronto Catalogue (1927), and Some Critical Comments." *Revue d'art canadienne/Canadian Art Review* XI, nos. 1–2 (1984): 79–96.

———. "Portraits by Lawren Harris: Salem Bland and Others." *Revue d'art canadienne/Canadian Art Review* V, no. 1 (1978): 21–27.

Plaskett, Joseph. *A Speaking Likeness*. Vancouver: Ronsdale Press, 1999.

Reid, Dennis. *Atma Buddhi Manas: The Later Work of Lawren S. Harris*. Toronto: Art Gallery of Ontario, 1985.

———. *Bertram Brooker*. Ottawa: National Gallery of Canada, 1979.

———. *A Bibliography of the Group of Seven*. Ottawa: National Gallery of Canada, 1971.

———. *A Concise History of Canadian Painting*. 2nd ed. Toronto: Oxford University Press, 1988.

———. *The Group of Seven*. Ottawa: National Gallery of Canada, 1970.

———. "Lawren S. Harris's Self-Portrait: Critical Milestone on a Remarkable Human Journey," *Journal of Canadian Art History*, XXXII: 1 (2011), 92–108.

———. *Our Own Country Canada: Being an Account of the National Aspirations of the Principal Landscape Artists in Montreal and Toronto, 1860–1890*. Ottawa: National Gallery of Canada, 1979.

———, ed. *Tom Thomson*. Toronto and Ottawa: Art Gallery of Ontario and National Gallery of Canada, 2002.

Robins, John. "Lawren Harris," *Canadian Review of Music and Art* 3, nos. 3–4 (1944): III.

Rosenblum, Robert. *Modern Painting and the Northern Romantic Tradition: Friedrich to Rothko*. New York: Harper & Row, 1975.

Silcox, David P. *The Group of Seven and Tom Thomson*. Toronto: Firefly Books, 2002.

Thom, Ian M. *The Cartoons of Arthur Lismer: A New Angle on Canadian Art*. Toronto: Irwin, 1985.

Thompson, Austin Seton. *Jarvis Street: A Story of Triumph and Tragedy*. Toronto: Personal Library, 1980.

———. *Spadina: A Story of Old Toronto*. Toronto: Pagurian Press, 1975.

Tippett, Maria. *Emily Carr: A Biography*. Toronto: Oxford University Press, 1979.

———. *Stormy Weather: F.H. Varley, a Biography*. Toronto: McClelland and Stewart, 1998.

Tooby, Michael. *The True North: Canadian Landscape Painting 1896–1939*. London: Lund Humphries, 1991.

The Transcendental Painting Group: New Mexico, 1938–1941. Albuquerque, NM: Albuquerque Museum, 1982.

Walker, Doreen, ed. *Dear Nan: Letters of Emily Carr, Nan Cheney and Humphrey Toms*. Vancouver: University of British Columbia Press, 1990.

Westfall, William. *Two Worlds: The Protestant Culture of Nineteenth Century Ontario*. Montreal and Kingston: McGill–Queen's University Press, 1990.

Whitelaw, Anne, Brian Foss, and Sandra Paikowsky. *The Visual Arts in Canada: The Twentieth Century*. Toronto: Oxford University Press, 2010.

Whiteman, Bruce. *J.E.H. MacDonald*. Kingston, ON: Quarry Press, 1995.

Wilson, Barbara M., ed. *Ontario and the First World War: A Collection of Documents*. Toronto: University of Toronto Press, 1977.

Zemans, Joyce. *Jock Macdonald: The Interior Landscape/A Retrospective Exhibition*. Toronto: Art Gallery of Ontario, 1981.

INDEX